White Elephants

To Mam, Dad, my brother and sister-in-law, my sister, Laura, and little Finn

White Elephants

The Country House
and the State in
Independent Ireland,
1922–73

EMER CROOKE

UNIVERSITY COLLEGE DUBLIN PRESS
PREAS CHOLÁISTE OLLSCOILE BHAILE ÁTHA CLIATH
2018

First published 2018
by University College Dublin Press
UCD Humanities Institute, Room H103
Belfield
Dublin 4
Ireland
www.ucdpress.ie

ISBN 978-1-910820-28-5

10 9 8 7 6 5 4 3 2 1

CIP data available from the British Library
The right of Emer Crooke to be identified as the author of this
work has been asserted by her

Typeset in 11pt on 14pt Fournier by Marsha Swan

Printed in Spain on acid-free paper by GraphyCems

Contents

Illustrations between pages 136 and 137

LIST OF ABBREVIATIONS

BTAHHC – British Tourist Authority's Historic Houses Committee
DoFF – Dept of Finance files
DoTF – Dept of the Taoiseach files
EEC – European Economic Community
ESB – Electricity Supply Board
EU – European Union
FOI – Freedom of Information Acts
HITHA – Historic Irish Tourist Houses Association
IGS – Irish Georgian Society
IHSA – Irish History Student's Association
IPA – Institute for Public Administration
IRA – Irish Republican Army
IT – Irish Times
ITA – Irish Tourist Association
NAI – National Archives of Ireland
NMAC – National Monuments Advisory Council
OPW – Office of Public Works
TD – Teachta Dála
UNESCO – United Nations Educational, Scientific and Cultural Organization

LIST OF ILLUSTRATIONS

1. Jenkinstown House, County Kilkenny by Robert French c. 1865–1914. Demolished. Courtesy of the National Library of Ireland.

2. Mote Park, Ballymurray, County Roscommon. Originally home to the Crofton family. Sold for demolition in the 1950s by the Irish Land Commission. Courtesy of the National Library of Ireland.

3. Erskine Childers, Minister for Lands, 1957–9. Courtesy of the National Library of Ireland.

4. Shanbally Castle, Clogheen, County Tipperary by Robert French c. 1865–1914. Sold for demolition in August 1957. Courtesy of the National Library of Ireland.

5. Slane Castle, County Meath. The castle is in family ownership to this day. Courtesy of the Centre for the Study of Historic Irish Houses and Estates.

6. Bishopscourt, Straffan, County Kildare, 20 August 1967. In private ownership. Courtesy of the National Library of Ireland.

7. Glenstal Abbey, Murroe, County Limerick. Photograph by Independent Newspapers (Firm), 31 May 1930. The abbey subsequently became a Benedictine Abbey and boarding school for boys. Courtesy of the National Library of Ireland.

8. Shelton Abbey, County Wicklow. Shelton Abbey is currently owned by the Irish Prison Service. Courtesy of the Centre for the Study of Historic Irish Houses and Estates.

9. Directors of Muckross House, 14 February 1964. L–R: Dr Frank Hilliard, Fr J. Sheahan, Beatrice Grosvenor, Seán O'Connor, Arthur Fairley, Fr Conleth and Edmund (Ned) Myers. Courtesy of the Trustees of Muckross House.

10. Muckross House, Killarney, County Kerry. Currently open to the public and operated as a museum. Courtesy of the the Trustees of Muckross House.

ACKNOWLEDGEMENTS

I am very grateful to UCD Press for their faith in me and in this project and in particular for the hard work and patience of Ruth Hallinan and Conor Graham, with whom it has been a pleasure to work.

I wish to thank my friends for their support and encouragement as well as my wonderful colleagues, past and present, from Maynooth, the Department of Finance and the Oireachtas who have made my career so far a very happy one and from whom I have learned so much. It has been a great privilege to work with you all and to work for institutions of which I am very proud. I also wish to thank Brian Kavanagh for the ongoing support and wisdom.

I am deeply indebted to Professor Terence Dooley for not only inspiring an interest in this subject in the first place when I was a student, but for being a constant and selfless mentor and friend. I would not have believed this book possible if he had not encouraged me to pursue this course; I am very grateful, Terry. I also acknowledge with deep gratitude the financial support provided by the Centre for the Study of Historic Irish Houses and Estates.

Most importantly, I wish to thank my family – my brother and sister-in-law and, in particular, my mam, dad and sister, Laura, and little Finn who have had to share a house with me as this project was undertaken. A thank you will never be enough to express how grateful I am to you for your love, kindness, generosity, selflessness, and unwavering belief in me. I am so thankful to have you as my family and know that I am very blessed to have such incredible people around me. You have shown me the true meaning of selfless love and the joy of family and I love you very much. This book is dedicated to you.

Above all else, thank you to God, for everything.

INTRODUCTION

The signing of the Anglo-Irish Treaty in 1921, which brought an end to the War of Independence, was not the last act in the story for an independent Ireland. In fact, the years that followed saw a resurgence of agrarian agitation, the eruption of civil war and the creation of a boundary with Northern Ireland. While all this took place, a nation state attempted to find its feet amid world war and an economic depression that defined the first half of the twentieth century in Europe and beyond. The newly independent Irish Free State paradoxically depended on much of the infrastructure left behind by the retreating British establishment – the arch enemy of old. Of particular importance was the staff of Dublin Castle, many of whom transitioned to the civil service of the Free State from the English administration and, in so doing, provided important institutional knowledge and continuity to a nascent political system. In fact, these officials were crucial to the formation of the Free State and its development and policies in the years thereafter.

The book that follows throws new light on the nuances of the politics and state-craft of establishing the Free State and the later independent Republic and how these were influential factors for the acceptance of the country house in Ireland. Those leading the first independent governments had been directly involved in the armed struggle for independence and had little parliamentary experience; for instance, the first Minister for Finance was Michael Collins. It was on the shoulders of these people that the burden of building a nation state fell. At the time they took over its governance, the country was an underdeveloped, agrarian-dominated society, with much of the population living in impoverished circumstances. The economic development of the state was stunted and soaring emigration continually bled the country of much of its youth. For a population facing these challenges, independence had been held up as the solution *par excellence*. In the aftermath of the revolutionary period, it seemed that the ideals it espoused would be proven true or false by the success of the Free State. The ideal new state being envisaged, however, was one that held little room for an Anglo-Irish, and predominately Protestant, elite and their country houses.

Land division was one of the most emotive issues both prior to and after the emergence of the Free State, with many rural families living as subsistent, migrant and seasonal workers or tenants on large landed estates. In fact, the independence movement had gained much of its momentum from agrarian disaffection. At the centre of the estate stood the country house, surrounded by the land of the demesne laid out as extensive parkland for the inhabitants of the house to enjoy. Many of the owners of these properties could trace their lineage back to plantation times: a far longer recorded history in Ireland than most of the population could claim. Poorer classes never had the luxury of record-keeping and lineage-tracing that the upper classes had.

Despite the length of time that a family had been resident in Ireland, they were a class apart from the population that surrounded them because of their identity as Anglo-Irish as well as the different economic, political, social, and, usually, religious spheres in which they moved. They socialised with other country house families at parties or in Dublin's exclusive clubs, and many supported the union of Britain and Ireland and looked to Britain as their natural home. Many, too, served in Britain's army and answered the call to fight in the world wars. This spelled the end of family ownership of a number of these properties, as heirs to these houses failed to return from front lines across Europe. The families' predominately Protestant faith, too, differentiated them in the largely Catholic, nationalist state that was being formed. All these factors contributed to the demise of the country house in Ireland and the disappearance of their owners from localities across the Free State.

However, even in countries like Britain where many of these elements were insignificant, the day of the country house as a dominant force and private residence was largely coming to an end. Certainly, the power of the country house and its ascendancy would never re-emerge. Built at a time when their inhabitants were a political and social elite, country houses survived almost solely on the rents of enormous tracts of land. Most gentlemen and ladies never worked and considered it beneath them to do so. They attended society balls and led hunts in local areas. Some were good landlords to tenants around them, others so merciless that they were vilified in popular perception for generations. Whatever their individual traits, by the early twentieth century their way of life as a class was dying out all over Europe as more democratic, equitable societies were championed. The fact that such families in Ireland were often of a different political leaning to the majority of the populace only served to increase their alienation and hasten their demise. Simultaneously, the culmination of the struggle for independence heralded the acceleration of the wholesale division of land on which many of these country houses survived.

This book explores the attitudes of the state and state bodies to the country house in independent Ireland from 1922–73, and the story of the state's role in the survival or demise of the country house in Ireland is both complex and nuanced. Allen Warren has argued that the state's attitude towards the country house is hugely influential for its survival even today. Stressing the non-exceptionalism of the Irish situation in this regard, Warren argued that 'The point for the future – in common across the three countries [England, Ireland and Scotland] – is that the relationship with the state and all it represents is likely to continue to be a critical factor in the survival and development of the historic house.'[1] Therefore, what the Irish state believed to constitute national heritage, how it legislated for this in action, and the reasons behind such inclusions or exclusions, are important aspects of the history of the country house and continue to be influential factors for their use and survival today.

As regards the term 'white elephants', these are defined as extravagant but ineffectual gifts that cannot be easily disposed of, or a possession that is useless or troublesome, especially one that is expensive to maintain or difficult to dispose of. The term finds its roots in the legend of the Kings of Siam who allegedly gave rare albino elephants to courtiers who had displeased them so that they might be ruined by the cost of the upkeep of the animals. Time and again when examining the files of government departments relating to country houses in Ireland in the early decades of independence, the phrase crops up. Similarly it is used by TDs and Senators in Oireachtas debates to describe a situation of the state either being gifted houses or being asked to step in to take control of the preservation and upkeep of enormous, often crumbling, mansions that could no longer sustain themselves on the landed income on which they had been built. Government departments shied away from taking on such enormous burdens and, even when they were offered as gifts, the state recognised that, financially, they were white elephants situated in a landscape and time for which they had never been built. The gifts were magnanimous gestures by their former owners, no doubt handed over with relief to the new state, though it was a state that was only finding its own feet and realising the extent of the financial challenges that lay ahead of it.

THE COUNTRY HOUSE AND THE STATE

The country house, often called the 'Big House' in rhetoric throughout this period in Ireland, was the rural residence of a landlord predominantly dating from the eighteenth and nineteenth centuries. Terence Dooley described how these were often imposing mansions 'built to inspire awe in social equals and, indeed, deference in the lower social classes'.[2] Furthermore, he pointed out that the term 'Big House', which is unique to Ireland, was also inflected with resentment as the houses were built on 'what most tenant farmers would deem to have been confiscated land',[3] a claim dating back to the time of the English plantations in Ireland. Dooley asserts that 'above all, and particularly from the 1880s, they inspired hostility'.[4] Prevailing historiography has argued that, by the advent of the Irish Free State, the country house was viewed with enmity or apathy by the Irish public and governments alike. Olwen Purdue, writing about the burning and destruction of the country house in the revolutionary period, contended that 'not only could the Big House be targeted for attack because it was seen to represent landlordism and imperialism but, following the formation and arming of the UVF [Ulster Volunteer Force] in which a number of land-lords took a leading role, Big Houses were seen as potential arsenals ripe for raiding'.[5] R. V. Comerford has also maintained that, for the first governments of the Free State, 'architecture from earlier times – particularly in the form of the stately home or Big House – was for long regarded as a relic of oppression and some kind of affront to the nation'.[6]

The burning of country houses during the War of Independence and Civil War appeared to confirm that the continued presence of the country house and its owners was not a welcome one in an independent Ireland; particularly one that was largely run, after 1921, by the very people who had fought in these wars. As the decades of the twentieth century passed with the demise and dereliction, sale and demolition of many country houses, the blame for the destruction of this aspect of the nation's built heritage, when indeed blame began to be cast, was aimed directly at the state. However, when the rental income from land that sustained these houses disappeared and when their symbolic meaning as centres of social and political power also declined, owners often sold or abandoned their properties. In the absence of their original owners and *raison d'être* it was difficult for the newly-founded state to ascertain how they could viably use these country houses for some national purpose.

The question that arises time and time again when country houses were in danger throughout the period of 1922–73 is whether the responsibility for preserving, maintaining or using such houses should fall to the state. In a country that struggled to provide the basic necessities of healthcare or employment for its citizens, the financial commitment of state intervention would have needed robust justification. Ideas were explored as to whether the country houses could be put to private use as schools, hotels or country clubs. From the 1920s to the 1950s some were acquired for large institutions, like convents and schools, but there was never enough demand to secure them all, and while an examination of the contribution of religious orders to save many country houses from destruction is needed, it falls outside the scope of this study. Another possibility was to use these houses as historical museums or local attractions. This was not given much sustained consideration by the state as the houses were not popular enough to make this a viable option, particularly in the early decades of independence. This contrasted with the situation in England where many owners opened their homes to day-trippers in the late nineteenth and early twentieth century. Furthermore, there was no significant domestic or international tourism in Ireland in the 1920s and 1930s and country houses would have been too expensive to maintain without some such industry to make them financially viable for the state.

In fact, it has been argued as late as 2011 that 'traditionally the audience for the historic house has been narrow, and recent research demonstrates that this is still the case'.[7] This is seen most visibly, even now, in estates like Castletown, County Kildare. The amenity of its parkland is used extensively by the local population, but fewer visitors come to tour the great house or do so more than once. In 2017, while 666,541 people visited Castletown's parklands, only 32,866 visited the house.[8] Thus, in the early decades of the twentieth century, with huge social, political and economic issues to contend with, the idea that governments should spend large portions of their budgets preserving country houses was a difficult one to justify. In particular, smaller to middling country houses would never have sustained themselves as tourist attractions and, after the loss of lands from the grander houses, these could not do so through farming or rental income either. The number of country houses that the government could have acquired, retained and used in rational economic terms was, in reality, very small, if indeed any could have met these criteria.

METHODOLOGY AND APPROACH

This study is confined to the area covered by the Free State and, after 1949, the 26 counties of the Republic of Ireland. A discussion of the country house in the six-county area is an entirely different study given the distinctive political, social and economic situation in Northern Ireland. Purdue has shown how many landlords, owing particularly to their strong connections to the Unionist cause as well as the Orange Order, retained their political importance and leadership roles in communities much longer than in the south where they were effectively absent from the politics and leadership of the Free State. This allowed for their perpetuation as a social group in the North. The political establishment was also radically different, with their involvement in the Second World War and, subsequently, the control of the area by the British administration.

Throughout this book, general discussions will be interspersed by case studies. The predominantly broad national approach aims to give the reader an overall perspective on government attitudes towards the country house while allowing for an examination of governments' actions in individual case studies. Furthermore, in an age of increasing micro-histories, it is still necessary to insert these specialised studies into wider national histories. Recounting the history of the Irish country house in this way, we could compare their story of commonality or exceptionalism with the stories of the country house in other jurisdictions such as Northern Ireland and Britain.

This book broadly follows a chronological structure to trace the story of the attitudes and actions of the state to the country house. However two chapters look specifically at the actions and policy of the Office of Public Works and the Land Commission toward the country house. The addition of these two thematic chapters is deliberately designed to provide a more focussed look at the two public bodies that were most important and influential in terms of the demise or survival of the country house during this period. The first, the Office of Public Works (OPW), is examined in Chapter Three, while in Chapter Five the actions of the Land Commission, a body that has attracted much criticism over its handling of country houses, will be appraised. While the latter chapter was difficult to formulate given the limited sources available on this contentious organisation and its important work, the chapter aims to piece together as accurately as possible the intentions of that organisation. When the Land Commission records are finally opened to researchers, more of the actions of this important protagonist in the story of the country house should come to light. It should be noted that, during the period under study, the portfolio for Lands was included in various departments. For the purposes of this book, where Lands was included with any other portfolio, it is simply referred to as the Department of Lands and the Minister for Lands.

An important theme that runs throughout this book is the changing acceptance of the country house as national heritage. This evolution was only possible because the concept of national heritage, and indeed the concept of the nation itself, is a fluid category, the boundaries of which can be set by those in control to suit the needs of a particular time. Benedict Anderson argued that the nation is 'an imagined political community'.[9] Therefore, if a nation is a deliberately-created construct, then its definition is changeable and can evolve to suit the demands of the present. Comerford has similarly discussed how defining a nation is, in fact, an 'ongoing process of invention', such that 'Irishness' is not an identifiable essence, 'but a category whose ever-changing contents need to be accounted for'.[10] In addition, it has been argued that 'preservation of historic buildings relates strongly to cultural nationalism'[11] and in Ireland the 'canon' of national heritage evolved over this period, so that by the 1960s the country house was increasingly considered eligible for inclusion. Yet, for much of this period, the country house was not thought to be of sufficient importance to the nation architecturally or historically to warrant protection as a national monument.

LITERATURE

The country house and its owners have always been a fascinating theme for writers long before the discipline of history paid it any detailed attention. Maria Edgeworth's *Castle Rackrent*, published in 1800, clearly shows the interest this subject held even at that time. Throughout the century, the works of Molly Keane portrayed the country house way of life and the stories that played out behind their walls. In 1926, Lennox Robinson's play *The Big House*, about a decaying and isolated country house family, was often performed on stage or on radio. In the 1930s, Brinsley McNamara's play, *The Grand House in the City*, which reflected the demise of the country house, was staged. The appeal has

endured even when the number of country houses had significantly declined.
The alienation of the family in the country house was portrayed in 1979 in
Brian Friel's *Aristocrats* and, in 1984, a new play by Richard J. Byrne entitled
Auld Decency was premiered at the Peacock Theatre, portraying the story of an
impoverished country house family forced to live in the cellar of their house.
The theme endured in literature to such an extent that the literary interest in the
country house was itself the subject of study. In 1991, *The Big House in Ireland:
Reality and Representation* by Jacqueline Genet was published, and only one
year later came Otto Rauchbauer's *Ancestral Voices: The Big House in Anglo-
Irish Literature*.

The discipline of history also began to turn its gaze to these houses and
their owners as worthy of study in their own right, but not until the 1970s and
1980s. Many books were published that both illustrated and fed into the growing
interest in the country house and highlighted aspects of the houses' art, architecture and history. As Dooley has noted 'despite their centrality to Irish history
(or possibly because of it!), it was not until the 1970s that Irish Big Houses and
the family and servant communities who occupied them began to attract the
level of attention from historians and specialists in art and architecture that they
merit.'[12] Since the 1970s, a significant body of work has been published on the
history of the country house, their art collections, architecture, or disappearance from the Irish landscape.[13] However, the first in-depth academic history
of the country house in Ireland was not published until 2001. Dooley's *The
Decline of the Big House in Ireland* brought a new dimension to the study of the
Irish country house by examining the reasons for its demise within the context
of economic, social and political developments. Since then, historiography on
the country house in Ireland has grown considerably. More recently Purdue's
The Big House in the North of Ireland examined the decline of the country house
and landed class, and, significantly, their determined survival in the region of
the six counties of Northern Ireland.[14] The work is an important analysis of
the situation in the North and provides a valuable comparative study to the
story of the country house in the south. Despite such a proliferation of country
house literature in recent years, Dooley stressed the need for an examination
of attitudes towards the country house in independent Ireland in a piece entitled: 'National patrimony and political perceptions of the Irish country house
in post-independence Ireland'.[15] This work highlighted some of the broader
contextual changes nationally that contributed to a progressive change in attitudes from apathy or antagonism to appreciation. It drew attention to the need
for a more detailed study of this area, emphasising how influential attitudes

towards the country house were for its survival. Warren has also argued for a timely reappraisal of the country house in Ireland, claiming that

> There is little to suggest any fundamental re-evaluation in the over-arching narrative of the decline and disappearance of the Irish landed class in terms of land, social relations and political or cultural power ... the dominant Irish chronological narrative seems so robust and self-evident with its emphasis on the land question, the symbolic and physical decline and destruction of the 'Big House', and the exclusion of the 'alien' families that had exploited their advantages over the previous three centuries.[16]

Hence, there is a need to analyse, in detail, the changes in attitudes, from early antagonism or apathy of the state and public towards these properties to a situation toward the end of the century when they were beginning to be widely regarded as an important part of the national heritage.[17] This study intends to address this part of their history, which will not only fill a gap in the historiography of this field, but still has relevance for how the country house is used, lived in, marketed and survives today.

SOURCES

This study has its basis in government papers and official records, the most informative of which were the files of the Department of the Taoiseach and the Department of Finance. The former, in particular, contain a large volume of primary source material concerning country houses, most particularly the offers of such properties to the state as gifts, as well as documentation detailing wider public pressure in terms of preservation, government responses, and overall attitudes to the fate of country houses. It appears that the reason the Department of the Taoiseach papers are so comprehensive in relation to some of these cases, and in certain instances contain all the papers from the other relevant departments, was because the Taoiseach's department took the principal role in these cases, at least until the 1960s. This was especially true in cases of country houses offered as gifts, since these offers were often addressed initially to the Taoiseach, and so responses were directed through this office. Even apart from these cases, the department was heavily involved in orchestrating government debates around these issues, corresponding in relation to and facilitating inter-departmental discussions and arranging cabinet meetings.

The Department of Finance files are also revealing and, while the number of papers on some of these issues is smaller, the information that can be gleaned is important. In most cases, apart from a few singular examples of the Taoiseach imposing his own opinion, decisions surrounding country houses, whether it be their preservation, use, or acceptance as gifts, rested primarily with the Department of Finance, which controlled government purse strings. In fact, the decisive factor in governments' decisions and policies toward country houses was economics and, in this regard, the Department of Finance held much of the power to act. Other significant sources are the OPW files. As the office was responsible for heritage preservation during this time, particularly under the 1930 National Monuments Act, an examination of the OPW files is extremely useful especially in relation to assessing what powers this body did or did not consider it had to preserve the country house and whether they used such powers. Unfortunately, the most relevant files of the Irish Land Commission, a body often implicated in the history of the destruction of the country house, are not yet fully available for examination. An enquiry was made to the Records Branch of the Department of Agriculture, Food and the Marine, where the records are held, but the Branch replied that the relevant files 'are not available to the general public for research etc., unlike other State documents in the custody of the National Archives'.[18]

The continuity in arguments advanced by government departments in relation to country houses over lengthy periods is notable, with little difference wrought by changes of government. This points to the fact that the most influential people were frequently not the ministers, who certainly fronted the department but changed periodically. Rather, many civil servants were a reliable constant over long periods and remained in their positions despite changing governments. They knew how various policies operated in practice and the constraints of departments in terms of legal powers and finances. These frequently unnamed or unacknowledged civil servants were deeply involved in the discussions that took place between departments on issues covered in this study, with government ministers often only entering the frame when approval was needed, if at all.[19] Attitudes taken by government departments were therefore also attributable to the civil servants who were recommending policy positions and priorities.

An interesting aspect of examining the files of government departments has been to consider how difficult it will be for historians to research this area in the future. Since the introduction of the Freedom of Information (FOI) Acts in 1997, the documents that are created as official records by departments are now carefully considered in light of possible future publication and public consumption. What is incredible to note in regard to the files examined for this book is that, during the period under study, FOI did not exist, and, for most of the period, neither did electronic filing or communication. These earlier records, therefore, represent an essential source of history with handwritten notes in the margin often offering the most revealing glimpses of the types of opinions and debates that were taking place, even within departments. On the other hand, they can be difficult to understand due to unintelligible handwriting or fading ink. Additionally, many documents are missing or absent from the correct file, or the handwritten notes or comments are either not signed by anyone or signed with a set of initials, making the real author difficult to recognise. The HR records of government departments and their organisation charts for this period are also difficult to come by; armed only with a set of initials, it has, at times, proven very difficult to identify staff. In the end, it is not significant to the broader history that a particular official in a department cannot be definitively identified. What matters is that, from their comments, we know, and can tell, that there were different opinions on the fate and importance of the country house among government officials, that staff felt they could voice different opinions, and that perhaps these opinions reflected the differences in the wider public's views on this issue as well.

Oireachtas debates from the Dáil and Seanad chambers are also fruitful sources for an investigation of political attitudes towards the country house. Unlike private government files, in parliamentary debates deputies were conscious of being quoted in the media and wanted to represent constituents on issues of local importance. Therefore, the debates are not only revealing in terms of political attitudes, but also obliquely shed light on public attitudes. Rhetoric in these speeches was almost always delivered with constituents and their views in mind: appeasing the populace to win popularity was then, as now, as important as debating in a realistic and rational way on emotive issues. Furthermore, opposition TDs had greater freedom to defer to hyperbole, while governments' views were muted somewhat by the facts that civil servants lay before them in briefs and memos. While the more robust and significant debates often took place in the Dáil chambers, it was important to examine the records from both chambers, as members of the Seanad were at times at greater liberty to discuss issues concerning these houses at longer length or in more detail. Furthermore, they provide a different perspective to the view of Dáil deputies, with Senators being drawn from a wider variety of backgrounds and, particularly in the early period of the Free State, a number being chosen from the landed class or members with an artistic or cultural background. This necessarily meant their views of the situation were different from the majority of deputies in Dáil Éireann who were drawn primarily from a predominantly farming or professional, middle-class background, which naturally moulded their attitudes. Elaine A. Byrne has argued for recognition of the importance of the early Seanad established in the 1920s as a 'non-partisan chamber' that provided an effective challenge to the government of the day as the 'de-facto opposition'.[20] The first Seanad was broadly representative of the many different religious and social groups in the Free State and included 36 Catholics, 20 Protestants, three members of the Religious Society of Friends (Quakers) and one Jewish representative.[21] In fact, while the Seanad has often been viewed in retrospect as a harmless attempt by the embryonic state to be seen to incorporate all aspects of society, Byrne has shown how important the chamber was. Cosgrave's government relied on the expertise of those in the Seanad, as the first government was composed of young, inexperienced deputies with no parliamentary experience at cabinet level. Similarly, only two of the 128 members of the Dáil elected in 1922 had any parliamentary experience.[22]

Wider public and media reports of, and attitudes to, country houses and the perceived role of the government with regard to them are evident in newspaper coverage throughout this period. It is interesting to note that sometimes in departmental files there are clippings on these issues from various papers, or discussions were brought up as the result of widespread or adverse media coverage, illustrating how departments were cognisant of the wider debates that were taking place in the media. They were also attuned to the public justifiability and impact of their decisions and policy-making. Debates over the destruction or imminent destruction of country houses often took place in the 'letters to the editor' sections of the papers where the widely varying view points of the public are evident. The most extensive coverage in relation to these properties was given in the *Irish Times*, possibly because of its history – it was considered at the time to be an upper-class publication. Originally founded in 1859 as the voice of southern unionism, after the Treaty the paper's natural constituency declined dramatically. In 1911, the Church of Ireland had 249,535 members in the 26 counties, although this had fallen to 164,215 by 1926 and to 145,030 by 1936.[23] Emigration to Northern Ireland and Britain, the withdrawal of the British army and their families, and the burning of a number of country houses all contributed to the decline. That said, circulation remained relatively steady: in 1920 daily sales stood at 32,500, by 1922 daily sales had reached 34,500 and by 1926 they stood at 36,500.[24] This indicates that readership of the paper was changing. Examination of the *Irish Times'* coverage of the challenges facing the country house in independent Ireland is also important to this study because it was the paper most widely featured among clippings in departmental files.

Some of the sources interspersed throughout the book come from oral history sources. While official historiography has often been critical of oral history, it does represent an invaluable source for revealing what people thought and felt about particular times and places. It gives life, colour and reality to the impacts of national legislative decisions and glimpses into how different sections of the population thought of each other and of themselves. Certainly, such sources must be approached carefully as to their veracity. However, that does not make them less valuable. History should be an attempt to faithfully describe a period of time and what it was like for the people who lived through it. The inclusion of snippets from oral history throughout this text is an attempt to tell this story as fully as possible and to give a voice to those who lived in the country houses and who are otherwise largely absent from the political debates and government files at the core of this work.

ONE

AFTER INDEPENDENCE, 1922–32

In 1923 the Irish countryside was dotted with stately houses that looked out on a land ravaged by the War of Independence, the Civil War and the deep scars of bitterness, division and resentment that they left in their wake. In most cases the houses were surrounded by small farmers, subsistence landholders and a landless section of the population in rural Ireland who felt that they had nothing in common with country house owners and who were increasingly anxious for the break-up of the estates and the redistribution of land. Terence Dooley has described how 'during these years [1919–23], landlords, largely because of their socio-political, economic and religious backgrounds, were to suffer outrage and intimidation on a scale the like of which their class had not experienced in living memory, not even at the height of the land war in the 1880s.'[1] The situation in which the country house found itself was as a result of the national, political and social context of this period. Nevertheless, in the scheme of issues that the fledgling Free State was faced with addressing, the problems of viability affecting the country house were not considered significant.

THE FREE STATE AT INDEPENDENCE

The year 1922 saw the establishment of the Irish Free State of 26 counties to be governed by its own parliament with dominion status under the King of England as a result of the 1921 Treaty following the War of Independence.[2] The first party that came to power in this new state was Cumann na nGaedheal under the President of the Executive Council, W. T. Cosgrave.[3] This government had a monumental task ahead of it. The country was still a relatively poor, predominantly agriculture-based economy. In Dublin much had been destroyed in the war and social conditions were generally poor. Unsafe and unsanitary tenements were widespread and the mortality rate of citizens high.[4] The economy also needed to be tackled as 'the resources of the Free State could come nowhere near funding social expenditure at the levels set by imperial Governments.'[5] In addition, as Mel Farrell has shown, the Cumann na nGaedheal party was not a unified whole but consisted of disparate elements that had joined together under the broad banner of pro-treaty nationalism.[6] Politically, the whole apparatus of the Free State was on shaky ground with a significant section of the elected representatives unwilling to join Dáil Éireann on account of the oath to King George V that was enshrined in the Anglo-Irish Treaty of 1921. To add to the difficulties faced by the first administration there was a split among politicians, revolutionaries and the general public, between those who were happy to accept the 26-county division and those who would settle for nothing less than full independence for the 32 counties and the severing of all links to Britain. This division led to the eruption of civil war in 1922, which plunged the country into chaos as the new state struggled to establish law and order; this was felt particularly in areas such as west Munster that were hotbeds of anti-Treaty activities.[7] The involvement of individuals in the War of Independence, the stance they took in the Civil War, and the bitter memories and recriminations that followed were to dominate political tensions for much of the first decade of independence.

DESTRUCTION AND DEFERENCE

The areas that saw the greatest anti-Treaty resistance were also the principal locations where most of the country houses of the Anglo-Irish landed class were burned.[8] While the burning of these mansions had begun during the War of Independence, the Civil War saw it become a much more prominent feature and weapon of retaliation. During the War of Independence, from January 1920 to the calling of the Anglo-Irish Truce in July 1921, an estimated 76 country houses were burned in the 26-county area of the present Irish Republic,[9] predominantly in counties most affected by violence, especially Cork where 26 were burned.[10] However, James S. Donnelly Jr has estimated that, including other types of dwelling such as suburban villas, the figure for Cork may be closer to 50, although it is difficult to arrive at exact figures.[11] In the Civil War that followed, significantly more were razed to the ground. An estimated 199 houses were burned between January 1922 and April 1923, nearly three times more than the figure for the War of Independence.[12]

The reasons for their destruction were numerous. Frequently, during the War of Independence, they were burned in retaliation for British attacks on citizens, particularly by the loathed Black and Tans. Agrarian issues – always of paramount importance in Ireland and one of the most significant driving forces behind the struggle for Independence – also led to the burning of houses by land-hungry farmers anxious for the break-up of estates and the redistribution of land.[13] Furthermore, throughout the War of Independence, some of these country houses were used as barracks or bases for training camps when commandeered by the Irish forces, so that when the Civil War broke out both sides destroyed houses that were rumoured to be considered for such use. After the establishment of the Free State houses were also burned because they were the homes of Free State Senators. Following the Free State's decision to embark on a policy of executing anti-Treaty volunteers, Liam Lynch, Chief of Staff of the anti-Treaty Irish Republican Army (IRA), issued a notice identifying legitimate targets, which included Senators of the Free State government and their residences. This order was effected through 'a campaign of intimidation, kidnappings, attempts on their lives and the destruction of their houses.'[14] Dooley has described how 'following Liam Lynch's order to burn the houses of Senators, a total of thirty-seven were burned, sixteen of which could be described as big houses.'[15] A number of the Senators in the first Seanad were of the landed class, in an attempt by the new government at inclusion of the former political, and usually unionist, elite. This policy meant that it was the section of Anglo-Irish country house owners who actually chose to stay in Ireland and contribute to the political life of the fledgling state who were the targets for arson. Many left Ireland, disillusioned by the reward meted out for their support for the new state, never to return. Sir Horace Plunkett, proponent and founder of the Co-operative Society in Ireland, whose house at Kilteragh in Dublin was destroyed, was one such exile. Other country houses were looted in the search for arms, some were attacked because of the historical reputation of landlords and local or historical grievances against them, while others were burned to the ground for no better reason than local hooliganism.[16] Then, as now, genuine social radicalism also attracts those simply intent on destruction. The fact that burning a country house was a greater statement than burning smaller houses of local loyalists was also an incentive to their destruction. Additionally, it was presumably easier for the largely Catholic nationalists to burn a house than to take a life to prove the strength of their arms.

Whatever the motivation, this campaign highlighted that country houses were viewed as an alien presence in Ireland.[17] Interestingly, in Jane O'Hea O'Keeffe's book documenting voices from the great houses of Cork and Kerry, most of the families contend that their particular house was not burned due to the family having had good relations with the tenantry around them, that they were good to the local people during the Famine, or that they were good employers.[18] While these testimonies must be viewed with a critical eye as to their accuracy, they remain an important source of oral history from those who lived in the country house. Maurice Hugh O'Connell of Lakeview House, Killarney, contended that the O'Connell home at Lakeview remained untouched partly because the family were Catholic and well-thought of locally, but also because many of the people in the local IRA either worked in the house or had relatives who did. This was a situation that must have been replicated all over the country and may have contributed to the sense of deference that was often reported by country house families of the arsonists, even when they proceeded to burn down the families' homes.

This is further illustrated in the fact that, unlike in Russia, for example, few of these landlords were physically harmed during this period, and they were usually informed that their house was to be burned down and were given time to evacuate.[19] The comparison is not unfounded and is also contemporary to the time, but where in Ireland the violence was minimal, relatively speaking, Douglas Smith has shown how the Russian upper classes were 'chased from their homes and their property expropriated, forced to clean the streets as a form of public humiliation, sent to labor camps, [or] killed with a bullet to the back of the head for the crime of their social origin'.[20] Smith has described the magnitude as well as the chaotic and violent nature of the campaign of terror against the elite classes in Russia as one of unfathomable scale, greater even than one of the greatest class revolutions in Europe, the French Revolution. While there are no accurate recorded numbers for the amount of people who died in Russia because of the class into which they were born, Smith describes how, by the 1940s, 'the nobility had been annihilated'.[21]

Given the passions involved in any battle for independence, the small number of the ascendancy class in Ireland killed during the War of Independence and the Civil War is a notable and exceptional feature of the Irish story. For example, Maurice Hugh O'Connell recalled how on one occasion, 'the IRA came looking for weapons at Lakeview … They were met by my grandmother, Mary Pauline, who recognised them and promptly told their leader to go home to his mother.'[22] Similarly, John Leslie, speaking about the survival of Tarbert House, County Kerry, during the revolutionary period, maintained that one reason for its survival was the fact that the leader of the local IRA was an employee of the house.[23] While this time was one of fear and destruction for country house owners when the dust settled on these spates of burnings, as Charles Lysaght contends, 'most aristocratic and gentry families were still in possession of their ancestral homes and still much better off than other sections of the population.'[24]

COMPENSATION

During the revolutionary period, while injury to persons was rare the damage and destruction of country houses was not. In the aftermath of this violence, the Free State government attempted to legislate for payments of compensation for property and damages inflicted during the Civil War. Those who had lost their houses could apply for compensation under the 1923 Damage to Property (Compensation) Act,[25] although the conditions that had to be met in order to be eligible for funding reduced many people's chances of being recompensed. For example, owners had to prove that they had attempted to defend and protect their property, something no non-resident owner could do. There was no compensation for the loss of contents and there was the question of market value for such a house, now in a climate where these mansions had outlived their purpose and had little sale value. Dooley has illustrated how for the majority of owners compensation was inadequate and slow to be paid, if awarded at all.[26] Most owners were awarded only a portion of the costs they had applied for and struggled with the terms attached to the compensation, such as a reinstatement condition. This was problematic when many did not want to build a house again in such proportions, could not afford to, or, given the violence and intimidation they had experienced – particularly from their own tenants or local area – did not want to remain resident in Ireland. They either left without compensation or attempted to rebuild, although this was difficult since payments were only made on completion of work and were slow in coming.[27] In fact, Dooley has concluded that 'after independence, Free State government policy, official and otherwise, was unsympathetic in terms of compensating country house owners for the losses suffered or in any way encouraging in terms of helping them to rebuild.'[28] However, this was a government severely constrained financially and also aware that there was little use in rebuilding such houses when they were no longer economically viable. In addition, many other sections of the population had also experienced trauma and destruction of property during the Civil War and were also looking for recompense.

Therefore, the problematic nature of compensation for country house owners was not a cause for great concern among a populace who primarily viewed owners as figures to be vilified, who were seen as disloyal to nationalist ideals or the Free State, and also who were perceived as a wealthy class given the size of their mansions that had been destroyed. In addition, much of the rest of the population had their own problems to be concerned with such as poverty, emigration and the political legacy of bitterness from the Civil War that divided communities and families. Thus, while many owners could not afford to rebuild a grand country house, the general perception was that they were a moneyed class, which did not induce many politicians to attempt to ease their financial burdens. In a debated motion by the Minister for Finance on compensation claims in 1922, Labour Teáchta Dála (TD) for Tipperary, Daniel Morrissey, made this clear when he claimed that, in the main, 'the destroyed property consists of mansions throughout the country, and really an extreme hardship has been imposed on the workers that have been thrown out of work as a direct result of this.'[29] It was the workers, rather than the owners, who were portrayed as the victims here. In reality, if he had spoken about the hardship of not having the money to rebuild a mansion he would not long have kept his seat in Dáil Éireann, either then or now. In the same debate, fellow Labour TD William Davin, elected for Leix-Offaly, went further when he promulgated the idea that 'the people who owned these mansions were, generally speaking, the remnants of England's loyal garrison in this country, who have cleared out to a more congenial home, and as far as I can gather, at least from newspaper comments, do not intend to return to this country.'[30] This view informed Davin's argument that 'they will take whatever will be given by the Irish people so far as money is concerned',[31] while his concern for the 'unfortunate' destruction of large mansions was mainly because they were 'places where a good number of people have got employ-ment'.[32] Naturally the views of the Labour deputies tended toward the concerns of the ordinary worker and can also be seen to represent them.

The benefit to the country of a reinstatement condition being attached to compensation for destroyed country houses was also considered questionable. In the Dáil, Dublin County independent TD Darrell Figgis argued:

> Instead of making this full re-instatement condition mandatory, there ought to be some provision in the Bill … by which this re-instatement condition may be put aside until it is actually discovered whether the amount of demesne land to be apportioned to such and such a landlord would really justify a house being built in the same large and magnificent proportions as the houses that, in some cases, were destroyed.[33]

The President of the Executive Council, W. T. Cosgrave, described rebuilding as 'an extravagance, an extravagance upon the person who would have to maintain such houses, and an extravagance upon the state in reconstructing houses of such dimensions' and he made a case for 'substituted dwellings or for a more useful class of house'.[34] Here, he was thinking of both the state and owners, as most of the latter were finding the maintenance of such houses a serious financial burden at this time. In fact, independent Senator Professor William Magennis maintained 'that for certain white elephant houses – great mansions – there might in the new regime be no market value at all.'[35] Similarly they were depicted by Labour TD for Dublin County, Thomas Johnson, as a 'burden rather than a benefit'.[36] Senator Sir John Keane, himself an owner of such a property, actually agreed with these sentiments and argued that owners in most cases did not want compensation to buy a 'white elephant' but to acquire suitable accommodation.[37] Despite this, the *Irish Times* reported that, in a Seanad debate on the Damage to Property bill, the Minister for Finance, Ernest Blythe, insisted that 'the Government was very anxious that people should rebuild, and that people whose houses were burned should remain in the country and rebuild their own houses.'[38] Conversely, the chairman of the Senate, Lord Glenavy, claimed in reply that 'nobody was anxious to have a building reinstated in its old form. It had grown out of their needs and they wanted a different style of architecture. They found that some of those houses had not been occupied as residences for a considerable period, and they were generally troubled as to what a proper estimate would be.'[39]

Even the payment of low levels of compensation for the loss of country houses was somewhat controversial. Farmer's Party TD for Tipperary, Michael Heffernan, declared during a vote on property losses compensation in 1925:

> A feeling exists that the owners of these mansions have got better terms in proportion to the losses suffered than people who had smaller houses and places which were very much less pretentious, destroyed. A mansion may have been built 70 or 80 years ago at

a cost of £100,000, and I need not point out to the Minister that if placed on the open market now it might be a white elephant; it might not be worth anything.[40]

Deputy Heffernan touched on an important point here, namely that some of these country houses were not very old by the early twentieth century – some were only 70, 80, or 100 years old, a similar age to many other buildings and homes throughout the country that were not deemed 'historical' properties. Against the resentment directed at compensation for country house owners vocalised by Deputy Heffernan, the *Irish Times*, undoubtedly with its own constituency in mind, strove to emphasise their local worth beyond the market value of the building and reported that 'anxiety is being caused in many directions by the serious economic disturbance due to the destruction of the mansions and country houses of the old gentry'.[41] The paper was presumably referring to demesne workers, as Dooley has illustrated how many of the staff employed by the country houses were from England, particularly those hired for the most prestigious posts. The 1911 census returns show that out of 767 servants returned, 470 were Irish and 'only 14 per cent were locally born emphasising the fact that landlords preferred to "import" their servants. Because of this, big houses were not of great economic benefit to locals seeking employment on a permanent basis.'[42] This also served to foster resentment with the local population with its implication that they were not to be trusted or that only an English or Scottish Protestant was worthy of working in the most important roles inside the house. Arguments like that advanced by the *Irish Times* above were in a minority with owners alienated as never before following the revolutionary period.[43] Nonetheless, Lysaght argues that while they may have been deprived of governmental power in the new state, in their own localities 'they still commanded and expected social deference.'[44]

LAND DIVISION

Country houses appeared now as buildings that had outlived their function, particularly with the land acts continuing to strip them of their estates. Legislating for the division of land was not a process that was initiated by independent Irish governments. This process began with the 1881 Land Law (Ireland) Act and the 1885 Ashbourne Act under the British administration. These land acts and later ones began to facilitate the transfer of land from landlords to tenant farmers. The 1903 Wyndham Land Act was one of the most influential in this regard, greatly expediting the process of land division. It induced landlords to sell by making available the payment of the entire purchase money in cash and a 12 per cent bonus on the sale of estates. It also made purchase a realistic goal for tenants and guaranteed that the annuity payable would represent a substantial reduction on their formal rent.[45] Many landlords availed of the opportunity and sold their land for a good return. In fact, the trustees of Carton received such a generous sum from the sale of most of the Leinster estate that 'the family might very well have prospered long into the future, but the coincidence of family tragedies and external forces (including the First World War and the ensuing worldwide economic depression), meant that this was not to be.'[46] The Wyndham Act began the significant re-carving of Ireland's landed estates, many of which passed from the hands of a minority elite to those of the majority tenant farmers. The British government introduced this legislation hoping that, by attempting to address the struggle for land reform, they would quash the demand for Home Rule.[47] However, it was also part of a wider phenomenon of a modernising Europe.

By 1914, over two-thirds of Irish tenants had become proprietors of their own holdings. Owning land was one thing, but being able to make a living from the size of that land was another; hence, agrarian issues continued to dominate the national agenda but became increasingly about viability rather than ownership as the twentieth century progressed. There were again outbreaks of agrarian agitation in the period 1917–23, in particular in the midlands and the west from the landless and small landholders. The agitation meant that the new government first dealt with land as its priority to try to return order to the countryside and because anti-Treaty proponents were feeding off the agrarian agitation to promote discontent. In any event, the land acts enacted before 1922 had not served to end landlordism in Ireland and so, with agrarian and political grievance inextricably linked to the Irish struggle for independence, land was one of the most important issues that the first Free State government was under pressure to address. As Olwen Purdue has argued: 'the increasingly widespread and aggressive nature of land agitation, particularly in the south and west, gave the Free State Government little choice but to quickly legislate for further land reform.'[48] They did so with haste, and in 1923 another land act was passed,[49] which was often called the Hogan Land Act after Patrick Hogan, the first minister with responsibility for land in the Free State. Under its terms

> All tenanted land wherever situated and all untenanted land situated in any congested districts county and such untenanted land situated elsewhere as the Land Commission shall, before the appointed day, declare to be required for the purpose of relieving congestion or of facilitating the resale of tenanted land, shall by virtue of this Act vest in the Land Commission on the appointed day ...[50]

So, while it was a land purchase act, it also introduced a much more dramatic and unprecedented policy of tackling the relief of congestion through the compulsory acquisition and redistribution of lands.[51] This policy, whereby land, which was owned by landlords, graziers and large farmers, could be forcibly taken from them by the state in return for compensation, was described by landed families as 'little better than expropriation'.[52] There were to be limited exceptions, such as land purchased under previous land acts, as well as home farms and demesnes, although these exceptions could be overcome by the Land Commission if it needed the land to relieve congestion.[53] However, the process was slow and hindered by the administration of appeals against land chosen for acquisition as well as the use of exemptions, such as the protection of demesnes, which allowed some landlords to hold on to much of their land. In fact, this was important as many of the houses that survived into the twenty-first century were those that had managed to retain their demesnes, since they could then be sold on to wealthy new owners seeking privacy, or hotels and country clubs seeking grounds.

A similar land act was passed in Northern Ireland in 1925,[54] so that 'by the end of the 1920s nearly all tenanted land in Northern Ireland had passed out of the ownership of the landed class and any remaining tenanted land would soon follow.'[55] Land division was a hugely complex procedure, so further land acts were needed not just to create new conditions to acquire land, but also to refine difficulties in previous legislation. The 1931 and 1933 Acts attempted to overcome the difficulties associated with the 1923 Act and speed up the process.[56] Patrick J. Sammon, who worked in the Land Commission for many years, has maintained that 1933 was an important year for the Land Commission. The 1933 Act stemmed from Fianna Fáil's commitment to increase land division to 100,000 acres a year.[57] Fianna Fáil had been successful in the 1932 election, not least because many were unhappy with the speed and scale of land division under Cumann na nGaedheal. A further act followed in 1936. These acts served their purpose as 'by the late 1930s, the old landed estates had eventually been broken up in Ireland.'[58]

After 1937, the rate of division had slowed down because most large untenanted estates had been divided. In the early years the non-residential estates of the landlord class were the primary targets of the Land Commission, but as land reform policy changed during the 1930s and 1940s, any large farm deemed unproductive or not creating enough employment was just as likely to be targeted. Naturally, this created an environment of hostility and suspicion around the Land Commission's work in rural Ireland. However, the 1933 and previous land acts were largely successful at dividing up the landed estates among tenant farmers, migrants and those on uneconomic holdings. While other land acts were passed in the following decades, these primarily refined the previously enacted legislation. 1965 saw the last land act passed by an Irish government, aimed at preventing the purchase of land by non-Irish citizens who would neither live on nor use it.[59] From this time on, the activities of the Land Commission – a body that was responsible for the biggest bloodless social revolution in Ireland – began to wind down.

The land acts were important for independent governments in terms of appeasing a voting populace who equated independence with the confiscation of land from the Anglo-Irish landlords and its subsequent division among 'native Irish' farmers. As these acts served to re-divide the Irish landscape, they proved to be the final nails in the coffin for the survival of many country houses on income generated from lands. For these mansions to be in any way self-sustaining, many more than 100 or 200 acres were needed. They were built at a time when the house was at the centre of vast estates of land with large rental incomes. Naturally, this could not continue in a newly independent – mainly agricultural and rural – state where so many had no land at all or holdings that were too small to be viable. However, it should be remembered that, even before the 1870s, landlordism was on the wane throughout Ireland, England and continental Europe due to a myriad of factors: falling property values, the emergence of new agricultural markets and political democratisation.[60] There were other influential factors in the Irish context too: the rise of the farming interest lobby group in the years after the Famine, and its political mobilisation after the agricultural crises of the later 1870s; disengaged managerial policies; an inefficient rent structure; the rise of a democratic society; and the crushing tragedies delivered by the First World War that saw many families and houses deprived of their son and heir. Alvin Jackson has argued that 'the most comprehensive blows to the landed position came – ironically – from the very policy which was designed as a rescue mechanism and which was embodied in a succession of acts from 1885 through to 1909: land purchase.'[61] Combined with the agricultural depression in the 1920s and the Great Depression, from 1929 onwards, the viability of the country house had all but vanished.

In spite of the land distribution initiated by the land acts up to 1923, Dooley has shown how the 1926 census, the first taken by the Free State, indicated that 'Protestants who made up only 8.4 per cent of the population of the Free State, owned 28 per cent of the farms over 200 acres in size'.[62] Nonetheless, the land acts passed by the British administration had started a process from which there was no going back and which had already left many country houses bereft of enough rental income to sustain them. Sir Cosmo Haskard of

Ardnagashel, County Cork, elucidated on how life had already become very strained for country house owners, even before the advent of the Free State. He said, 'Life at Ardnagashel for the Hutchins family during succeeding years became more difficult. Resources were dwindling and the economic situation took its toll. Rental income had all but ceased due to the disposal of lands and the sale of tenants properties following the passing of the five British Land Acts between 1870 and 1909.'[63] When country houses were divorced from their original purposes and stripped of their demesnes through the land acts, they soon became 'anachronisms in the Irish countryside'.[64]

ISOLATION AND VIABILITY

After independence, the demesne walls had become increasingly symbolic of a divide between the inhabitants of the house and the local populace. This was also a consequence of owners' desire to remain separate from local communities with whom they had rarely deigned to associate. The lines of division between the landed class and the population continually remained an issue in Irish life throughout the twentieth century. As early as 1848, John Mitchel wrote in the *United Irishman* that 'the time for conciliation of the landlord class is past ... I believe rights of property as they are termed must be invaded.'[65] Comerford has also elucidated how their status as a landlord class wrote them out of the new definition of Irish nationality that was being created. He argued: 'much of the rhetoric of nationality is concerned with justifying possession of the land ... in modern Ireland, the lords of the soil were supposed to be of different stock from the rest of the population. In the 1880s, the Irish nation was re-imagined so as to exclude them.'[66]

Any arguments that emphasised the positive effects of having such a class remain in the country came from their own ranks and were primarily articulated in the Seanad, where some of the Anglo-Irish class were still able to expound their views on the issues of the day. Thirty out of sixty Senators were appointed by the President of the Executive Council with particular regard for those groups not adequately represented in the Dáil. [67] Through this political outlet, some country house owners decided to take an active political role in the new state. Free State Senator, poet, author and medical practitioner— who had been a supporter of Sinn Féin – Dr Oliver St John Gogarty, was one such figure. He maintained that, despite historical associations, the houses and establishments rented for the hunting season, primarily by the gentry, were financially important to the country.[68] His own residence in Connemara, Renvyle House, was burned to the ground in 1923 owing to his position as a Free State Senator. In a 1929 Seanad debate on game preservation, he ironically encouraged a realistic, rather than idealistic, view of the nation when he proposed that 'even the Gaeltacht to some extent depends on the circulation of money.'[69] He highlighted the economic dangers when vacant houses were being left, instead, to decay, but was aware that it was not a popular concern, commenting satirically that 'as long as we are going to consider that the salt of the earth lives in the Gaeltacht it may be possible to allow a number of gentlemen's houses in the country to fall into ruins to further our patriotism.'[70] Similarly, in a 1923 debate, independent Senator Colonel Maurice Moore argued that he would like to see the derelict mansions and demesnes built up again, despite the fact that 'the society and people of those times have passed away'.[71] He went on to emphasise his belief in the necessity of having this class in society. He was also careful, though, to base this necessity on their role and value to the country and not as a preservation of privilege, emphasising: 'I think it is necessary to have a leisured class in this country, able by their money and the extent of their land to do a good deal in the way of setting an example, trying experiments in agriculture, and affording an object-lesson to the people of the district around them.'[72] In the final analysis, however, these opinions were being voiced in a chamber whose deliberations did not reach far beyond its own benches and to an audience of which many had a vested interest in the preservation of this way of life.

Therefore, the country houses were in a precarious position in the early decades of post-independence Ireland, with decimated rental income and advancing age making them ever more expensive to maintain. In addition, the 1929 Wall Street Crash, worldwide economic depression and the decline in value of stocks and shares, in which many owners had invested money, all contributed to owners' inability to maintain their houses.[73] The fallout was manifold, with many forced to sell if possible, move out, abandon the property or possibly continue to live in the house, although in much reduced circumstances and with little money to invest in the property's upkeep. When the income-generating lands were confiscated, contents were often sold to pay the bills and the country house itself usually followed.[74] Many houses that were sold were turned to new uses. Religious orders bought and saved a number by converting them into convents, religious institutions or schools, such as Emo Court, County Laois, which was bought by the Jesuits from the Land Commission in 1930 as a novitiate. In fact, before 1935, 'Battersby and Sons alone had sold at least sixty country houses in Ireland including Bishopscourt; Kilashee; Kylemore

Abbey and Ravensdale.'[75] Nevertheless, there was little sustained market for these houses that were predominantly difficult to sell. This proved to be the case for many mansions acquired by the Land Commission during the course of their division work, so that demolition or ruin were often the only options left for these once grand houses.[76] Burton Hall, County Carlow, was one such house, which was sold to the Land Commission in 1927 and subsequently demolished in 1930. Dooley has argued that 'the coincidence of the break-up of estates, increased taxation and the economic depression in the 1920s and 1930s, sounded the death knell for so many Irish big houses.'[77]

However, the decline of the country house was lived out by a small minority of citizens who resided in private mansion houses. Owners' claims that they were now far from wealthy were not taken too seriously in popular perception, given that an impoverished gentry may have lost some of the fortune they once had, but many were still in a wealthy, or at least perceived wealthy position, compared to a large proportion of the population. In the first decades of independence, then, the perception that these ostentatious properties were now burdens rather than luxuries was not one that had widespread currency or appeal and popular opinion believed that life within the demesne walls was continuing in all its extravagance. In a 1931 Dáil debate on the Intoxicating Liquor Bill, Fianna Fáil TD for Cork-East, William Kent, embodied such sentiment by arguing that the government should be targeting 'the people in stately mansions and banqueting halls who spend thousands of pounds in costly liqueurs, champagnes and crushed port'.[78] Others attempted to counter this with the newly cultivated idea, close to reality for some, of the impoverished owner. In a Dáil debate in July 1924 on the Finance bill, Major Bryan Cooper contended: 'persons who own such houses need every concession and would be glad to get it even if it were only a five pound note.'[79] The heavy burdens of taxes and death duties were not the only expenses involved in ownership of a country house in this period, and the increasing costs of maintenance and preservation, combined with decreasing income from the land, contributed to the sale, abandonment or destruction of many properties that were no longer economically viable. Ursula Leslie remembered that on her first visit to Tarbert House, County Kerry, before her marriage into the family, her father cautioned 'those old houses are like vultures … They flap their wings and they suck the blood out of young people. Then, when you get old, they start to look at the next generation to see what they can do for them!'[80]

Dooley has shown how the Free State inherited its rates of death duty from Britain which had, particularly since Lloyd George's 'People's Budget' of 1909, risen significantly and hit landowners hard. Previously, the low rates and exemptions for landowners in proportion to those of the rest of the population amounted to what Dooley terms 'impressive privileges'.[81] Under Free State governments, they also rose and by 1950 the rates had increased dramatically, rising progressively from 6 per cent to 41.6 per cent in the intervening period. Simultaneously, from 1925 to 1930, a total of £5 million was paid in death duties in Ireland and this amount rose to a total of £13.4 million for the period 1945 to 1950.[82] The same 1909 budget had introduced a super tax on gross incomes over £5,000, a tax the Free State also inherited; although, 'in 1923, the rate of super tax in Ireland rose progressively from 1s 6d in the pound for incomes over £2,000 to 6s in the pound over £30,000.'[83] Likewise, the Free State government inherited ordinary income tax rates from Britain, although these rates also fluctuated in the following years. Furthermore, high rates payable on houses led to their decline as a dismantled house was rate-free, thus leading many owners to remove the roofs from houses, leaving them to ruin.[84]

Purdue has studied the situation in Northern Ireland, where by 1939 the upper level of taxation had risen to 60 per cent for properties valued at over £1m. This meant that 'for someone inheriting a big house, taxation at these levels were, at best, a problem – at worst, ruinous. There was hardly an estate in Northern Ireland that was not seriously affected by the payment of taxation and, in particular, death duties at some stage. On those estates where the actual margin of income was small, such payments simply could not be met.'[85] Taxation, and particularly death duties, could be the making or breaking of estates. Purdue described how 'there were estates in Northern Ireland, the Free State and throughout the British Isles where the payment of death duties brought a family to such a state of financial ruin that they had no alternative but to sell or simply abandon their property.'[86]

Nonetheless, she emphasised that most remaining Northern Irish families were able, through careful planning, to avoid such significant duties or were able to manage their payment successfully while keeping their property going as a viable concern.[87] This is notable as it was not the case for many country house families in the south. Rates, taxes and duties were similar in Northern Ireland, but through careful management and prudent planning, country house families were able to survive as a powerful elite up to the 1960s and beyond. In the south, many lacked the necessary business and legal acumen required to manage and minimise losses from taxation, while others simply no longer had the desire or motivation to keep the house going through such difficulties. In 1931, these country houses were described as 'white elephants' in the *Weekly Irish Times*, which went on to report: 'to be burdened with a house with rooms that are never occupied is like holding a private museum, in which no one is interested. So that there is nothing to envy in the individual who has a big house and nothing else to live on!'[88]

WIDER SOCIAL CONDITIONS

It would be difficult to call the decreasing wealth of country house owners anything like hardship in a country where genuine poverty and destitution was rife. Dublin had its own slum tenements at this point and the country continually lost a proportion of its population. *Émigrés* were anxious to leave an Ireland where opportunities for employment or raising one's economic position were scant. Dermot Keogh has shown that 'rank poverty in the countryside in the 1930s continued to force young men and women to suffer the indignities of the "hiring fair" … Others sought seasonal work abroad. About 9,500 went to Britain in 1937.'[89] Similarly, for the first independent governments, emigration was the issue of high priority, although little practical action was taken. The scale of the emigration was enormous. Nearly 700,000 people left independent Ireland between the end of the Second World War and the early 1970s.[90] Enda Delaney has argued how this level of mass migration underlined the obvious shortcomings of the independent Irish state and was the source of 'much embarrassment' for politicians. This was driven home by the fact that Britain was the destination for the majority of emigrants who left after 1921.[91]

The country house, however uneconomical – as a private home and as symbolic of the British administration in Ireland – was not a prime concern for the government in economic or indeed heritage terms. In fact, a similar point was made decades later by Chris Hammett in 1975, the year of European Architectural Heritage. By this time, Ireland had joined the European Economic Community (EEC) and thus heritage preservation became a necessary and broader concern than simply national interest and pride. There was now a responsibility on the state to preserve the landmarks of the country as part of a wider European inheritance. In Ireland, the Minister for Local Government established a National Committee who ran a schedule of events. In one seminar, the question of who benefits from conservation was debated and Hammett argued that 'Conservation should not be considered alone, or in purely architectural terms, but in the general context of housing need. The question of who gains and who loses must constantly be kept in mind.' He elucidated further that that this did not mean conservation was redundant, but that 'someone living in a slum is probably far more concerned with getting a decent place to live in than with the preservation of our historic legacy.'[92] This sentiment has resonance in the debate surrounding the preservation of such houses and more generally heritage and the arts, even today. Heritage will always lag behind other societal issues in terms of import, particularly during financially straightened times, and yet there is value in it that should be upheld. However, it should always be balanced with the needs of the citizen and, in particular, should be of benefit to the population. Christopher Ridgway has also touched on this point about public benefit and access to these houses as being important, not just from a sustainability perspective, but also so that there is 'public value' in the endeavour of the preservation of the house, estate, and even the families who inhabited them.[93] This is important, as while the destruction of country houses was lamentable, it must be remembered that the Irish economy did not really take off until late in the twentieth century. There were, naturally, more pressing claims on the public purse in the first half of this century. The question of 'heritage' should be able to answer the question of who should pay its price and why.[94]

THE NATIONAL MONUMENTS ACT

Up until 1930, the state was tackling more pressing social issues than heritage preservation and so the legislation that controlled this area remained the same as legislation enacted by the British administration. National monuments could be vested in the Commissioners of Public Works or given to their guardianship by the Commissioners of Church Temporalities, the Ancient Monuments Protection Acts, 1882 and 1892, and the 1903 and 1923 Land Acts.[95] As such, prior to the 1930 Act, the commissioners were charged with the duty of maintaining ancient monuments under five different statutes.[96] Aware of the absence of any specific legislation for the national heritage, in 1924 the Royal Irish Academy and the Society of Antiquaries of Ireland sent a memorandum to the Department of the Taoiseach on proposals for a suggested National Monuments Act. They stated that if such an act were passed, the Irish Free State would take its place among the other nations of Europe in terms of such legislation. They emphasised:

> In Ireland, such preservation is doubly necessary: first because education in the past has not been such as to develop in the people at large an understanding of the value of ancient monuments; and secondly because of the great importance of Irish antiquities for an understanding of the early civilisation not merely of Ireland, but also of Europe.[97]

Their draft act thus specifically focused on the preservation of 'ancient monuments' which were defined as: 'all remains bearing upon the racial characteristics, or the social, political, artistic, or religious history of the Irish people.'[98] To make this clear, it outlined: 'the year 1800 A. D. shall be fixed as the limit of date before which all such be deemed "ancient", except in the case of manuscripts in the Irish language, when its limit shall be 1850 A. D.'[99]

While the government may have been inspired by these proposals, they did not act on them immediately, but five years later proposed their own legislation. In a 1929 debate on this National Monuments bill, Hugh Law, Cumann na nGaedheal TD for Donegal, argued for the protection of 'the historical mansions' and highlighted 'the destruction that is going on, every day that passes without adequate protection being afforded brings about the ruin and, it may be, the disappearance of monuments which are of the deepest interest to all Irishmen.'[100] However, this claim was not backed up by many other politicians' concerns, nor was it specifically legislated for in this act. It was 1930 when this act – the most significant legislated for by an Irish government in terms of heritage protection until the 1995 Heritage Act – came into force. The 1930 National Monuments Act made provision 'for the protection and preservation of national monuments and for the preservation of archaeological objects in Saorstát Éireann.'[101] For the purposes of this act, a 'national monument' was defined as a monument or its remains 'the preservation of which is a matter of national importance by reason of the historical, architectural, traditional, artistic, or archaeological interest attaching thereto'.[102] The 1930 Act also established the National Monuments Advisory Council (NMAC) for giving advice and assistance to the Commissioners of Public Works in relation to the enactment of this legislation, and was to include among its members the Keeper of Irish Antiquities at the National Museum and an officer of the Commissioners of Public Works, as well as other nominated members.

Mairéad Carew has argued that this act only legislated for the preservation of a 'native' past. She maintained:

> The National Monuments Act 1930 was a very important piece of legislation in terms of consolidating national identity in Ireland through the protection of its material culture. Those archaeological monuments deemed to be 'national' could be used in the service of the new state and in the enunciation of its official history. Those deemed 'anti-national' could be allowed to decay or a blind eye could be turned to their destruction, as they served no purpose other than as a reminder of a past which was perhaps, from a particular political perspective, best erased.[103]

However, the National Monuments Act did not specify any particular date for the limits of its powers and was, in this sense, theoretically much broader in its wording than the proposals which the Royal Society of Antiquaries in Ireland with the Royal Irish Academy had submitted to government in their draft 'Ancient Monuments Protection Act' of 1924. This draft act had defined qualifying ancient monuments as only those dated before 1800. Their proposed act would have therefore restricted absolutely, by legislation, any monument built after this time. The government's 1930 National Monuments Act changed the focus of preservation from being solely on ancient monuments to being on all monuments that could be considered of national importance. By not defining any date for qualification as a national monument, the act left it open to the commissioners' discretion to decide whether or not any buildings built after 1800, such as country houses for example, could be preserved under this act by virtue of their architectural interest or other merits. Technically the country houses of Ireland could have been preserved under this act, although Chapter Three will show that, predominantly, they were not. This discretion was important and was the purview of the OPW as it was the body charged with its implementation. The OPW's commissioners' and inspectors' attitudes and opinions on what should be covered under the protections of this act were of crucial importance, as was the question of what the Office's budget or resources allowed.

The 1930 Act was not without its limitations. Within a few years of the enacting of the legislation, these limitations had already become so apparent that the NMAC recommended amendments. Suggestions included giving local authorities the ability to transfer the ownership of a national monument from their care to the ownership of the commissioners and the issuing of temporary preservation orders where a national monument was in immediate danger of destruction. In addition, it was recommended that powers be given to inspect monuments still in private ownership or on private lands and to excavate at reported archaeological sites without waiting for a license.[104] In spite of this, the OPW concluded that most of the suggested amendments were scarcely necessary and that the present act was adequate, suggesting that its staff did not consider most of the 'limitations' that the NMAC had pointed out to be overly important.[105] The first proposed amendment, that is, allowing local authorities to transfer ownership, was the only one considered of sufficient importance to warrant the introduction of an amending bill, but they thought that the absence of this amendment was not so destructive as to merit the early introduction of legislation 'particularly at a time when the government's legislative programme is so large and includes matters of so much greater importance';[106] an unusual admission from a department specifically concerned with the importance of preserving heritage. The act was not amended until 1954.[107]

The implementation of the 1930 Act by the Commissioners of Public Works reflected the new state's desire to preserve and promote its own native traditions and heritage. While no date limits were specified in this act, most monuments preserved under this legislation dated prior to the seventeenth century. In fact, the Inspector of National Monuments from 1923–49, H. G. Leask, advised that an architect with a knowledge of early and medieval architecture was required for the role of inspector, as such architecture constituted 'the great bulk of the National Monuments in State care and a very high percentage of those buildings which will in future be taken over.'[108] Furthermore, in relation to a letter from the Tourist Board enquiring about the possibility of preserving country houses under the National Monuments Act, a civil servant in the OPW argued that the buildings referred to were 'of modern date and construction and would not, save in very exceptional circumstances, be suitable for preservation under the National Monuments Act.'[109] In response to a similar query from Tipperary District Council in 1944, the OPW proposed replying that the 'old places' referred to were mansions or houses of comparatively modern date and construction, and these would not, save in very exceptional circumstances, be suitable for preservation under the Act.'[110] It was predominantly ancient monuments that were preserved under this legislation, such as round towers and the monastic settlement of Glendalough; monuments that, deliberately or not, comfortably embodied a native Gaelic tradition that the state was seeking to embody.[111] Preserving and promoting this heritage also created a lineage from which the state was seen to have been 'born' and one which was untainted by centuries of British control. On the other hand, the country house was symbolic of precisely the colonial history that the state had no wish to venerate.

This raises an important question: at what point in its history does a building gain eligibility to be called historical or historically important? Furthermore, while this was the first attempt by the new state to create some policies around, and control over, national monuments, their budget for heritage was not a large one. Ruins of monasteries or ogham stones were more realistic propositions for maintenance. They required a low budget to preserve, often only needing the erection of a fence and a sign to secure such a site as a national monument in the commissioners' eyes – very manageable with a small field staff. Conversely, a country house was meaningless as a ruin. Its historical importance and integrity lay precisely in its maintenance and grandeur as a home, the decoration of its rooms, its art and architecture, the preservation of which would have proven a colossal expense for the commissioners. The houses were often also over two centuries old and so had many problems with dry rot, leaking roofs, heating and plumbing. This would have made them hugely expensive to maintain in good condition. There was also no widespread interest in preserving country houses and so the government would not have been providing a popular visitor or amenity site for locals, nor would the houses have proved economically viable to the government in terms of tourism revenue. These considerations were to the forefront of the government's agenda when they were offered Russborough House, County Wicklow, as a gift to the nation in 1929, just before the passing of the 1930 National Monuments Act., discussed later in this chapter.

GIFTS TO THE STATE

Across the water, the English National Trust was enabled by the British government to accept gifts of country houses, not least to avoid embarrassing situations of offers to government that they did not want to accept. Nevertheless, during the 1920s 'the Trust was finding it difficult to scrape together even the £2,000 needed to pay death duties on its gifts from Lord Curzon, Bodiam and Tattershall Castles.'[112] In fact, the economic position of the government in England, without the country house bearing any of the weight of colonial associations placed on its Irish counterpart, had been just as antagonistic to the survival of the private country house in the first decades of the century, if not more so. Their motivations were instead ideals such as economic and class equality. Peter Mandler revealed that 'when Labour's fiscal policy of taxing the land materialised in 1930 – the top rate of death duties went back up to fifty per cent and a Land Valuation bill was announced – a few landowners also came out in favour of the State taking over their agricultural and amenity functions.'[113] He described how, under Labour and the National Government, these arguments did not evoke sympathy. The Treasury was opposed to giving tax relief to private citizens and 'predicted a public outcry if private houses were subsidised in this way just because they were "historic"'.[114] The Treasury were similarly uninterested in taking on the ownership of houses or estates, perhaps dissuaded by the experience of the offer they had received from Sir Charles Trevelyan of his house and estate at Wallington, Northumberland. Trevelyan offered the property as a gift to the nation 'if some public use could be found for it'.[115] However, similar to many of the case studies examined here for the 26 counties in Ireland, 'no Government department showed any interest in this gift … At most, the Treasury was willing to consider legal changes that might make it easier for the Trust to accept gifts such as Wallington, free of estate duty, to spare the state embarrassment.'[116]

Concessions to the Trust in England at this time were influenced by the fact that the country house problem was one the state did not want to take on. Enabling the National Trust to do so freed them from any obligation they had to accept houses for which they had no use and little appreciation at this time. When Neville Chamberlain became Chancellor of the Exchequer he was willing to look at the question in a different way long before such suggestions were heard in Ireland. Mandler has argued that, while Chamberlain agreed with the Treasury's objection to reliefs or benefits for private historic house and estate owners, he was willing to consider the concept of concessions to the Trust 'if private owners submitted themselves to closer public control.'[117] Similarly, the government and its departments considered that if the country house were going to be accepted as part of the national heritage, then it warranted and required national planning, 'not some hole-and-corner, case-by-case negotiation with the National Trust'.[118] In contrast, the question of a National Trust was not on the Free State's agenda at this time and, therefore, any such gifts of houses were the responsibility of the government itself.

THE CASE OF RUSSBOROUGH HOUSE

In 1929, Russborough House, County Wicklow, described by Mark Bence-Jones as 'arguably the most beautiful house in Ireland',[119] became one of the first country houses offered as a gift to the state. Such houses were often presented for ostensibly patriotic and philanthropic reasons, though it was also an option for owners anxious to rid themselves of a property that they could not sell. For whatever reason, the offering of country houses to the Irish state continued up until the 1970s, and these cases can be particularly revealing of owners' positions and governments' attitudes behind closed doors. The case study of Russborough House is one that in many ways typifies the discussions surrounding the offers of country houses to the state throughout the entire period of examination in this book. This is notable, given that Russborough was one of the earliest instances of such offers. Russborough also offers a glimpse into the differing attitudes that surrounded the value of such properties to the government at this time, from the interest it created and the visits that cabinet members took to view the place, to the more nativist bias displayed by the Secretary of the Department of Finance.

Russborough House is a large Palladian mansion, built in the 1740s for Joseph Leeson, afterwards the first Earl of Milltown, and designed by Richard Castle. In 1929 it belonged to Lady Turton, having passed to her on the death of her husband, Sir Edmund Turton. At this time, the Hon. Sir Edward Eliot, Lady Turton's nephew, began investigating the possibility of her gifting the property to the nation, confiding to Sir Walter Nugent, an acquaintance and Free State Senator, that 'Lady Turton cannot afford to keep up the house as it ought to be kept up and it appears that it would be very difficult at the present time to find a purchaser.'[120] It had occurred to Lady Turton that 'it might be possible for the house to be made use of in some worthy way for the good of the Irish nation.' While Eliot wrote that 'its distance from Dublin would be against any such scheme', he maintained that the house itself would make 'an admirable museum or art gallery'.[121]

Two months later, the decision had been taken and Eliot wrote to Nugent, presumably as his only contact within the Oireachtas of the Free State, officially declaring: 'on behalf of Lady Turton, I am now authorised to make a definite offer of Russborough to the Irish nation.'[122] He outlined that the gift would include the whole of Russborough demesne, with the exception of a piece of land known as Ballydallagh, and the contents of the house.[123] The demesne consisted of approximately 432 acres of land let for grazing. It was under-stood that these rents would be received by the state if the gift were accepted, although they were not thought to be very material.[124] He wrote:

> Lady Turton's motive in making this offer of a gift is from her love of Russborough and her love of Ireland. The only conditions which Lady Turton would wish to attach to the gift are that some undertaking should be given that the house and estate should be maintained and that the house should be used for some worthy national purpose.[125]

He also thought that Lady Turton would be 'very much gratified if the nation, in the event of it deciding to accept the gift, would make some provision under which the house should be open at reasonable and convenient times to the inspection of visitors.'[126]

Sir Walter Nugent became the middleman between Eliot and the govern-ment, informing the latter of this offer. The government acted quickly and just a month and a half later President Cosgrave wrote personally to Nugent informing him that he and two of his colleagues had been to Russborough and 'were very much impressed by its beauty of architecture and situation and are very grateful indeed to Lady Turton for her generous and patriotic offer.'[127] He explained that the difficulty in reaching a decision was largely financial, writing:

'as I think I already mentioned to you, we have been compelled, very reluctantly indeed, to refuse generous offers of similar mansions on at least two previous occasions', although he noted that 'their distance from Dublin was considerably greater and a big additional disadvantage was a complete absence of furniture and pictures'.[128]

One of the mansions offered to government just a few years previously, in 1925, was Glenstal Abbey, County Limerick, built in the 1830s by the Barrington family. Home in 1925 to Sir Charles Barrington and his wife, Glenstal Abbey had been left with less than 1,000 acres after the land acts and was becoming increasingly difficult to maintain. However, the event that hastened the Barrington's desire to leave Glenstal was the shooting dead of their only daughter, Winnie, in 1921. She had been travelling in a car with a Black and Tan officer which was ambushed by the IRA. Nonetheless, when they decided to leave in 1925, Sir Charles eschewed bitterness by writing to the Free State government offering Glenstal as a gift to the Irish nation. He suggested its suitability as a residence for the Governor-General, who remained as a figurehead of the British administration in Ireland. Cosgrave and Tim Healy, then Governor-General, visited Glenstal in July 1925, and 'were astonished at its magnificence, which far exceeded our expectations'.[129] Despite this, restricted by the tight finances of the new state, Cosgrave had to inform Sir Charles that 'our present economic position would not warrant the ministry in applying to the Dáil to vote the necessary funds for the upkeep of Glenstal' and it subsequently became a Benedictine monastery.[130] Interestingly, 17 birch trees were recently planted in one of the gardens at Glenstal Abbey to commemorate the 16 leaders of the 1916 Rising who were executed and another in memory of Winnie Barrington.

Cosgrave re-emphasised to Eliot in 1929 how disappointed they had been to have had to refuse the gift of Glenstal. In the same letter on the subject of the offer of Russborough, Cosgrave wrote that he knew a certain portion of the contents of Russborough were included in the late Lady Milltown's gift to the National Gallery and were on loan only for the duration of Lady Turton's lifetime. He assumed that she did not wish to have them removed from Russborough. While he did not know what proportion these articles were in relation to the total contents, Cosgrave wrote that if it were considerable and should Lady Turton want them removed

> The cost of re-furnishing on a scale suitable to the house would be large and would be a very important factor in our minds at the present time when we are endeavouring to economise all round. This consideration would be of almost equal importance whether

it was decided to retain the house as a museum and art gallery – a doubtful proposal in view of the distance from Dublin – or whether it was found possible to utilise it as a national guest house for which it should be very suitable.[131]

Economy was certainly the order of the day as the Wall Street Crash of October 1929 had far-reaching effects worldwide. Cosgrave asked if Sir Walter could ascertain Lady Turton's intentions in this regard and added that it would also be helpful to know the present letting value of the grazing on the demesne. Once he had this information, the OPW could inspect the property 'with a view to suggesting the best method of utilising the gift should it materialise', as well as preparing an estimate of preliminary expenditure required and the net annual maintenance charges for the Finance Minister.[132]

Cosgrave, accompanied by Lady Turton, Eliot, two members of the Board of Works and the Minister for Finance, Ernest Blythe, again visited Russborough in February 1930.[133] Eliot stressed: 'Lady Turton is anxious that we should accept. She is of Irish extraction and mentioned that she did not like … the idea of selling the property and taking the proceeds out of Ireland.'[134] However, Eliot had earlier confided to Nugent that she was making the offer precisely because she could not find a buyer for Russborough. The fact that Cosgrave made time for a second visit to the property illustrates the personal interest he took in this case. At this time, Eliot compiled a memorandum on Russborough for the government to consider, including a detailed schedule of the contents and particulars of the gift.[135] Illustrating how seriously the government considered accepting this gift, further inspection was deemed necessary and the OPW informed the Department of the President on 2 April that they were sending a member of their architectural staff to make a survey of the building with a view to preparing an estimate. The value of the gift, and these properties in general at the time, is revealed in the clarification that the OPW sought on the matter, writing:

> With regard to the exact value of the house, we should be glad to be informed in what sense the word 'value' is to be understood. The house is, we understand, a very fine and beautiful eighteenth century mansion; it has probably no sale value because no one would be likely to buy it except perhaps for demolition. The land can be valued on its profits if let for grazing, and the furniture on its sale value.[136]

What is clear here is that, in 1930, no matter how beautiful the architecture of a country house, it had no market value except in terms of salvage value from its demolition. However, hindsight should not judge this comment as the antagonistic view of a philistine government department. It was the reality, in monetary terms, of the time.

In July 1930, the OPW had completed their examination and the reports on Russborough were forwarded to the Department of the President. These included a report by the OPW's principal architect, Mr Byrne, on the extent and cost of necessary works of repair and improvement and estimates for annual charges for maintenance of the mansion; reports by the assistant superintendent of the Phoenix Park, Mr Pearson, on the cost of restoring and maintaining the grounds of the house; a report by the OPW's chief valuer, Mr Robinson, on the valuation of Russborough House and demesne; and a report by the furniture clerk of the OPW, Mr Curnow, on the value of the furniture and pictures in the house. All reports considered the possibility of using the house either as a residence or as a museum as requested. T. Cassedy, Secretary of the OPW, noted that they had not been asked to advise on the fitness of the place as a residence and, if not considered for that purpose, its preservation 'as a museum specimen of the class of eighteenth-century Irish mansions, to which it belongs, would be extremely desirable if the government is prepared to meet the cost'.[137] He suggested consulting the National Monuments Advisory Council, which had been established under the 1930 National Monuments Act. It is interesting to note here that, as early as 1930, the OPW thought it would be 'extremely desirable' to preserve the mansion as an example of an Irish mansion. Early in this period this official clearly showed an appreciation for the value of this mansion in itself and its importance to Irish history. Importantly, this was only desirable if the government were prepared to finance it out of exchequer funds, not the OPW's budget.

Attached to this letter was the report of Mr Byrne on Russborough House, which began: 'the mansion ... is an interesting example of an [eighteenth] century nobleman's seat', adding 'the house and its demesne seem worthy of preservation as an example of by-gone time and fashions'.[138] He wrote:

> If the mansion is not to be regularly occupied (say in some such manner as is Chequers by the British Prime Minister) but the principal part is retained as a specimen of an 18th century nobleman's seat, and, with suitable contents, exhibited as one of the national museums, the costs of structural repair and of annual maintenance would be reduced.[139]

This is interesting, as Chapter Three will show that, in almost all cases of country houses brought to their attention over this period, the OPW recommended against their preservation. Furthermore, the mention by Byrne of Chequers in England is notable and points to the dynamics at play among some politicians and those in state bodies who, on the one hand, may have rejected the country house because of its associations with British rule and, on the other, continued to be influenced by, and look to, Britain in terms of the running of the state. Returning to their estimates, the OPW's principal architect reported that if works were confined to the centre piece and curved arcades of the house, leaving the wings and flanking buildings without repair, they estimated incurring a cost of £6,500, excluding lighting and drainage.[140]

In September 1930, the Assistant Secretary at the President of the Executive Council's department requested that the Minister for Finance, Ernest Blythe, have his department examine the matter and return a recommendation.[141] The President wanted the issue dealt with urgently as he had received 'enquiries on behalf of Lady Turton as to the government's attitude in the matter.'[142] In spite of this, there does not appear to have been any urgent decision taken, as, over a month later, on 15 October, the Private Secretary to the President asked Eliot to convey to Lady Turton his regret that there had been 'so much delay in dealing with her generous offer'.[143] He explained that the Minister for Finance had almost completed his examination and would 'shortly be in a position to make a recommendation'.[144] This shows the importance of the recommendation of the Department of Finance, which the government required in order to decide on the gift, presumably on the basis of what the department was prepared to allow. The letter concluded: 'the President would like to assure Lady Turton that he himself is keenly interested in the project and will endeavour to secure as early a decision as possible.'[145]

On 24 October, James John (J. J.) McElligott, Secretary of the Department of Finance, informed the Private Secretary to the President that the Minister for Finance recommended declining the gift.[146] He considered it probable that all the figures quoted by the Commissioners of Public Works for state expenditure would be found in practice to be too low. In his experience, particularly with regard to the acquisition of Leinster House for the Oireachtas and the acquisition of old mansions for preparatory colleges, he noted that:

> Adaptation and renovation of old buildings are extremely costly, that preliminary estimates are almost invariably largely exceeded, and that when renovation commences the opening up of work, or, failing that, the experience of actual use, reveals defects previously unsuspected which can only be set right at heavy expense.[147]

It was anticipated that in the old building at Russborough there would be considerable outlay both on external and internal reconstruction and improvements to make the place 'serve adequately as a modern residence'.[148] It is notable that the Department of Finance did not believe the estimates of the Commissioners of Public Works were correct, even though this was their area of expertise.

J. J. McElligott was one of the most influential civil servants in the Department of Finance and served as Assistant Secretary from 1923 until 1927. He was then promoted to Secretary, the most powerful position within the Department, where he remained until 1953, thereby influencing government policy in relation to finance for a very considerable period of time. McElligott was, and remains, the longest serving Secretary General in the Department of Finance. Interestingly, both McElligott and his predecessor, Joseph Brennan, had worked in the British civil service where they learned the discipline of public administration. McElligott had also fought in the Easter Rising and was imprisoned in England for a time thereafter, indicating his passionately nationalist outlook. In the Department of Finance, his belief throughout the period was that 'Government should spend as little as possible, keep taxation low, and rely on the unhampered flow of the market to ensure maximum profits for farmers and businessmen.'[149] This was important because the permission of the Department of Finance was required before the cabinet could approve any proposal that required spending, although the Taoiseach could override this stipulation if he felt it absolutely necessary. This practice was followed by all governments up until the 1960s and 'naturally gave the Department of Finance great power over the total business of Government, a power which its long-serving Secretary McElligott was keen to use.'[150] While some have been critical of McElligott's tight control of budgetary purse strings, his enormous contribution to the state should not be ignored. In his role in the Department of Finance, he helped restore the public finances and guided the country through many crises, including the Great Depression and the Emergency, while funding significant initiatives such as the Shannon Hydro-Electric Scheme.

On the subject of Russborough, McElligott noted that the Minister for Finance – who had most likely been briefed by McElligott – was convinced that the figure of £450, which had been quoted as the figure for the ordinary maintenance of the Russborough buildings, would be exceeded when compared with the government's 1930–1 estimates for buildings in their charge. McElligott contrasted the proposed annual cost of £830 for the upkeep of the grounds and gardens with the Phoenix Park which, 'while not quite seven times the size of Russborough demesne costs about £18,000 per annum in maintenance'.[151] However, a Department of the Taoiseach official did not consider this 'a just comparison'.[152] McElligott noted that the figures quoted by the Commissioners of Public Works took 'no account of establishment charges', such as staff wages, maintenance, renewal of furniture, supply of coal, gas and electricity, provision of police and military protection, or cost of entertainment.[153] Again, comparison was made with the total annual cost of the Governor-General's establishment, the vice-regal lodge, which required only yearly maintenance and no structural improvement and was still given £16,000 per annum by the government. The Governor-General was believed to supplement this with substantial sums from his £10,000 salary. These examples were included as an indication 'of the scale of outlay which would be involved in the maintenance of a residential establishment in a style in keeping with the dignity of the state in a large old mansion such as Russborough.'[154]

As to the alternative proposal, the Minister for Finance did 'not gather that anyone seriously suggests that Russborough House would be suitable as a museum'[155] McElligott emphasised that its distance from Dublin – 20 miles – and from any other large population centre made it inaccessible to the general public, and so ruled out the idea. He noted that this consideration had been acknowledged by Sir Eliot.[156] Moreover, the department believed that the Commissioners of Public Works' report made clear 'that the present contents of the mansion are of no special interest as museum specimens.'[157] Therefore, the minister did not consider it necessary to make a serious examination of the costs involved in using the place as such and was satisfied that, if Russborough were examined, it would be found unfavourable.

McElligott then addressed the idea of treating the mansion itself as a historical monument, a proposal which the Commissioners of Public Works supported. In the Department of Finance's opinion this amounted 'simply to treating Russborough House with its contents and demesne as a national monument, to be preserved and maintained at state expense, and the gift as simply a request from the owner of a national monument that the state should take it over and preserve and maintain it'.[158] The department noted that the costs incurred through such a use would be much less than those of an official residence, since if the rooms were used as display rooms for museum objects, it would only be necessary to preserve the building, contents and grounds from actual decay. Caretakers could also be employed to 'show round any persons sufficiently interested to visit the place'.[159] Large outlay on sanitary works, heating or lighting installations would also be avoided if the premises were on display in daylight only. Even still, the Department of Finance again found the Commissioners of Public Works' estimates for this proposal quite inadequate as the figures postulated that only the central block and arcades of the building would be preserved, with the wings being allowed to decay and the gardens and ornamental grounds dropped and used for grazing. They also included no provision for caretakers' wages, cleaning, maintenance and rates on lands and buildings, which it appears even they would not be relieved of paying.

In addition, the Minister for Finance did not consider it practicable for the state to allow the wings go to ruin and 'the dropping of the gardens and ornamental grounds would, in his view, defeat the whole idea of preserving the mansion as a specimen of a country house of its period.'[160] The fact that this was proposed by the commissioners would suggest that the cost of maintaining the whole building and gardens was prohibitively expensive and therefore, to preserve any of the house, priorities would have to be determined on what could realistically be maintained. The Department of Finance estimates were £5,000 initial capital outlay on the restoration of buildings, grounds and gardens, plus approximately £1,500 a year net on current establishment expenses for the 'lowest standard of upkeep tolerable under state control'[161] after deductions of grazing receipts. McElligott again emphasised:

> The Minister remains of the opinion that the gift should be declined on the ground that its value to the nation when so used would not be worth its cost. So far as the Minister has been able to gather neither Russborough House nor the family connected with it has ever been associated with any outstanding events or personalities in Irish history. Accordingly, the interest which the place possesses is only its interest to connoisseurs of architecture, plus whatever interest it has as illustrating a certain phase of social life in Ireland. Opinions differ as to the aesthetic merits of the Georgian as a style of architecture, but, the period being relatively modern, good specimens of it are sufficiently numerous both in this country and in England to render state action to preserve this one superfluous.[162]

Demonstrably, it was thought, at least by the Department of Finance, that the preservation of Georgian architecture could be achieved by maintaining a number of examples rather than individual cases. While this was certainly not a decision that was appreciative of the architectural merits of each individual house, it was one that was based on a limited budget in relation to preservation. It was also a decision made in 1929 when there was not a keenly developed sense of the importance of preserving such houses, a public interest in their preservation, an awareness of their individual merits, or a tourism industry which could support them. In addition, Minister for Finance Ernest Blythe, TD for North Monaghan, was known for attempting to keep state expenditure low. He had also been a volunteer in the War of Independence thereby undoubtedly influencing his views toward the country house.

Aside from the economic reasons behind the recommendation to decline, McElligott also gave the Minister's opinion on the value of the gift, particularly to the Irish nation, and his attitude towards whether the government had a responsibility to preserve these country houses. He wrote:

The Minister is informed that Georgian architecture is better represented in the city of Dublin than in any country house in Ireland, and several of the best Georgian buildings in Dublin are already in Government hands and used as public buildings. He is informed, moreover, that Russborough is not the best specimen in the Saorstát of Georgian country house architecture, that it is only the central block which has real architectural distinction, and that even there the distinction belongs to the interior rather than to the exterior. Even if this house were the best specimen of Georgian country house architecture in the Saorstát, which, as stated, it is not, the Minister considers that its taking over for preservation by the Saorstát Government would not be justified unless it stood very high amongst houses of the kind all over the British Isles, because Georgian is not an Irish style of architecture, and there seems no point in an Irish Government preserving, as a national monument, a building not distinctively Irish, which will present itself to overseas visitors as only second rate of its kind.[163]

Evident here is a definite bias in favour of 'native' monuments rather than those which could be considered 'foreign'. The implication was, therefore, that the government of Ireland had no duty to care for these monuments and that they would be of no importance to Irish people as they were not thought to be an intrinsic part of Irish history. While the independent state was seeking to define itself in the decades following independence, it naturally sought to distinguish itself from the empire of which it had once been part and to create differences that would simultaneously justify and bring to fruition the separation of England from Ireland, as a post-colonial state seeks to in the first stages of decolonisation. Perhaps, too, the Minister was genuinely thinking of overseas visitors who could see outstanding examples of such architecture in Britain and may have come to Ireland to see more traditional or 'native' Irish monuments.

The letter continued:

Turning to the interest which Russborough possesses as illustrating a certain phase of social life in Ireland, apart from the fact that that phase is sufficiently illustrated by numbers of other mansions in the country in private hands, there is again the point that that phase of social life had nothing distinctively Irish about it, the social life of country magnates in the 18th century within a wider radius of Dublin being patterned upon the life of the corresponding class in England of the same period. The National Monuments Act, 1930, defines a national monument as one the preservation of which is a matter of national importance by reason of the historical, architectural, traditional, artistic, or archaeological interest attaching thereto. It would require much special pleading to bring Russborough in any reasonable way within that definition.[164]

It is very difficult to see here how McElligott was not blinded by prejudice from his active service in the nationalist cause by denying that Russborough had *any* national importance either architecturally, artistically or historically, whatever its potential financial burden. Russborough remains one of the most striking and beautiful examples of Palladian architecture in the country today. However, financially, the burden of the acquisition of Russborough was too great. The total outlay by the Commissioners of Public Works on the preservation of national monuments for several years had averaged, including outlays from endowment funds, some £2,800 a year. Acquiring Russborough, therefore, would, apart from the initial £5,000, raise annual state outlay on national monuments by over 50 per cent for one property. McElligott added:

> When one considers the number, the nature, and the enormous national and indeed world interest of the monuments covered by the £2,800 – the structures of pre-Christian antiquity at New Grange, the round towers, the churches at Glendalough, the Rock of Cashel ... the project of spending over one half that total upon this one place, which, by comparison has neither any national nor world interest worth speaking about, seems quite out of proportion. So far state intervention to preserve old monuments has not gone beyond those belonging at latest to the Middle Ages, and to initiate now a programme of preserving eighteenth century buildings would be quite a new departure which could not fail, by making a heavy inroad on the scanty funds which can be made available for such purposes, to prejudice the preservation of real national monuments, of these remain a large number belonging to the Middle Ages or to antiquity which the state may feel called upon to take over and preserve.[165]

This makes it clear that despite no date being specified in the National Monuments Act, it had been the practice of the OPW to only preserve those ancient monuments dating prior to the Middle Ages and not beyond the seventeenth century. Department of Finance officials were afraid of the number and burden of country houses that could be placed on them to preserve if they made a precedent with Russborough. However, economically speaking, their attitude to the gift was rational when over 50 per cent of their annual budget – a considerable proportion – would have been swallowed up by the maintenance of one property. The fact that the gift of the house came with no financial endowment to cover its upkeep was also an influential factor for the government. McElligott explained that the Minister believed that without this: 'the value of the gift, per se, is a minus quality. The Minister is less disposed to recommend state intervention to relieve private owners of the expense of maintenance of 'white elephants' since the state itself is already in the position of having more old buildings on its hands than it knows what to do with.'[166] This reference appears to be to Dublin Castle, the Royal Hospital Kilmainham which remained 'to be disposed of', the Royal Hibernian Military School, also described as 'something of a problem' and several military barracks, notably the large one at Newbridge, which were all 'empty and idle'.[167]

Financial strain was the main concern of the Department of Finance in this letter and its estimates were based on realistic previous experience. Nevertheless, even taking this into account, the Minister and his departmental staff, most particularly McElligott, were less than appreciative of the property's aesthetic or architectural value, with no mention that the house or its contents were worthy of any particular merit. They discounted its value as a historical specimen, or as an object of public interest, not only because there were other examples of this but also because it was not sufficiently Irish. Another factor influencing Department of Finance opinion is evident from internal department notes on the matter which deal with the indecision about how Russborough might be of use to the state. One minute noted 'The file suggests that nobody knows for which of the two purposes the place ought to be used. If a man does not know for what purpose he needs a thing that is pretty good evidence that he really does not need the thing at all, and the same, I presume, applies to a nation.'[168] A handwritten note on this file to the Secretary General agreed 'that the proposed gift of Russborough House and demesne to the nation will be practically useless and certainly entail great expense and that it should consequently be declined.'[169]

The report of the Department of Finance was influential, as cabinet minutes of 2 December 1930 record that 'having regard to the initial expenditure and cost of maintenance which acquisition of the house and grounds would involve it was agreed that the offer could not be accepted at the moment.'[170] On 5 December President Cosgrave wrote to Eliot apologising for the delay and stating that, while the majority of the Executive Council

> had the opportunity of visiting the house and were very much impressed by its architecture and the beauty of its situation … It is with sincere regret that we have been forced to the conclusion that financial considerations render it impossible to accept the gift at the present moment. The cost of the initial works which would be required and of the subsequent maintenance could not, if the house and demesne were to be kept in a suitable manner, be brought down to a figure which in the present condition of our finances we could justify including in our expenditure, the more so as the state has already on its hands a number of residential buildings which it maintains at a loss.[171]

He asked that Eliot convey to Lady Turton the government's gratitude for her very generous offer and wrote:

> We appreciate highly the interest which she has always taken in this country and the love of Ireland which has motivated her offer. She may rest assured that our decision

has been dictated by necessity and has been arrived at after anxious consideration and with much reluctance and regret.[172]

It was not until ten days later that the Commissioners of Public Works were informed of the government's decision in a letter which stated: 'you are doubtless aware that … the government decided that they could not accept the offer'.[173] This highlights that it was the Department of Finance, not the Commissioners of Public Works, which made the final call on the refusal of Russborough. Notably, the more nationalistic discussions regarding Russborough's importance are not mentioned in any of the external communications on the matter; rather, financial considerations, a more palatable and understandable reason for refusal, was what was relayed to Lady Turton. On 15 January, Cosgrave explained to Eliot what was meant by the phrase 'at the present moment' in his original letter declining the gift. He clarified:

> The position is that we have a number of residential and other buildings left over to us from the British Government times which are expensive to maintain and rather too large for our requirements. None of these, of course, would fulfil the purposes for which Russborough would be ideal, and it may be that if the economic situation generally became brighter, it would be possible for a future Government to accept Lady Turton's offer. At the moment, however the prospects of this seems remote and it would be unfair to suggest to Lady Turton that she should refrain from making other arrangements regarding Russborough because of the likelihood of any early variation in the decision to which we were reluctantly forced to come.[174]

Eliot replied: 'I do not know at all how she proposes now to deal with the house, but should she decide to keep it and an opportunity should occur at any future date, we might perhaps renew the negotiations.'[175]

However, in June 1931, the *Irish Times* reported that Russborough House, 'one of the first early Georgian mansions in Ireland', had been purchased by Col. Daly, a British army officer.[176] This was a Col. Denis Daly, a relative of the Dalys who owned Dunsandle House, County Galway, which will be discussed in Chapter Three. The *Irish Times* made clear its admiration for the property, stating: 'Russborough House, situated in the midst of some of the most beautiful scenery in Wicklow, was formerly one of the show places in the County.'[177] After Daly's ownership, Russborough passed to Alfred and Lady Beit in 1953 and is currently in the possession of the Alfred Beit Foundation. Fulfilling Lady Turton's original wishes, the house and grounds are open to the public and the website elucidates on Russborough's colourful history and the tenacity of its various owners that led to its survival, overcoming two forced occupations of the house in 1798 and 1922, two fires in 1964 and 2010, and four robberies.

Despite the odds, Russborough 'continues to be one of the most stunning Irish houses open to the public'.[178]

In the end, government officials expressed their regret that they had to refuse this offer for economic reasons. While the Department of Finance did discuss Russborough's minimal interest due to its lack of nationalistic associations – and this belies a lack of appreciation for the importance of this architecture in its own right and its integral place in Irish history, even if in a negative role – what it appears to have been most concerned about was the expense involved in accepting and preserving Russborough House. The Minister and Secretary of the Department of Finance immediately recommended against acquisition, noting the vast sum of the budget for national monuments which this single building would take and their concerns that estimates for costs involved would have to be substantially revised upwards. It was only later in their letter that they discussed its merits for consideration under the National Monuments Act or its possible use to the public or the state, outlining that it was not in itself an exceptional example of Georgian architecture and that its use to the state would be minimal. The Department of Finance had to decide between preserving this single country house as a museum piece in itself – which they had no use for and were not aware of any public interest in preserving – or spending the same budget or less on protecting all the ancient monuments they listed which came under the scope of the National Monuments Act, including round towers, ogham stones, and even Newgrange. It is also worth remembering that the Department of Finance were not aware of any plans to demolish the house; in fact it was sold afterwards by the owner. The ultimate decision, it seems, was whether the government needed to, could be justified in, and, most significantly, could afford to accept and preserve these country houses. In the case of Russborough, the Department of Finance stated definitively that the answer was no. Undoubtedly, if the house had greater association with the nationalist history being espoused by the new state, the decision would have been more difficult to take, although, given the financial constraints under which the government was operating, the final outcome may have remained the same.

CONCLUSION

In the period 1922 to 1932, the first Cumann na nGaedheal Free State government was confronted with establishing law and order, overcoming the anti-Treatyites in the Civil War and laying the foundations of a newly independent state. As such, heritage preservation was not their main concern. In relation to houses damaged or destroyed during the Civil War, compensation under the 1923 Act was difficult to obtain and slow in coming; both factors combined to dissuade owners, who originally wanted to stay in Ireland from doing so. The Department of Finance was also necessarily running a very tight budget at this time; even attempting to establish the state on a secure financial footing was a considerable task. As such, the payment of large sums to owners to rebuild ostentatious mansions that no longer had any market value did not make sense to the economically bound administration. Thus, to tax the wealthy, or perceived wealthy, classes with high levels of death duties on large incomes and to charge rates on large houses made sense to a government and a populace who had no desire to perpetuate an elite wealthy class. The owners of such houses were much better off than a large proportion of the population in the 1920s who lived in 'rank poverty' and so, in theory, higher rates for larger houses made sense in terms of social justice. Nationalism undoubtedly played a role as well, and many of the leading politicians of the time had come from a militant republican background. Local councils too, which set the rates payable, were now dominated by local middle class and farming interests that had no desire to allow any privileges to the country house. Arguments for an easing of the financial burdens towards this class were therefore rare and usually voiced by the owners themselves, who were attempting to cultivate a new idea that they were now an impoverished ascendancy. While this may have been true in some cases it was also a useful image that made them more acceptable in a state grappling with poverty.

The difficult economic situation in which the new state found itself necessitated that the government naturally focused on issues that affected the very mortality of the majority of its citizens, in terms of sanitation and adequate housing, or attempted to tackle emigration, rather than the narrower concern that country houses were being sold on or destroyed. In fact, governments have always had to grapple with the limited budgets of the state. In 2008, reflecting on the challenges which governments had to overcome when faced with the destruction of country houses, Dr Garret FitzGerald recalled that while he tried to persuade his cabinet colleagues to offer a scheme that would allow country house owners maintain and retain their houses, he admitted that '[t]he economic situation in the 1970s and 1980s made this impossible'.[179] Furthermore, in this period Dooley has shown how the 1923 Land Act was an enormous financial burden on the new state, costing £30 million in comparison to the £10 million figure they had raised through the issuance of the First National Loan to fund government day-to-day expenditure and capital projects. In order to finance the Land Act, Cumann na nGaedheal had to seek a loan from Britain – recent political if not economic enemies. Ultimately, the sheer scale of the finances required to achieve this scheme for land division and distribution 'undoubtedly constrained the ambitions of Cumann na nGaedheal and, indeed, their expenditure in other areas of social policy', let alone heritage preservation, even if they had been sympathetic to this area.[180]

Even still, the 1930 National Monuments Act did legislate for the preservation of national heritage. One can see from departmental correspondence that, while no limiting date was specified in the act, it was usually only implemented for monuments that were dated pre-eighteenth century and not of more 'modern' construction. This may have been for a number of reasons and once again budget was paramount. The Department of Finance revealed in the discussion over Russborough that the OPW's annual budget for 1929 was £2,800, a small budget for the preservation and maintenance of all national monuments. As such their focus was on older sites and ruins that required no heavy maintenance expenditure, while the enormous maintenance costs involved in preserving a country house would take a huge portion of this budget. Furthermore, given the number of owners anxious to leave Ireland at this time, the government did not wish to make a precedent of taking on such properties. This consideration of expense was also the primary reason the Department of Finance recommended declining the offer of Russborough. In their estimate, it would have cost £5,000 in initial acquisition costs and over half the annual budget of the OPW to maintain, making it almost impossible for them to acquire and certainly disproportionately expensive in relation to other monuments perceived worthy of state care. Whether the government also exhibited nativist bias in the case of Russborough is not in question. Department of Finance officials spoke about the fact that Russborough was not particularly Irish and therefore less worthy of preservation, if indeed that had been possible.

The department's views should also be considered in the context of the time. The Department of Finance was administrating the finances of the country on behalf of a populace who appeared to have no interest in preserving the country houses and were primarily concerned that the land of such estates be divided. The issue of acquiring or using these mansions and other buildings left over from the British administration in Ireland was one of a publicly sensitive nature, and governments were aware of this when deciding on their future use and the amount of public finances that they would expend on their preservation and upkeep. Public opinion differed widely on whether they should be preserved or to what use they should be put – and some groups were deliberate in showing

the government their feelings. On 17 December 1932, for example, the Frank
Lawlor Cumann (local branch) of Fianna Fáil from Irishtown, Dublin, wrote
to the President of the Executive Council to inform him that they unanimously
passed a resolution stating 'that the most fitting use to which the late Viceregal
Lodge could be converted would be that of a Patriot Pantheon', and, therefore,
the former residence of British Viceroys would be 'purged of its evil associations.'[181] Given the difference in public opinion on such buildings, the department may have felt that they had no public mandate to expend so much public
money on a property like Russborough. This was particularly important when
its value to the public would at this time have been negligible. Moreover, the
Department of Finance argued that international tourists would go to Britain
to see such architecture, expecting to visit more native examples of the built
heritage in Ireland. In addition, the fact that Russborough was deemed 'too
modern' to be preserved illustrated the weaknesses of the conditions around
preserving monuments. The idea of vernacular architecture, particularly in
terms of ancient monuments, could not extend even as far as thatched cottages,
none of which were preserved under the 1930 Act either. In fact, as late as 1976,
in a Seanad debate on the Planning and Development bill 1973, Fianna Fáil
Senator Séamus Dolan suggested that

> Owners of houses of architectural value, if they are unoccupied should not have to pay
> rates ... These old houses have a value and character of their own. If we preserve them
> we will be doing something we might be thanked for in years to come. They would be
> a tourist attraction.[182]

Interestingly, Dolan recommended the same preservation for thatched cottages,
suggesting that the government's reluctance to preserve was a wider issue than
just undervaluing historic houses, particularly as he mentioned the 'stigma' that
had been attached to thatched cottages as the homes of the 'ancient Irish'. Until
the latter decades of the twentieth century, the state was not anxious to celebrate the fact that so many of its citizens had lived in poor, traditional housing
for so long.[183]

   Land division in this period under the 1923 and 1931 Acts cut off one of the
final air supplies to the country house and signalled the end for many. However,
an even more destructive period for the country house was on the horizon and,
as the Cumann na nGaedheal party was ousted from power in the 1932 election,
the country house problem would fall to a new government in a period when its
disappearance from the Irish landscape seemed inevitable.

TWO

THE COUNTRY HOUSE ABANDONED, 1932–48

In March 1932, Cumann na nGaedheal were defeated in the general election and Fianna Fáil assumed power under President of the Executive Council, Éamon de Valera.[1] This government remained in office until 1948, a period that saw an economic war with Britain, the enacting of the Irish Constitution and Irish neutrality during the Second World War. It was also a time during which the destruction of country houses and their abandonment became commonplace throughout the countryside. The visible and striking nature of the destruction and dereliction of these houses became a catalyst for stirring public concern. The government was prompted into action to investigate whether these country houses could survive in the new state by adaptation to new uses when they were no longer being maintained as residences by their owners. This chapter will examine why this concern developed, who articulated it, how the government responded, and what impact this had for the fate of the country house. An illustrative case study of Hazelwood House, County Sligo, will also be examined to assess how all these factors played out in an individual case.

SOCIETAL AND POLITICAL CONTEXT

In October 1936, *The Irish Press* recounted the story of a mother living in a tenement in George's Place, Dublin, who had seen five of her children die there.[2] This was one of a series of articles published in the paper that year that highlighted the deplorable conditions in the many slums in Dublin and in other cities throughout the country. According to the census of 1926, 22,649 Dublin families were living in overcrowded tenements.[3] Sickness and death rates in slum areas were almost twice what they were in the city's suburbs.[4] Furthermore, as late as 1938, the Citizens' Housing Council, a private body set up in response to the conditions in Dublin slums, published a report stating that there were, at the time, 9,440 families living in unfit houses, in comparison with the 7,967 families listed in this position in the 1913 Housing Inquiry,[5] illustrating that, nearing 1940, conditions for the poor in Dublin city were deteriorating. It also puts the issue of the 'impoverished gentry' and their decaying country houses into a broader sociological context; a context in which the government had to consider the question of the survival of the country house.

In addition, tensions between the British and Irish governments were heightening. The destruction of a statue of King George II in St Stephen's Green, Dublin, 1937, in response to the coronation of King George VI in England was also illustrative of the continuing anti-British sentiment felt by some sections of the public.[6] The incoming Fianna Fáil Government, elected in March 1932 under Éamon de Valera, reinforced a sense of separation and antagonism with Britain.[7] Fianna Fáil owed much of their success in the 1932 election to the disillusionment of the populace who had seen little change in their economic situation following independence. This government was also largely made up of those who had a hard-line nationalist stance on political matters, did not accept the Anglo-Irish Treaty of 1921 and had refused to join the First Dáil. One of the government's initial acts was to suspend payments of land annuities due to the British government owing from the various land acts passed under the British administration.[8] This refusal breached the terms of previous agreements between the governments. Economics aside, this was seen as a politically motivated move by de Valera to try to distance Ireland from Britain. In return, the British administration imposed emergency taxes on Irish agricultural exports. With Britain as Ireland's largest export market, this reaction from the British government was swift and harsh. The British response was also politically motivated, their aim being to so adversely affect Irish farmers that the Fianna Fáil government would be ousted and a more conciliatory Cumann na nGaedheal would return to power. In reality, the Economic War benefitted Fianna Fáil politically.[9] R. F. Foster has argued that 'de Valera used the "economic war" to brilliant political effect in domestic Irish terms. Traditional Anglophobia responded to the Fianna Fáil rhetoric of sacrifice in the face of foreign oppression; the snap election that returned Fianna Fáil in 1933 was largely fought on this basis.'[10] The Irish government reacted equally harshly and increased Irish protectionism by imposing restrictions on British imports to Ireland. In addition, the end of the 'war' was seen as a victory for Ireland, since, in 1938, when restrictions were eased by both sides, the land annuities that the Irish Government owed were exchanged for a £10 million once-off lump sum; far less than the estimated £100 million due for land annuities. In addition, naval ports on the Irish coast which the British had retained control of after 1922 were returned to the Irish state, thus enabling de Valera to declare neutrality during the Second World War, which began in 1939.[11]

The government, driven by de Valera's nationalist agenda, also enacted the Constitution of Ireland, *Bunreacht na hÉireann*, in 1937.[12] This document set out to define the Irish nation state. Dermot Keogh has maintained that the Constitution was 'the embodiment of the Catholic nationalist tradition' which de Valera 'personified in his public life'.[13] It also stated explicitly that no titles of nobility would be conferred or recognised, without government permission, by the Free State. This move directly targeted some country house owners' claim to status through their titles.[14] Most importantly for de Valera, the monarch and the Governor-General were now written out of the constitution. In addition, the government enacted a budget which made it harder for country houses to survive, due to increases in taxation rates and death duties on substantial houses, estates and wealth. This budget had such an effect on Lord Powerscourt that in 1932 the *Irish Times* reported that he had decided with 'regret' to part with his ancestral home, Powerscourt in Wicklow, owing to the burden of increased taxation. The paper feared he was only one of the first owners to realise that the position in the Free State 'under the recent budget ... [for] landowners and others living on invested capital' may simply be untenable.[15] They added that the 'most unfortunate feature about the matter is that many people who in the past have earned livings on big estates will find themselves deprived of living and friends as well'.[16] It was Lloyd George's 'People's Budget' of 1909 that actually introduced a 'super tax', calculated on gross incomes over a certain figure, which, along with interest rates, fluctuated throughout this period.[17] The Irish Free State inherited this tax and its rates of death duty from Britain, 'but by 1950 the rates had increased dramatically rising progressively from 6 per cent to 41.6 per cent in the intervening years. While from 1925 to 1930, a total of £5 million was paid in death duties in Ireland, this amount rose to a total of £13.4 million for the period from 1945 to 1950.'[18] Furthermore, a high ordinary income tax rate of 6s. in the pound was inherited by the Free State government, who in fact lowered it to 3s. in the pound in 1928.[19] However, Terence Dooley has shown that 'in the face of economic depression and the Economic War with Britain, it rose from 3s. 6d. in the pound in 1932 to a high of 7s. 6d. in the pound in 1942' so that 'over half of earned or invested incomes of over £10,000 per annum was lost to taxes by 1950'.[20] This was particularly detrimental to former landlords' income since most had invested income or bonds, received in return for the acquisition of land under the land acts, hoping they would be a similarly sustaining source of income.[21] This was also the case in Northern Ireland by the early twentieth century when, after the sale of estates, the predominant source of income for country house families changed from rental to investments.[22] Invested incomes had already proven disastrous in some cases for families who lost large portfolios resulting from the 1929 Wall Street Crash and the subsequent depression.[23]

In 1932, the *Irish Times* was keen to place the entire blame for the demise of the house on the state's taxation policy. Its report declared:

> The dead hand of the state lies heavily on the great houses ... A great house, whether its history has been good or bad, possesses a soul that vanishes with its owners ... Sentiment, however, cannot stand against the pressure of hard facts ... The money which would have kept the soul in a great house must pass to-day into the coffers of Governments and it is better that the estates should pass into other hands than that they should be compelled to go to ruin in the hands of their impoverished owners.[24]

The political and cultural leanings of the *Irish Times* must also influence how one reads their coverage of such issues. John Healy was editor of the *Irish Times* at this juncture; he was the longest-serving editor and was in this position from 1907–34. One reporter described Healy as 'a man of remarkable inflexibility of mind' and, during his time at the helm the paper, 'still clung to its old attitudes'.[25] The same reporter described how Healy 'clung jealously to the few links that still bound the two nations [Ireland and Britain], and watched with sadness the gradual loosening by Mr Cosgrave's Government and their virtual destruction under the Presidency of Mr de Valera'.[26] Furthermore, Healy was characterised as 'a west British pedant ... who could not accept the fact that the establishment of the Free State represented a major change in Irish relations with Britain' resulting in the claim that, at this juncture in Irish history, the paper was read 'almost exclusively, by Church of Ireland clerics, Trinity dons and the remaining occupants of the "big house" and their minions'.[27] All the factors mentioned above meant that the passing of the country house from generation to generation within families already living in much reduced circumstances was very difficult, causing the destruction or desertion of many country houses in this period.

SALE, ABANDONMENT AND DESTRUCTION

In the absence of robust data, figures for the destruction of country houses are very difficult to arrive at, but the demolition of 15 houses, at the very least, took place between 1930 and 1950, predominantly the period when this Fianna Fáil administration was in government. This is not inclusive of those houses that were abandoned to dereliction and ruin.[28] This figure is a very rough estimate, in the absence of concrete quantitative data, from the 1988 revised edition of Mark Bence-Jones's *A Guide to Irish Country Houses*, which listed some 2,000 country houses. The criterion for inclusion in this volume was that the house was a country house, not a town property, 'which, at some stage in its history, was the country seat of a landed family or at any rate of a family of some standing in the locality'.[29] An analysis of the houses mentioned in Jones's book and their fate at the time of its publication is inaccurate, but necessary, in order to get a sense of broad estimates when figures for the numbers of houses demolished, ruined, abandoned or otherwise in this period are scant or non-existent. Therefore, it at least gives a sense of the most destructive periods for the country house in these decades, despite the difficulties with providing precise figures from this work.[30] Using estimates from this book, the decade between 1950 and 1960 appears to have been the most destructive period for the country house in Ireland, far outweighing the other decades under study here in terms of demolition of buildings. By an approximate estimation, over 200 houses were demolished, ruined or abandoned between 1920 and 1970, as listed by Bence-Jones, although this number is likely to be revised significantly upwards if detailed quantitative analysis on this issue were ever undertaken in future.[31] Approximately 254 of the 4,500 country houses compiled on the National University of Ireland, Galway's landed-estates database which covers the provinces of Connacht and Munster, are listed as demolished, only about five per cent of the total. Furthermore, over 50 houses were taken over by religious orders as convents, novitiates, schools and so on.[32] These included Mount

Anville, County Dublin, which was transformed into a girls' convent school; Moore Abbey, County Kildare, which became a hospital run by the Sisters of Jesus and Mary; Gallen Priory, Offaly, which was converted into a convent; Loftus Hall, County Wexford, which also became a convent, and Kylemore Abbey, County Galway, which was turned into a convent and school, among many others.

By estimate, out of the 2,000 houses listed in Bence-Jones' work, only approximately 10 per cent were definitively destroyed, ruined or abandoned. Even allowing for the fact that this is a rough estimate and no fate was recorded for many houses, this is still quite a small proportion. Furthermore, Bence-Jones has since argued that only 10 per cent of the 2,000 properties recorded in his book are still in the hands of the original owners. Therefore, if only 10 per cent of country houses are still owned as homes by their original owners and over 10 per cent were destroyed, it seems probable that the majority of country houses were sold to new owners or put to other use by the state, private businesses or religious orders. While there may be debates about the damage such transformations do to the historical integrity of such a property, one can see from the evidence above that perhaps as many as 80 per cent of the 2,000 country houses documented by Bence-Jones survived through such trans-formation, in contrast to the 10 per cent still in the hands of original owners. Hence such adaptations may account for the survival of most country houses in Ireland today. The difficulties for the survival of the country house in the twenty-six counties in this period were similar to those faced by the country house in Northern Ireland and Britain. This challenges the idea of exception-alism with regard to the destruction of Irish country houses. Olwen Purdue has maintained that, while similar, the position of the country house in the 26 coun-ties in the first decades of the twentieth century was worse. She wrote that big houses disappeared in Ireland 'through the inability of the owner to maintain them, through violent destruction, or because, no longer having any role in the new Ireland that had been created to exclude them, their owners simply closed the door behind them and left'.[33]

By 1943, Anglo-Irish Free State Senator Sir John Keane was drawing atten-tion to the position of the owner who was 'struggling to live on his demesne', being 'overhoused', with 'no surplus cash income'.[34] Keane was also quick to point out that the loss of a country house would result in unemployment in rural localities, demonstrating his awareness of the necessity to appeal to the value of maintaining these properties by highlighting their economic importance.[35] Furthermore, he emphasised that he was not talking about wealthy demesne owners, as they 'do not deserve very exceptional treatment'.[36] Rather he was speaking of owners who were now struggling financially and called them 'a very deserving class in the community ... They are very poor, a new genteel poor'.[37] In relation to a reduction of rates on country houses, he asked the Minister for Finance 'not to cling too rigidly to the official point of view of his advisors, but really to consider the human aspect of these cases which, I think, has never appealed so far to his departmental advisers.'[38] In reply, the Fianna Fáil Finance Minister, Seán T. Ó Ceallaigh, maintained that if an individual made a case, he may have the value reduced,[39] although it belied an unwillingness to change the general official line towards these houses and owners. Exceptions may be made in particular circumstances to a rule that, in itself, made it increasingly difficult for owners to survive. However, rates on houses were a burden on every member of the community; therefore, the government would have made a very unpopular move if they had reduced rates only for people living in the historic mansions of Ireland.[40]

Such was the decline in the number of country houses held by original owners that in 1946 the *Irish Independent* argued: 'in Great Britain, as in Ireland, the Big House is passing. Perhaps it would be more accurate to say it is changing character ... the crushing death duties which have been, in effect, a series of capital levies on successive owners, have made the rich poorer without making the poor richer'.[41] Clontarf Castle was one such property, which was sold in 1957 as a result of the onerous death duties incurring on the death of John George Oulton. Sarah Connolly-Carew also remembered the effects of death duties at her family home, Castletown House, County Kildare. She recalled how:

> Uncle Ted's funeral came two years after our Scottish Grandfather's unexpected death at sea, and the Connolly-Carew and Maitland families were caught in a double round of Death Duties and Inheritance Taxes. I wonder if he knew that after his death, the great estate would start crumbling around us? I pray not. Almost immediately, even to us children, it became obvious that the woodland rides were no longer cut back and tidied every year, the numbers of farm workers were drastically reduced, and the number of servants in the house cut from twelve to six.[42]

Still, duties were not so exorbitant that residence in a country house was impossible and, in fact, the position was seen to be better than England, where the house bore none of the historical baggage that its Irish counterpart did. In 1946 the *Nenagh Guardian* reported on an influx of a wealthy elite to Ireland. They described how the 'monied classes' in Britain, fearing the new Labour government, were instead decamping to country houses in Ireland that had been 'vacant since the exodus at the Treaty time' and were being 'snapped up at fabulous prices'.[43] Harristown House, County Kildare, was one such property. Formerly belonging to Percy La Touche, it was purchased by a British army general for £44,000.[44] In July 1938, the *Irish Times* described the reaction to such a situation in England where, at a conference there, one of the speakers suggested it was 'a national duty' to retain landed families on their properties and so 'safeguard the pride of Britain' by considering proposals such as exemptions from taxation, rates and death duties.[45] The paper reported that in Ireland the problem was exacerbated as owners left their houses vacant, and indeed, left the country as well. Once the country house was untenanted for a long period, the Land Commission stepped in to divide the estate, as it was unused and unlived on. The paper wasn't reluctant, however, in blaming the state for the demise of the country house, stating that 'while in England the destruction of the landed families is probably unintentional, in this country it is part of a deliberate policy.'[46] The fact that taxation policies in both countries were very similar and that there are no Irish government files suggesting that they deliberately sought to end this way of life, questions this assertion by the *Irish Times*. What is undeniable, though, is that the break-up of estates in order to divide up the land was a policy pursued by this Fianna Fáil government.

THE ACQUISITION OF MUCKROSS HOUSE AND ESTATE

Interestingly, one of the first acts of this government on this issue was to accept the offer of Muckross House and estate as a gift to the nation by Senator Arthur Vincent in 1932. There appears to have been little or no discussion of the merits of the gift in government. With little hesitation, on 5 September 1932, Conor Maguire, the Attorney General, wrote to the owner, Senator Vincent:

> I am now in a position to inform you that the Executive Council is in favour of accepting on behalf of the state the offer of the Muckross estate. It is hardly necessary to say that the President and council appreciate the spirit in which this splendid gift is being offered to the nation ... Irishmen everywhere will rejoice that a demesne famous for its beauty and so rich in historical associations is about to become national property.[47]

It is clear that the government's attraction to the gift was primarily in the demesne, which would provide, in many ways, greater amenity value and wider appeal than the house. The gift was subject to the conditions that the estate would be known as the Bourn Vincent Memorial Park and that Mr Bourn would have the right to erect a monument to his daughter in the park.[48] On 16 November 1932, the solicitors for Vincent wrote to the Attorney General enclosing an announcement they had formulated for the press, which he forwarded to the Minister for Finance.[49] The announcement was entitled: 'Great new national park; the Muckross Estate, Killarney, to be given to the nation' and explained that the gift had been assured to the government through the generosity of Mr William Bowers Bourn of California, who had originally bought the property from the late Lord Ardilaun, and settled it on his son-in-law, Senator Arthur Vincent.[50] It reported that the government would take over the property as a going concern, acquiring all effects necessary for the occupation of the house, the retaining of the famous herd of Kerry cattle, the boats and the farming implements and machinery from the estate.[51] Arthur Codling, Assistant Secretary to the Minister for Finance (and an Englishman), added a paragraph to the announcement which read: 'we feel sure that Irishmen, not only in this country, but throughout the world, will learn with great pleasure of the generous gift of the donors. The beauties of Killarney are world-famed. Henceforth they can by no mischance become the monopoly of a privileged few; they are part of the heritage of the nation.'[52]

It is clear that the land of this estate, particularly in the famed scenery of Killarney and its amenity value to the public, was the primary reason the state took over this property, rather than for the preservation of the country house. The acceptance of this gift did not mean the government viewed these houses as worthy of conservation in their own right, particularly when owned by the 'privileged few'. The demesne land remaining with the property was an incredibly important aspect in the survival of the country house. Public parks, golf clubs and hotels all depend on the land more than the house, and it was the attraction of this land that in many cases saved the houses at the centre of such estates. This is illustrated further by the fact that, after the passing of the 1932 Bourn Vincent Memorial Park Act, the government took possession of the estate and opened it to the public, although Muckross House itself lay idle until 1962 when eventually it was opened as a museum in a joint venture between the trustees of Muckross House and the state. The government's original focus on the demesne is important as later statistics illustrate that many more people benefited from that amenity than from the house. The National Parks and Wildlife Service noted that the number of paying visitors to Muckross House in 2003, at its peak, was 200,632, while the total number of users for the demesne and national park (the land total was added to since the gift of Muckross) was over one million.[53]

Many estates were primarily acquired for their land, arboretums or amenity areas. One example is St Anne's in Raheny, Dublin, where the house burned down in an accidental fire when in state care. It was the land of the estate that was considered valuable for providing housing and amenities to Dublin city. Similarly, in the case of Kilmacurragh, County Wicklow, the arboretum was the draw in discussions surrounding its acquisition – the house was barely mentioned. Later when Fota estate, County Cork, was considered for purchase, all the public pressure on the government to acquire the estate, even in the early 1970s, was focused on the preservation of the land as an amenity for Cork city. Apart from An Taisce's submission to the government on Fota, the only other letter that even mentioned the preservation of the house, and again suggested its use as a museum, was from Liam Irwin, Secretary of the Irish History Students' Association (IHSA). He wrote to the Taoiseach to inform him that the IHSA's AGM had unanimously passed a motion supporting An Taisce's proposal that the government acquire Fota Island for the nation.[54] The concern in all of the other letters that the government received was that the land on the island would be made available as public amenity space, including golf courses. This attitude was mirrored to an even greater extent in England, where Mandler has shown that many country houses were acquired by local authorities in order to use the land for housing and amenity development in suburban areas. In such cases, 'the houses often came as unwelcome baggage with a property desired for its recreational value.'[55] One such example was Temple Newsam and its 600-acre park, which was sold to Leeds Corporation on very easy terms in 1922, again primarily for the amenity value of its lands.[56]

Ironically, it was land that was also behind most negative perceptions of country house owners, considered by many as the descendants of usurping land-lords who had unjustly acquired land that belonged to the 'native' Gaelic Irish. In a Dáil debate on the 1933 Land bill, which became the 1933 Land Act, Fianna Fáil's Minister for Defence, Frank Aiken, speaking on behalf of the Minister for Lands and Fisheries, stated: 'derelict residences shall no longer protect lands required for division',[57] while Mícheál Cleary argued that it was 'the duty of the state to step in and say that the men whose forefathers were evicted from these lands should be restored to them'.[58] The 1933 Land Act introduced by Fianna Fáil gave the Land Commission more far-reaching powers to compulsorily acquire land than they previously had when residential land was excluded.[59] This was an exemption in previous land acts, which was used by many land-owners to include outlying lands or farms, even if it only contained a residence unoccupied, derelict or ruined. The 1933 Act was specifically designed to stop these practices. Furthermore, the Land Commission could now acquire land when the owners did not live in the area or use the land as ordinary farmers. Dooley has shown how effective this 1933 Act was, writing: 'by the late 1930s, the old landed estates had eventually been broken up in Ireland. The Free State Land Acts had vested 113,800 holdings on just over 3 million acres in the Land Commission for £20.8 million'.[60] He has argued that as a result 'the reduction of retained land below a viable level began a downward economic spiral that was impossible for big house owners to reverse. It was tantamount to ruin especially with the rise in taxation.'[61]

The division of land and the subsequent break-up of the demesnes upon which the houses were centred was seen as the natural culmination of an agrarian and national struggle that had been fought since the Land War of the late nineteenth century. The demise of the landed class was thus also sought and presumed to be part of this land division process. In a 1939 land bill debate, the Minister for Lands, Gerald Boland, elucidated that 'it is a great pity that the landlords did not take the advice given to them by Thomas Davis a century ago; that they could have been a force in this country for good'.[62] He did allow that there may have been exceptions, astutely tipping his hat to a number of senators who had been members of the landed class, including Sir John Keane. Nonetheless, he maintained his unabashed antagonism towards them because generally 'they were a poor lot and they let their opportunities go, and the less we say about them now the better.'[63] In the same debate Senator Christopher Byrne embodied similar attitudes towards this class as unjustifiably owning land and wealth when he argued: 'we are not going to stand by and allow one-fourth of the people to own three-fourths of the land, while the three-fourths have to live on the one-fourth', thus expressing the view that the landed class unjustifiably held Irish land and wealth.[64] In fact, this did not apply to most of the former ascendancy after the land acts of the early twentieth century. The Irish landscape was changing, and its new image, as it was being constructed by this government and its ministers, was no longer centred on the country house, their vast estates or the elite class who owned them. As they disappeared, the dramatic sight of derelict and demolished country houses throughout the Irish countryside began to garner significant attention for the first time. Arguments were voiced, calling for these houses to be put to use rather than demolished. This concern was first expressed by the public, the media and other politicians, not the sitting government.

Illustrative of this growing interest in the country house, and fuelling it further, was the *Irish Times*. In May 1936 the *Weekly Irish Times* began a series entitled 'Historic Irish Mansions' by James Fleming on the subject of country houses with original families still in possession.[65] This series continued for five years until 29 November 1941 when it had covered 291 houses. The amount of houses featured reveals the number of mansions that were still owned by original families. In addition, this was a high-profile feature on many houses and families that may have been previously unknown, coming as it did little more than ten years after the targeting and burnings of country houses that took place during the Civil War. Perhaps it was considered that such a danger had passed, or owners realised that the readership of the *Weekly Irish Times* were interested in their houses solely for their historic merit. Either way, this was a long-running series that proves that there was interest in the history of such houses as early as the 1930s.

It is worth asking why public interest and concern around the destruction of the country house was awakened at this time. Was it because the country house had growing novelty as something that was being 'lost', a much more sentiment-inducing motif than the maintenance of a private home of which there were many? Certainly, the visual poignancy of the destruction of country houses garnered more attention than abandonment or gradual dereliction could evoke. This was again the case when, in 1974, 'The Destruction of the Country House' exhibition opened at the Victoria and Albert Museum in London. It charted the disappearance of the country house in Britain to great and stark effect and inspired groups to focus on the country house and the preservation of the built heritage, like SAVE Britain's heritage, which was founded the following year. It also served to stir public consciousness. In 1989 a similarly deliberately stark and emotive exhibition, 'Vanishing Country Houses of Ireland', sponsored by Christies – paradoxically a company responsible for the sale of much country house contents from Ireland – began running at Powerscourt House, County Wicklow. The calls for a halt to the demolition of such houses during the 1930s and 1940s were also predominately motivated by the consideration that these buildings could be put to alternative use within the community, rather than being motivated by concern that the house as a private residence should be preserved. In fact, it is worth noting that any concerns voiced during this period, when such concerns tentatively began to be voiced, were for the houses as grand buildings, not as ancestral homes of former landed families.

The importance of attitudes towards owners in terms of influencing wider opinion is a theme that remains constant throughout the period covered in this book. As the original owners sold, left or abandoned their houses, the minority who remained became more isolated than ever, and were considered the remains of a departed ascendancy on the shadowy margins of Irish life. Dooley has described how:

> It was difficult for those who remained in Ireland to integrate into the political, social or cultural mainstream of Irish life. Most families attempted to keep a foot in both Ireland and Britain. They continued to look to British public schools, Oxbridge and military colleges for their education, They continued to serve Britain as soldiers and in Britain as politicians ... However, attempting to keep a foot in both countries did not help these families to become fully integrated in either Ireland or Britain. In Ireland, they were generally perceived as being British; in Britain they were generally perceived as being Irish.[66]

In independent Ireland, the owners' drift into oblivion went either unnoticed, was considered indifferently, or was presumed to have already taken place. Elizabeth Bowen, the writer who lived in Bowen's Court, County Cork, recognised this divide and stated in 1941 that if country houses were to survive, barriers on both sides of the demesne walls would have to be broken down.[67] Interestingly, the late Egerton Shelswell-White of Bantry House, also in Cork, has commented that when he was a child, 'the estate wall seemed like a prison keeping me in, not just keeping other people out.'[68] While this period did see the literal destruction of the estate walls by land division, the psychological, cultural and social barriers that separated Anglo-Irish owners from the rest of the population actually appeared to grow. As their houses were being dismantled, the landed class were portrayed as disintegrating. In fact, by 1942 Independent Wicklow TD Patrick Cogan referred to them as already extinct. For the remaining members, this rhetoric served to utterly negate their identity and presence in the country. Cogan stated that previously 'we were inclined to denounce and freely denounce, the old landlord class who ruled our rural areas. We got rid of them.'[69] This was presumed as a given, even as he highlighted the positive contribution this class made to society and regretted their loss. He gave lip service to the popular critique of landlords, but also asserted that 'some of them were not so bad and, in clearing out that class, we destroyed a section of it who contributed far more to the development of the land than we have been able to contribute under our own democratic administration.'[70] Meanwhile, the necessary changing lifestyle of this class was caricatured by the *Irish Times* in 1934 when it reported: 'the duke, pursued by the income-tax collectors, has gone to live in a London mews. His daughter is a waitress in a tea-shop, and his son sells motor cars to the wealthy descendants of men who held horses in the yard fifty years ago.'[71]

NEW USES

Many of the country houses were now empty and therefore also 'emptied' of
symbolic association with the Anglo-Irish landed class, so they could be put to
use in the new state. Public committees and politicians wrote to the government
suggesting that these houses be used as schools, hostels, hotels or TB sanatoria. In the absence of information on their suitability for such adaptations,
the houses were simply thought of as large, well-made buildings which would
be expensive to erect again and therefore should be put to some public use.
For the first time in such numbers, concerned parties wrote to the government
suggesting that the responsibility to preserve and use these houses was the
government's, not the choice of private owners. Empty, these houses could be
made to play a new role in the state, but only if the government was motivated
to transform them to do so.

Public opinion differed widely on their possible new adaptations. In a 1939
Dáil debate on the Tourist Traffic bill, Fianna Fáil TD for Leitrim, Bernard
Maguire, argued that

> Many of these mansions could be utilised at very little cost and turned into very useful
> hostels or hotels … I believe these old mansions which, in most cases, are white
> elephants on the hands of the Land Commission, and in many cases are being pulled
> down at public expense, could be utilised and thus continue to pay rates to the local
> authorities.[72]

In 1943, Fine Gael TD for Leix-Offaly, Dr Thomas O'Higgins, suggested using
some of them as TB sanatoria. He emphasised that every county had 'splendid
mansions' that are 'in the custody of either the department of Defence or the
Minister for the Co-ordination of Defensive Measures' and asked for discussion with 'whatever department controls those beautiful empty mansions' as
they would be ideal centres for evacuees.[73] Alternatively, in 1938, Fine Gael TD
for Donegal East, Daniel McMenamin, suggested that a number of 'very fine
mansions' that were semi-derelict be taken over as domestic training schools.[74]

Peter Mandler has shown that the situation in England was similar and
that the thinking of the time was, 'short of demolition, white elephants might
be converted to some remunerative use. When this occurred, sentimentality
was rarely an issue, more a grim determination to exploit all available assets
to their fullest.'[75] The emphasis on using these houses for some public good is
understandable in the context of these decades of economically straightened
times in Ireland and Britain, and remains a reasonable argument today. If these

houses cannot be used for some public good then should public funds be used to preserve them? That public good may not be turning them into a hospital but may well be preserving the house for future generations to enjoy as a museum or aspect of architectural history, but the public good in doing so, and the value of the preservation to a significant body of the population, should be considered. In 1933, the *Irish Times* also reported that the fate of the country house in Ireland was being replicated in Britain, where:

> The 'Big House' is being turned from its old functions to services for which it was never intended, but for which it seems to be completely suited ... Lord Northbourne has let his Kentish seat to be a preparatory school and the famous Maidwell Hall ... has just been sold for another school. Among famous English houses which have been converted into schools in recent years are Stowe, Canford Manor, Maiden Erleagh.[76]

A similar pattern was being woven in Ireland, where the 1939 acquisition of Donamon Castle, County Roscommon, by the Divine Word Missionaries continued a trend of religious orders acquiring country houses.

There was also concern in 1941 about another aspect of the destruction of country houses. However, the argument was not for their preservation, but rather that dismantled and demolished country houses should be used by the government for their raw materials. Lead, for example, had become a very valuable commodity during the Emergency, from 1939 to 1945. Houses were bought for demolition by speculators interested in selling off valuable slates or lead from their roofs, while the Land Commission also demolished some houses on acquired lands, from which they could use the materials to build factories and roads. Country houses had become far more valuable and useful for their parts than when they were standing. In April 1941, in the Dáil, Deputy Seán Broderick, Fine Gael TD for Galway East, urged the Minister of Local Government and Public Health, Mayo North TD Patrick J. Ruttledge, to recognise that country houses had 'good roofing' and 'the finest of slates, which could be used on houses again' and he asked the Minister to work with the Land Commission to use these materials instead of allowing the houses to be sold for a paltry sum, when their 'timber and roofing' was subsequently sold on 'at a huge profit'.[77] Yet even the virulently nationalist Fine Gael TD for Meath-Westmeath, Captain Patrick Giles, did not agree with Broderick, although preservation was not quite on his agenda either. He stated that when large estates are divided, the '"big mansion" was always a problem', claiming that such houses were built of the best of granite, with stabling and lofts that any man would envy'. 'Unfortunately,' he went on, 'under the blind policy of the Land Commission', they had been sold and 'men have come with axes and crowbars, have torn them down and made roads from the material, while people in the country are crying out for granaries for the storage of grain.' He believed that the Land Commission should be required to leave an adequate supply of land around the houses on sale to ensure that they could be taken on by someone and viably maintained. He argued:

> They may be monuments of inequity in the past, built on the sweat of slaves, but they are there at present, and they are Irish property, and the Land Commission should think twice before tearing down even one of them. I ask the Land Commission to realise that they are more valuable than as material for making yards and roads. Let them be utilised for something.[78]

Twenty years later, however, this hot-headed TD blustered: 'those old houses should be blown sky-high. They were built with slave labour and the blood of decent men. Two or three of them were blown up by the Land Commission in County Meath and I was delighted.'[79]

The influence of the Minister for Lands on the Land Commission's policy in relation to houses they acquired with land could be significant if the minister were interested in making his mark, as will be discussed in Chapter Five. Fianna Fáil TD for Cork North, Seán Moylan, who was Minister for Lands from June 1944 to February 1948, certainly had strong views on the matter. He had been very influential in the struggle in Cork during the War of Independence and no doubt this shaped his opinion. On the subject of country houses acquired by the Commission, Moylan stated his view clearly that

> The Land Commission, of course, and every other Department have permitted the destruction of certain houses, with which I do not agree. But, in general, the majority of these big houses that I know, and I am very familiar with them, are not structurally sound, have no artistic value and no historic interest. From my unregenerate point of view, I choose to regard them as tombstones of a departed ascendency and the sooner they go down the better – they are no use.[80]

Dooley has also cited Moylan as an example of how: 'after independence, Free State/Irish Republic Governments were slow to show any type of sympathy or concern for the plight of country houses. There was little appreciation in government circles for their cultural heritage value.'[81] He argued that Seán Moylan illustrated such attitudes when, in February 1944, Seán Flanagan, TD, asked Moylan as Minister for Lands, if he would hand over the country houses situated on Land Commission-divided estate lands, instead of allowing them to fall into decay or to be demolished. Moylan replied: 'residences on lands acquired by the Land Commission for division which are not suitable for disposal to allottees may be demolished in order to provide material for building smaller houses for allottees or may be sold by public auction, at which it is open for such bodies as the deputy mentions to bid for them.'[82] Moylan only spoke, here about the destruction of houses which were of no use, but he also embodied the views of this Fianna Fáil government who, despite growing public and political concern, viewed the position of the country house with apathy or indifference. Its destruction was considered to be the concern of private individuals or even a natural consequence; an inevitable by-product of reclaiming the land of Ireland for the 'Irish', which the government was intent on being seen to do, and which their voting constituencies were eager for them to live up to.

This attitude also seems to have been pervasive in local authorities which allowed no relief on rates due on these houses, even when put to new uses by national organisations. An Taisce, the National Trust for Ireland, which was created in 1948 by Robert Lloyd Praeger, was restricted in its work because it was not given exemptions from rates or duties on properties. Furthermore, in 1944, the *Irish Press* reported that a great barrier to the extension of An Óige, the Irish Youth Hostel Association founded in 1931, was a lack of hostels, but country houses could only be taken on for such purposes if there was a reduction in rates.[83] The article described how, all over Ireland:

> There are to be found, in various states of preservation, fine Georgian structures that were formally seats of the landowners. Many have already been razed to the ground; others are in danger of suffering a similar fate. There must surely be a sufficient number which could be adapted as hostels for youth and it would be hard to find a better use for them.[84]

A few days later the paper reported that their suggestion that disused mansions be converted into youth hostels had been 'warmly commended' by leaders of An Óige and the Irish Tourist Association (ITA), which was a voluntary organisation that promoted tourism in the Free State.[85] This article quoted David Barry, Secretary of the ITA, who had said that the paper's suggestion was very good if the mansions were in holiday districts and that the conversion of a number of the old mansions would meet the need for more accommodation, and some might even be set aside for holiday hostels for adults.[86] J. J. Waldron, National Secretary of An Óige, had replied that 'the big empty houses in these areas would ... be ideal for hostels, but if they were made available on free loan there would have to be some concession in the matter of rates, as in Britain and other countries.'[87] Assistant Secretary of An Óige, Seaghan O'Brien, also welcomed the suggestion and pointed out that, within its limited resources, An Óige had recently purchased Aughavannagh House, County Wicklow, former home of John Redmond, for the bargain price of £350. Furthermore, a trustee of An Óige said that the suggestion was timely as 'a large house which they had been using near New Ross had been bought and demolished for scrap.'[88] This is particularly notable, as this mansion was not lying derelict but being put to good use by an organisation who required it, and yet still it was demolished. This illustrates how much more valuable these houses were at this time razed to the ground for their scrap materials, particularly during the Emergency, than left standing, lived in, rented or derelict. The paper added that this type of mansion was successfully being used for youth hostels in Britain and European countries.[89]

Aside from youth hostels, local corporations were also imaginatively exploring possible uses for these unoccupied mansions. In 1944 the *Irish Independent* reported that they were glad to see that Limerick Corporation was leading the movement to explore the possibility of acquiring a country house for a temporary TB sanatorium. Somewhat naively, the paper commented: 'coincident with this announcement appears the offer for demolition of two more big mansions. One of them seems to be in perfect order and the other boasts splendid dance floors. Surely a dance floor is just what is needed to accommodate a row of hospital beds.'[90] The reporter wrote that, when one considered the amount of time it would take the ratepayers to provide the £50,000 to £100,000-type of building that was the present 'grandiose standard for institutions of this kind, the demolition of solidly-built mansions that one would not now build for the price of an institution, seems the height of foolishness and vandalism'.[91] She believed country houses were ideal for agricultural demonstration centres, rural educational and recreation centres, district farm and cookery schools, convalescent homes, holiday homes for workers and children, and sanatoria, all of which, she argued, would be out of the question if they had been newly-built, concluding: 'such mansions present so many possibilities for the recreation and the welfare of the people that their destruction should be stopped without delay'.[92] The article appeared to ignore the expensive works that would be needed to restore many of these properties and also to convert them to the innumerable new uses mentioned. Similarly, the *Irish Times* also believed that 'some of the large empty country houses would make excellent sanatoria'.[93] In contrast, the *Irish Press* reported that three surveys of disused mansions had been made in recent years, and 'from the viewpoint of adopting them as sanatoria, the results have been most disappointing'.[94]

However, one mansion, at least, did appear to be suitable, as in 1944 Ballinderry House, County Westmeath, was bought by Westmeath County Council as a temporary sanatorium, thereby proving, despite government reports, that such adaptation was possible.[95] Westmeath County Council appear to have been particularly opposed to the destruction of the country house, as in June 1944 the Secretary of Westmeath County Council wrote to the Taoiseach, Éamon de Valera, sending him a resolution that had been passed unanimously by the Council that 'We, the members of Westmeath County Council protest against the demolition of mansions in Co. Westmeath.'[96]

In reality, apart from being converted to large schools, novitiates or convents, there were not many other purposes to which these houses could be put, particularly by the state. As Allen Warren has argued: 'these houses were never businesses, more objects of consumption to enhance power and status'[97] and therefore usually unsuitable for adaptation to other purposes. Dooley has emphasised that, by the 1940s, 'abandoned and disused mansions were considered only in terms of how they might be used as hospitals in a bid to eradicate the tuberculosis health crisis in Ireland and at another stage how they might be used for the advantage of such organisations as An Óige, the Irish Tourist Board or the Youth Training Body.'[98] The Irish Tourist Board was established under the Tourist Traffic Act, 1939, a precursor to Bord Fáilte and Fáilte Ireland. The Irish Tourist Association already existed before this time, but without any state support. After the passing of this Act, it received an annual grant to continue its work and the Association embarked on a project in the early 1940s to record the assets of localities in Ireland from a tourism perspective, including architectural heritage.

The focus at this time on whether these country houses could be put to some public good is understandable, as it was the only way they could be used and therefore preserved, even in the practical terms of being lived in, heated and maintained. In reality, only a minority were ever put to use and this period was one of the most destructive in terms of the decline and disappearance of the country house in Ireland. This situation was mirrored in England. David Cannadine has argued that between '1945 and 1955, four hundred country houses were destroyed, more than at any other period of modern British history' as they were 'too big, too uneconomical and often damaged beyond repair, the setting for a life and for a class now generally believed to be extinct'.[99]

GOVERNMENT RESPONSE

In 1943 the Irish government responded to increasing public concern over the destruction of houses by commissioning a report on the issue to be carried out by the Department of Local Government. Cabinet minutes of 30 September 1943 record that it had been decided that the department should have a survey made of disused country mansions and should examine the question of their utilisation in consultation with other concerned departments.[100] A note of 8 December reported that the department had 'circularised County managers for a list of disused country mansions and that when the reports were received the houses would be inspected by the department and housing inspectors' and a memorandum would be prepared for government.[101] It was 17 May 1945 when the Department of Local Government and Public Health compiled this memorandum. The department's housing inspectors carried out the survey and submitted reports on 330 buildings. Copies of the reports were forwarded to the Departments of Defence, Industry and Commerce, Lands and the Office of Public Works. The Department of Defence had replied that 'the experience gained by the use of such buildings for the accommodation of troops during the Emergency indicates that they are quite unsuitable for military purposes, and accordingly that the department is not interested in their future use.'[102] The OPW stated that it was very unlikely that any of the premises could be economically useable for their accommodation or office requirements, illustrating that this report was only assessing whether country houses could be used as accommodation for government departments or state bodies, rather than as part of the wider brief of heritage preservation. As with the thrust of public agitation on the issue at this time, for the government too, the practical use to which such houses could be put was considered paramount. The Department of Lands had no observations to offer on the reports, while the Department of Industry and Commerce forwarded the reports to the Irish Tourist Board, which had taken the particulars of a number of houses which could have been of possible interest to the Board, although they considered many of the houses as 'suitable only for demolition and salvage'.[103] They were interested in this aspect of the question as the salvaged materials could have been used to construct holiday camps, for example. This is particularly interesting as the body responsible for the promotion of tourism in Ireland at this time concluded that these houses were not important as tourist attractions, presumably based on their figures and experience. However, the Irish Tourist Board had acquired one such house, Monea House, County Waterford, and proposed to acquire Glenart Castle, Courtown

House and Marlfield House, County Wicklow, and Classiebawn Castle, County Sligo. It appears that Monea House was turned into an Irish college and therefore its primary use was a large building for classes, not as a historical attraction on its own merits. Furthermore, the Board's plans to acquire the other houses did not come to fruition in many, if any, cases.

A number of the buildings included in the Department of Local Government and Public Health's report were also considered for adaptation as accommodation for TB patients, but were ultimately deemed unsuitable. The memorandum concluded that the net result of the investigations into the possible usefulness of these mansions was that five (as a provisional number) were suitable for accommodation and 325 were unsuitable for any public purpose.[104] Thus the enquiry into the usefulness to the state of such country houses for conversion to other uses was overwhelmingly negative. Given that the focus of the report was on the suitability of country houses for the purposes of the workings of the state – the primary ends of which were office accommodation for government departments, hospitals and schools – it is hardly surprising that these buildings, which had been designed as homes and centres for entertaining, were considered unsuitable. The report appears to have been quite black and white in this regard. Of course, the significant number of houses taken over as schools, convents and monasteries by religious orders at this time proves that, with adaptation, these houses could be made to serve new uses. The fact that most of these houses are still in use by those religious orders or have been sold on today also illustrates that their purchase, conversion, use and preservation may have been a worthwhile investment.

This memorandum was sent to the various government departments on 23 May and was to be considered at the next government meeting.[105] It was examined when the government met on 29 May although no decision was taken on the findings of the report other than to note its contents.[106] Dooley has explained how: 'in the end only a handful of big houses passed into government hands at this time' such as those adapted as agricultural training centres, namely Johnstown Castle, Wexford, acquired by the government by an act of 1945 and Ballyhaise, County Cavan.[107] This was because the government, while displaying enough interest to conduct a report into their possible use, concluded that it was not possible for the state to preserve any significant number of these country houses by putting them to new use. In none of the responses recorded in the report, including that of the Irish Tourist Board, was the possible value of their historic, architectural or aesthetic importance mentioned. They were solely considered by all departments in terms of possible departmental use.

The results of the report appear almost shocking in retrospect. On the other hand, it is important to remember that there was very little tourism in Ireland at this time and the government was, like the press, not aware of the possible potential of these houses as valuable attractions. Similarly, in England, Mandler has argued that 'the general public's near-total indifference to the fate of the country house in the 1920s and 1930s – callous and inexplicably philistine as it may seem today – is fully intelligible in its proper context. There was, first of all, little concept of "the country house".'[108]

The government could not afford to take on even a portion of over 300 financially draining old mansions for which they had no need, use or demand. This problem was so immediate at the time because, as Dooley has argued: 'it was not the destruction of a minority of big houses, probably less than 10 per cent, during the revolutionary period that was most significant, but rather the abandonment and/or demolition of a much higher proportion in the decades that followed.'[109] A similar situation was facing the English country house. Mandler has shown how, among various adaptations of country houses in England, some were advertised for letting, such as Knole and Levens Hall. Another, Montacute, failed to sell at an auction in 1929, but was saved from an inglorious fate by Ernest Cook who gave it to the National Trust 'which accepted its first major country house with some reluctance, alarmed by the potential maintenance costs'.[110] However, he maintained that while such an arrangement could be mounted for a few of the greatest olden-time mansions, it was neither possible nor desirable to do the same in the cases of the vast majority of large country houses, now surplus to requirements. Hundreds of them were demolished; by one estimate, '7 per cent of the total stock of country houses' in England.[111] Mandler also argued that, in England as in Ireland, the abandonment and destruction of the country house was not solely caused by governments' policies. He wrote:

> Insofar as culture and history remained concerns of the aristocracy, few could afford any longer to attach these qualities to large country houses. Not only were big houses ruinous to maintain, heat in straitened times, but they were just not consistent with modern standards of good taste and comfort. Lord Crawford himself granted that, were it not for the presence of his beloved art and book collections, Haigh Hall would be 'uninhabitable'. Many owners both of town and country palaces laid them down with relief.[112]

DERRYNANE HOUSE

Another such house was Derrynane, County Kerry, former home of Daniel O'Connell. Following the offer from its owners to dispose of the property to the state in April 1945, the government did investigate possible uses for the house if acquired, spurred on by de Valera, in an apparently more eager way than for other properties. The Department of the Taoiseach believed 'that the house might be acquired by the Tourist Board and preserved by them as a memorial of Daniel O'Connell, that the Land Commission should consider the question of the best use to which the lands might be put, and the forestry division of the Department of Lands consider the utilisation of part of the lands for afforestation purposes.'[113] A memorandum on the case prepared by the Taoiseach's department outlined that the Tourist Board had said they saw 'no possibility of the board purchasing the property and maintaining it as an O'Connell museum, as they could not certify … that the proposal would be "a work of profit-earning character" for the purpose of their act'.[114] Nevertheless, they did agree that Derynane House, also known as Derrynane Abbey, was one of a number of properties which should be preserved for the nation through state acquisition and maintenance and suggested that 'this should be done by means of a body set up under state auspices on the lines of the National Trust in Great Britain'.[115] In May the Department of Industry and Commerce had informed the Taoiseach's department that they understood the Tourist Board would submit a report, at a very early date, on the creation of a National Trust in this country. The Trust would have powers to acquire properties, such as Derrynane, which should be preserved for the nation.[116] Furthermore, cabinet minutes from July 1945 recorded that 'it was decided that the question of the establishment of a National Trust should be actively pursued.'[117] In spite of this, the suggested establishment of a National Trust does not appear to have developed further, with the Department of Industry and Commerce and the Department of Finance going back and forth over whose responsibility it was to even investigate the possibility: neither department was eager to do so.[118]

In September 1945 the Commissioners of Public Works wrote to the Department of Finance in relation to the possibility of acquiring Derrynane Abbey under the National Monuments Act. They stated that 'there could be no question of our acquiring any more than the house, its site and such portion of an adjoining site as would be required to provide the necessary means of access and to cover in or fence the monument or preserve the amenities thereof.'[119] This would have excluded about 315 acres of the total 332 acres. Therefore, they believed that, unless the original suggestion to establish a National Trust was pursued, then the acquisition by the Land Commission of the entire estate would be the preferable course. The Land Commission could have then transferred to them the house as a national monument and any land surrounding it that would be important to its preservation.[120] This would also have meant dispossessing the then owners to adhere to the terms of the 1930 Act. It also shows that the Commissioners were limited to the conservation of buildings or monuments, not land, by the legislation under which they operated. This would also have made the preservation of country houses under the 1930 Act difficult, as acquiring the house alone, without any of its demesne land, would have deprived the house of its greatest amenity and a significant part of its value and beauty.

As a result of the Commissioners' views on Derrynane, the Department of Finance wrote to the Taoiseach's department indicating that it was apparent 'from the terms of the report that the Commissioners of Public Works do not regard the taking of action under the National Monuments Act in regard to the acquisition of the property as either feasible or desirable'.[121] Similarly, the suggestion that action be taken by the Land Commission 'would not appear to be practicable in view of the report of the Department of Lands on the subject'.[122] Demonstrably no state body, again, was anxious to set a precedent of becoming burdened with the preservation of country houses. The bottom line for the Department of Finance, either way, was the excessive cost involved, just as it had been in the offer of Russborough; this, despite Derrynane's association with O'Connell and the Taoiseach's views. Their letter concluded: 'in view of the uncertainty as to the purchase price, the capital expenditure involved in putting the premises to rights and the large recurring expenditure entailed in maintenance the minister does not favour state acquisition by way of special act.'[123] Furthermore, the department official emphasised: 'the Minister considers the establishment of a National Trust for this purpose as wholly objectionable.'[124] Although no reason was given, the establishment of a National Trust would have inevitably led to either considerable expense in endowments or loss in terms of reductions in rates for the Department of Finance and other government departments.

In contrast, de Valera was obviously still interested in trying to acquire the property, and in a minute of 9 October, the Taoiseach's department suggested: 'if the matter were approached in a sympathetic manner it should be possible to convince one's self that it would be necessary to acquire all the land adjoining the house in order to preserve the amenities thereof.'[125] This illustrates that, when they deemed it desirable, some members of the Department of the Taoiseach thought the National Monuments Act could be stretched to suit a need. They also commented that the cost of maintenance and repairs estimated by the OPW were not excessive, as an immediate expenditure of £2,000 would be sufficient to put the old buildings into a good state of repair, while the annual maintenance charges were estimated at £100.[126] The minute concluded: 'the taking over of the property by a National Trust would probably be the ideal solution, but even if it were decided to establish a National Trust in this country a very considerable time must elapse before it would be in active operation.'[127]

The Finance solicitor agreed, writing on the subject of Derrynane: 'I do not think, in view of its long association with O'Connell, that there could be any difficulty in classing it as a "national monument" as defined by the act.'[128] While in other cases the relatively modern construction of country houses was given as a reason against their acquisition, here it seems that the over-riding association with O'Connell meant that the country house itself could undoubtedly, in the opinion of the Finance solicitor, come under the protection of the National Monuments Act. This contrasts starkly to McElligott's opinion on Russborough's eligibility for protection under this Act discussed in Chapter One. However, the solicitor made clear that if the owners intended to present the abbey to the state, it could be done under section ten of the Act, but the lands would be excluded.[129] This was precisely the problem that the Commissioners of Public Works had highlighted. The solicitor added that 'the Land Commission could, of course, under their statutory powers, acquire both lands and house, subsequently vest the house in the board as a national monument and dispose of the surplus land for their own purposes or by way of resale.'[130] He doubted they would favour such action as the land was primarily unsuitable for their purposes.[131] Therefore the solicitor concluded that, while the house could be considered a national monument, he found it difficult to see how Derrynane Abbey with its entire lands could be dealt with under the 1930 Act beyond making a preservation order in respect of the buildings.[132]

Despite such difficulties, the Department of the Taoiseach, presumably on de Valera's instructions, wanted to discuss possible *ad hoc* legislation which would make the preservation possible, but the arguments of the other departments, undoubtedly Finance's being paramount, were obviously persuasive. The state did not act to put forward such legislation and the house was taken over by a group of interested parties who formed the Derrynane Trust, under the leadership of Denis Guiney.[133] Ownership was later assumed by the state from this Trust and the house is now in the care of the OPW.

THE CASE OF HAZELWOOD HOUSE

Hazelwood House, County Sligo, an eighteenth-century house designed by Richard Castle, was another country house whose fate garnered a lot of press attention. It is an interesting case for illustrating public concern and government reaction to the decline of country houses during this period. This case study is particularly illuminating as it embodies many of the factors that contributed to the decline of country houses, such as the sale of the house and its value for demolition rather than residential use, the lack of public interest in its fate, the minority, including the *Irish Times*, who were attempting to champion its cause, and the varying attitudes displayed by the government, which, in the end, resulted in no action. What this case also highlights is the class and cultural divide that means the country house was, and continues to be, a contested space.

In 1946 Hazelwood House was put up for sale and demolition by the Land Commission. The Land Commission was concerned with the division of land on such estates and had no use for houses that came with the land and no remit with regard to these houses. The *Irish Times* covered the case extensively and, on 12 January 1946, ran almost a full page spread on the house entitled: 'Historic County Sligo mansion to be sold for demolition'.[134] Despite this level of coverage, suggesting public concern or at least interest, the paper began their article: 'Hazelwood House is going to be demolished, and the people of Sligo, with few exceptions, do not care.'[135] Like other publications, it believed that Hazelwood was one of the finest mansions in Ireland, although the article described the residents of Sligo as 'not interested'.[136] The reporter wrote that he had discussed the demolition of Hazelwood with 'several prominent' Sligo residents who concluded that no one in Sligo cared what happened to Hazelwood and that it appeared to be no use to anyone. Only one person in the locality reported to have felt strongly enough about it to protest and he suggested that Hazelwood might be used as a sanatorium and taken over by the Department of Local Government and Public Health.[137] The paper recounted that the house had been sold to the Land Commission some years previously and, during the war years, had been used by the army. The paper questioned what its future use might be: suggestions had been made to turn it into a hotel, boarding school, a hospital or a sanatorium. It reported that the building had deteriorated a good deal during recent years, though it was still in a basically sound condition and had been fitted with a lighting plant, a pumping plant and a modern sewerage system. A builder commented: 'undoubtedly, it would cost quite a considerable sum to convert the house into a hospital, but it does seem a pity, in these times when many new buildings are urgently needed, to pull down a good, solid structure like this.'[138]

In general the paper reemphasised that local people were not interested, reporting:

> People in Sligo who know the house say that it is too low-lying for a sanatorium, and they already have a hospital in Sligo, anyway. They say that it is too big and too far out for a school. They say that the place has not sufficient amenities for a hotel. They do not even seem to think seriously about it; they just say 'there isn't really anything you can do with Hazelwood,' and leave it at that.[139]

This was an attitude replicated in England where Mandler has shown how:

> The larger houses of the eighteenth and nineteenth centuries had been so consistently depreciated from all quarters that they had become almost completely emptied of meaning. They resembled 'hotels or hydros rather than private residences,' wrote one correspondent to *The Times* ... Another writer condemned as 'foolish' the idea that because these buildings are old, they are necessarily beautiful ... Clough Williams-Ellis, in calling for preservation of the 'honest-to-God stately homes of England', stressed the need to cut them off in the public mind from 'the considerable tail of merely large or pretentious houses'. G. M. Trevelyan granted that an empty palace was 'a somewhat melancholy affair', difficult to insinuate into the public's affection.[140]

The *Irish Times* seemed to underplay the fact that the government could find no use for Hazelwood, no one would buy it, and even the local people were satisfied that it should be demolished. The article concluded despairingly that, owing to local apathy, 'within the next couple of months a historic old mansion in one of the loveliest settings in Ireland, ideally situated for a hotel – similar mansions in much less attractive surroundings have made very successful hotels – will be pulled down and carried away brick by brick.'[141]

The paper also devoted its 'Irishman's Diary' section to the topic. The column indicated that the *Irish Times* believed local indifference to the fate of the house was, to some extent, based on a prejudice towards the property because of its associations with landlordism. It stated: 'the Wynnes may have been planters. In fact, they were: for the first of them came across to Ireland with King William and took part in the Battle of the Boyne. But what does that matter?'[142] The next section was addressed directly to the Minister for Lands, Seán Moylan, and read: 'surely, Mr Moylan, this act of consummate vandalism cannot be allowed to happen ... Will you allow such a house as Hazelwood to be demolished – no matter how much lead the vandals will find on the roof?'[143] The diarist claimed: 'there are many uses to which such a house could be put. One, may I suggest, is to establish it as a youth hostel, for it is in almost ideal surroundings. The Tourist Association could find a use for it. It could be made into a convalescent home for children – anything but demolished!'[144] None of these conversions, it should be noted, could have been undertaken by the Land Commission, which had a specific remit outlining its functions. In an attempt to urge the Minister to consider Ireland's reputation internationally in terms of cultural heritage, the diarist lamented that 'Yeats's *Lake Isle of Inisfree* is little more than a stone's throw from Hazelwood. He would turn in his lonely grave if he knew the fate that is being prepared for one of the finest houses of its kind in Ireland.'[145]

Not all were in agreement with this paper's stance, however, and four days later a letter to the editor of the *Irish Times*, signed 'Oliver Cromwell, Dublin', portrayed a different view of the situation. Anticipating the demolition of Hazelwood, he stressed to the editor that this was 'an excellent opportunity of putting your principles into practice'. He suggested that if the editor and all the other 'art connoisseurs' pooled their resources they would be able to 'outbid the "vandals" and so preserve for ever a historic monument of Ireland's struggle for freedom!' He concluded that even if they did not manage to save Hazelwood, there were many more mansions throughout the country with historic associations 'waiting to be saved' and offered sarcastically that if they were the 'wonderful adaptable structures' they were suggesting, then they would be a great investment, even apart from the 'praise-worthy cause of preserving good examples of architecture'.[146]

The letter was written in this sarcastic tone throughout. Nonetheless, in the next paragraph 'Cromwell' did not limit his negative views to the subtleties of irony and stated: 'unfortunately, one must not allow an enthusiasm for art preservation to warp one's judgment of the practical uses of these whited sepulchers'.[147] The next remark is where the letter becomes particularly interesting and is presumably why the cutting was contained in the OPW's files on old mansions. It appears that, from all the signatures at the side of this clipping, all important officers and clerks in the department saw the extract. Written on the clipping was the question, 'a Minister of State?', which may have been motivated by the next section of the letter:

> As one who has taken pleasure in ordering the entire destruction of scores of these large, neglected mansions and castles, may I inform you that, however suitable these buildings may be for museums, they are absolutely useless from a utility point of view. If you could have obtained the services of a few thousand prisoners from Belsen or some other continental slave camp, it might have been feasible, but in this land of acute domestic shortage, these mansions are useless.[148]

While admitted that it was true that they could be renovated and converted, 'the outlay would be excessive and the result far from satisfactory. Far better to start afresh when materials are available and give some promising young architect an opportunity of designing a building to suit its particular purpose, to be labour-saving, to please the eye, and to fit in with the surrounding countryside.'[149] This section is most revealing as one would assume, as the OPW evidently did, that if the writer of this letter were one who had ordered the demolition of scores of historic houses, then it was must have been someone in a position of power such as a Minister for State, or even the Minister for Lands, Moylan, who had been directly addressed in the 'Irishman's Diary' a few days previously. If this were the case, it was evidently not good practice for a government minister to address the issue with so little cover of identity in a virulent and ironic letter to a national paper, in a manner that did not justify governmental decisions in reasonable terms but instead chose to reveal the fact that he took pleasure in ordering the destruction of mansions. The comments regarding concentration camps are hardly believable for the contemporary reader. The writer concluded that it was too late to talk about saving the Irish country house because, since the Land Commission began its policy of dividing large estates, 'the Irish mansion was doomed'. He argued it was then that preservation action should have been taken by interested parties, not when the construction trade in the country was stunted due to a lack of raw materials as a result of the Emergency. In such an environment, the writer claimed that the 'timber, slates, lead and fittings, which were salvaged from mansions were immediately put into use, and numbers of urgent factory extensions and commercial buildings owe their presence to mansion demolition activity.' Touching on the societal conditions in the country more generally, he threw a last punch, writing 'It is interesting that there are people who wax indignant over the destruction of a useless empty country mansion with one hundred rooms, but remain complacent about some of our town "mansions" with ten persons living in each room.'[150]

This comparison was not misplaced, as the discussion of the slum tenements of Georgian Dublin at the beginning of this chapter has shown, and, at this time, there does not appear to have been as much concern about the historical preservation or integrity of these urban buildings compared with their rural counterparts. In fact, wide-scale concern was probably first mooted only in the late 1950s and early 1960s when the government was embroiled in controversy over their decision to allow the ESB to demolish the Georgian townhouses in Fitzwilliam Street in Dublin and erect a new office block in their place. This case provoked widespread attention, drew varied opinions, and highlighted the issue of the preservation of these urban houses for the first time in a significant way.

Returning to the case of Hazelwood, on 18 January the *Evening Mail* reported that the sale by the Land Commission of Hazelwood had been cancelled. The paper highlighted how the original advertisement for sale had 'pointed out that there was a high proportion of lead in the roof, and stipulated, on the instructions of the Land Commission, that the purchaser "shall demolish the building and remove all materials, clear and level the site".'[151] The *Evening Mail* claimed that Hazelwood House was 'one of the finest mansions in Ireland' and added their belief that the public were concerned, reporting: 'since the advertisement appeared, people all over the country have been asking why this fine historic house should be demolished, and why the government could not find some use for it as an hospital or an hotel.'[152]

Despite the cancellation of sale pending the investigation of tentative offers for purchase that had been made to the Land Commission,[153] debate continued to take place over the subject in letters to the editor of the *Irish Times*. Hubert Butler, writer, essayist, and a member of the Protestant population of southern Ireland, argued in a letter to the paper that in more populous countries, these houses were used by a National Trust or converted into museums, rest homes or youth hostels.[154] However, he admitted that Ireland had not the public support for these solutions. Despite this, he suggested the houses might allow for several different uses simultaneously.[155] In this respect, he referenced the preservation of Temple Newsam, Yorkshire, although he realised such a project in Ireland would have to adapt to a smaller population and resources, and would need to be associated with other similar projects. He described how Temple Newsam was now more alive than ever and, in the summer, was swarming with interested visitors.[156]

In reality, finding viable uses for these houses proved difficult in England too. In contrast, another writer believed: 'the responsibility for the preservation of Anglo-Irish historic houses rests primarily with the Anglo-Irish. They do not, in Éire, appear to take it very seriously.'[157] While this statement certainly bears traces of a nativist prejudice, the fact the owners of many of these properties, the subject of so much political and public discussion, had sold the houses voluntarily to the Land Commission or demolition squads, or abandoned them completely to their fate, is rarely addressed – something Moylan stressed. Although some may have done so reluctantly, given the amount abandoned, it can be inferred that many others left the new state by choice and sacrificed their Irish residence to concentrate dwindling resources on their other, usually British, property. Others may have been unconcerned with what fate befell the house after their departure. Admittedly, the survival of the country house had become difficult, with little or no land to keep the houses viable and servants increasingly difficult to obtain, to say nothing of the rates and taxes which were driving owners themselves to pull the roofs off their houses and abandon them to ruin. In some cases too, gambling debts or ostentatious living had left a legacy of ancestral debt from the eighteenth and nineteenth centuries that could no longer be fed by the house and estate. Hazelwood House, however, was not demolished at this time. Instead, it was bought in 1947 by the Department of Health for use as a psychiatric hospital before again being turned to a new use in 1969 when purchased by an Italian business group, SNIA. This proved that, as a structure, it could be adapted, although in later years its historical integrity was severely compromised.

CONCLUSION

The Fianna Fáil government under Éamon de Valera, who succeeded to power in 1932, was undoubtedly more protectionist and republican than its predecessor, Cumann na nGaedheal, and less conciliatory toward the British government and any remains of their authority or representatives in Ireland. They were also less concerned with the protection of heritage, and no act was passed with the aim of heritage protection during this period. Furthermore, while Muckross estate was acquired, primarily for the amenity value of its parkland, no country house was procured as a national monument. Land division was also pursued relentlessly. The 1933 Land Act continued, and in many cases completed, the redistribution of land from great estates to former tenants and landless men and resulted in the destruction, isolation or sale of the associated country houses.

Country houses were also abandoned during this period because of the expense of rates and taxes imposed by the government – primarily inherited from the British administration – or simply the apathy of owners themselves. Country houses, starkly neglected and going to ruin in the Irish countryside, began to stir public consciousness for the first time in the 1940s and arguments were voiced in the media and in the Oireachtas that the government should acquire these houses to put them to various uses as schools, hospitals or sanatoria. The houses, emptied of their owners, were now seen by the public to be acceptable to adopt as part of the Irish government's concern, if they could be of some practical use. The government responded to this pressure by commissioning a report into their possible usefulness to the state. However, no department found that they could be adapted for such purposes, and so the government could not justifiably acquire houses after the emphatic results of this report. Nevertheless, their policies did not make it any easier for houses to avoid the point of abandon either. In fact, during this period, owners found their financial positions even more perilous, although their houses gained value for the first time in years due to their salvagable materials.

Hazelwood embodies several of the difficulties facing the country house in this period. It was advertised for sale and demolition in 1946 when many such houses were being put on the market. Unlike the 1920s and '30s, by the 1940s, particularly during and after the Emergency, there was a ready market for their lead and other salvage. This material had helped to build factories and roads in the country, for example, when raw materials were in short supply.[158] Furthermore, there was little public interest in saving Hazelwood from demolition. It was primarily the *Irish Times*, accompanied by those from the landed class, or aesthetes such as Hubert Butler, who led calls for its preservation. Even so, these appeals realistically proposed that Hazelwood could only survive if put to alternative use as a youth hostel, school or tuberculosis sanatorium. In spite of this, the government's conclusive report into the usefulness of such properties was echoed in Moylan's statement that they were primarily unsuited to such purposes. While this may have been true in many cases, depending on the condition of the house on sale, Hazelwood proved by its use thereafter that it was at least possible to adapt these houses to other functions, although their historical integrity was, in most conversions, compromised. Nonetheless, use was often the only salvation for the many houses that were pouring onto the market by the 1950s when governments were unwilling and unable to preserve them on their own merits, and no substantial section of the public was pressurising them to do so. The complexities behind this governmental attitude will be examined in the next chapter.

THREE

THE OFFICE OF PUBLIC WORKS, 1930–60

The Board of Works, established by an Act of Parliament passed in 1831, continued to function after independence. Throughout this time, the office was called either the Office of Public Works or the Board of Works, until the former eventually took precedence in government documents and as its official title.[1] The office primarily functioned under legislation from the previous administration until the Free State Government passed the 1930 National Monuments Act. An examination of the OPW needs to be addressed on its own and in detail as the only body with a specific responsibility and mandate to act in relation to monuments it deemed eligible for preservation under this act. This is also necessary because it appears the office worked on the issue of national monuments and historic houses relatively independently of government ministers. Rather the OPW's officials, commissioners and the Inspector of National Monuments for most of this period were the most important figures in relation to decisions and action taken, while changing ministers were rarely mentioned. The office worked in this way because this was not an area that any government was particularly concerned about or in which they sought to make a mark; the preservation of national monuments was never an 'election issue' and always languished behind more pressing social concerns in terms of interest and funding. It is also an area of work that needs expertise, so changing ministers

often trusted the OPW's staff implicitly. The OPW's interpretation and implementation of the 1930 National Monuments Act throughout the period from
1930–60 will be examined in this chapter to assess what their attitudes towards
country houses were, whether they deemed them worthy of preservation, the
reasons behind their decisions, and how this impacted on both their actions
and the fate of country houses brought to their attention during this period. A
case study of Dunsandle House, County Galway, will examine how the OPW's
policies influenced their action in an individual case.

POWERS

The primary means through which the OPW had power to preserve country
houses in this period was under the National Monuments Act 1930, which
made provision 'for the protection and preservation of national monuments
and for the preservation of archaeological objects in Saorstát Éireann'.[2] For
the purposes of this act, a national monument was defined as a monument or
its remains, 'the preservation of which is a matter of national importance by
reason of the historical, architectural, traditional, artistic, or archaeological
interest attaching thereto'.[3] The 1930 Act also established the NMAC for giving
advice and assistance to the commissioners in relation to the enactment of this
legislation, and it was to include the Keeper of Irish Antiquities at the National
Museum and an officer of the Commissioners of Public Works, as well as other
nominated members.[4] While the 1930 Act was the first act regarding heritage
preservation enacted by the newly independent state, Harold G. (H. G.) Leask,
Inspector of National Monuments for much of this period, argued that the 1930
Act had changed little regarding the primary function of the service, which
remained preservation and conservation, not restoration.[5]

It needs to be remembered that the OPW was not specifically charged with
the preservation of historic buildings or, more particularly, country houses; it
was its interpretation of the National Monuments Act that could have made
this a possibility for them. In fact, no government body had specific responsibility for preserving these buildings, which frequently fell through the cracks
between the duties of departments and organisations. The OPW was the office
in the best position to manage their preservation, but this was dependent on
their officers' interpretation of their own powers under legislation, their brief
and remit and, most significantly, the limitations imposed on them by their
resources of both personnel and finance. Furthermore, the OPW was a state

body answerable to the government and the Department of Finance and this may also have influenced their attitude or freedom to act on this issue, particularly in relation to budget.

In 1953, the *Irish Independent* drew attention to the gap in terms of responsibility or power to act in relation to the protection of the country house and historic buildings. An article on 20 October examined whether any particular body was 'charged with the sole responsibility of maintaining or preserving for the nation buildings of historical value'.[6] Reportedly, there were at least four bodies with some responsibilities in relation to historical buildings, namely, Bord Fáilte, the Land Commission, the Board of Works and An Taisce (the embryonic National Trust for Ireland which had been founded – by private interested parties – in 1948). The *Irish Independent* believed that the functions of all of these bodies in relation to the preservation of historic buildings lacked definition 'with the result that there is some confusion as to the ultimate responsibility' regarding the preservation of country houses such as Tinnehinch, County Wicklow, former residence of Henry Grattan. This had recently been partially demolished.[7] They explained that a section of the Tourist Act under which Bord Fáilte had been set up the previous year had empowered the Board to protect and maintain national monuments and historic buildings, sites and shrines and places of scenic or historical interest to the public. Despite this, a spokesman for Bord Fáilte was unable to say whether the interpretation of this section was wide enough to permit them to acquire and preserve buildings, which were in danger of destruction, such as Tinnehinch, and 'would be a total loss to the nation'.[8] All Bord Fáilte had been enabled to do thus far was to provide amenities at places like Newgrange. Interestingly, the Tourist Traffic Act 1952 did allow Bord Fáilte 'to accept gifts and donations, and to undertake and carry out trusts which may be lawfully undertaken by the Board, and may be conducive to its objects'.[9] The Commissioners of Public Works had a statutory responsibility for the preservation and maintenance of what were described as 'scheduled national monuments which were of first importance historically as ancient ruins'.[10] However, the *Irish Independent* emphasised: 'they have no function or responsibility in the acquisition of historical buildings', although where the paper had got this information from is uncertain.[11]

In theory, the 1930 Act allowed for the preservation of historic buildings, but perhaps the *Irish Independent* was reporting on how this was implemented in practice by the Commissioners. The report explained that, occasionally, various properties with land attached could be acquired compulsorily or otherwise by the Land Commission, but not for historical reasons. Furthermore, the paper emphasised: 'neither is it obliged to preserve any building of a historical character which it acquires; and not infrequently such buildings are disposed of in other ways. Some have gone to the Forestry Department and others to the Department of Agriculture. Others have been demolished, the permission of the local authority having been first obtained.'[12] In the view of the *Irish Independent*, the only one of the four bodies mentioned that had any clearly-defined functions and responsibilities in this area was An Taisce, whose memorandum of incorporation as a limited company entitled it 'to acquire by gift, purchase or grant, any lands, buildings or property of value to the nation for their historical associations or natural beauty'.[13] It was also entitled to protect and improve such properties. An Taisce, however, was little more than advisory in capacity at this time as it had no funding from the government to exercise its powers, unlike the English National Trust, which had wide powers, government recognition and financial assistance. In contrast, An Taisce had to depend on 'the support of its members, the interest of the public, and the goodwill of local authorities: but it has never received any official recognition'.[14]

H. G. Leask is an important character in this story. He began working in the OPW as a temporary Assistant Surveyor, but by 1923 was appointed Inspector of National Monuments. He was passionate about architecture, archaeology and Irish antiquities and was also a member of the National Monuments Advisory Council. Leask remained on the Council after his retirement from the OPW in 1949 and continued his interest in heritage until his death. He has been described as a particularly honest man, with a conscientious nature and an obvious passion beyond employment for the architectural heritage. This necessitates that his appraisal of cases of country houses that were brought to his attention should be viewed with a consciousness of the limited economic and human resources available to the OPW at the time. In his position as Inspector of National Monuments, Leask advised the Commissioners of Public Works and was directly responsible to them.[15] Anne Carey has shown how Leask's main role concerned the conservation of national monuments, although, during his tenure, the workload of the role grew so great that, in 1946, Leask highlighted that the assignment was too heavy for a single officer.[16] The sheer volume of work, coupled with limited resources at local and national government levels, as well as 'the absence of a clear policy regarding the conservation of roofed structures', undoubtedly affected Leask's views on the preservation of country houses during this period.[17] In fact, in 1935, Leask explained that the preservation of country houses was a work so large as to be 'impracticable' and that the Commissioners' policy of only selecting the most interesting specimens of country houses reported to them as worthy of preservation, rather than preserving every structure brought to their attention, was 'the only possible one'.[18]

WIDER INTEREST AND CONCERN

As the previous chapter has documented, when public concern began to be raised in the 1940s regarding the destruction of the country house, interested members of the public saw it as the government's responsibility to act in relation to their preservation. More specifically, it was thought that this was the duty of the OPW, to whom such concerns were primarily addressed by members of the public or forwarded to by other government departments – emphasising that the latter also saw this issue as one the OPW could or should address.

Around this time, the possibility arose for the OPW to preserve Tinnehinch House, County Wicklow. In January 1943, Allen and Townsend Chartered Surveyors wrote to the OPW to inform them that they were instructed to offer for sale Tinnehinch, the residence of the late Sir Henry Grattan Bellew, which comprised a mansion house and lands. They noted that the buildings were in poor condition but wrote that before offering the property elsewhere, they wished to enquire whether the OPW would be interested in the property.[19] In response, Leask, as Inspector of National Monuments, wrote to Division C of the OPW stating that, apart from the historic association of the house with Grattan, he did not see that the place had any special interest from the national monuments point of view.[20] He added that 'it is not one of the great Georgian mansions for which the country is remarkable'. Division C of the OPW was principally the drainage division although, judging by this correspondence, staff of this division were also involved with the issue of national monuments.[21] In Leask's opinion, Tinnehinch House was 'not particularly distinguished', adding, 'The house does not appear to be one which could be treated as a national monument.'[22] In March the surveyors were informed that the OPW was not interested[23] and by July the *Irish Independent* reported that Tinnehinch had been bought in trust by Messrs. Hardman and Sons.[24] Ten years later, it was partially demolished by its owners without permission. Since that time, a new house has been built on the site where only the crumbling outer walls of the original structure remained.

As a result of the frequency of such cases, in 1945 Leask and J. Raftery, Joint Honorary Secretaries of the NMAC, wrote to the OPW to say that the Council had discussed:

The wholesale demolition of 18th and 19th century mansions which has taken place in recent years. These houses represent an important phase in the country's politico-social and cultural history and the council deplores the fact that a large number of them have been destroyed without any records of their features having been made.[25]

They went on to say that, while the Council was of the opinion that there was no effective method of taking preventative action in cases of threatened destruction in the absence of special legislation, they considered that 'in the cases where such houses are vested in or under the control of the Land Commission that that department might be asked to give notice of intended demolitions in order to give an opportunity for having surveys and records of any which may possess features of artistic interest'.[26] They requested this be brought to the attention of the Land Commission. The reference to special legislation is important and Carey has shown how Leask understood the National Monuments Act as giving powers of conservation only, not restoration, and was stringent in ensuring that the OPW kept to its legislative boundaries in this regard.[27] The OPW was willing to enquire into the feasibility of the suggestion of the NMAC and, in April 1945, the OPW wrote to the Land Commission enquiring if they would comply.[28] The Department of Lands replied that they would 'in future give them notice of any demolition of 18th and 19th century mansions contemplated by the department'.[29] The Department of Lands and the Land Commission were demonstrably willing to agree with such a request to create a record of these mansions, even though it would presumably delay their staffs' plans or work on the demolition or sale of the structures on their hands.

They very quickly lived up to their promises too. On 3 May 1945, Karl L. Schorman of the Forestry Division of the Department of Lands wrote to the NMAC to inform them that, after consultation with the Department of Local Government and Public Health, the department proposed to 'pull down, with a view to the sale of the materials, the mansion known as Jenkinstown House, County Kilkenny'.[30] He described how the building was, up to a recent date, in the occupation of the military authorities and was 'generally in a very bad state of repair'.[31] This house was only one of many that had been occupied by the military during the Emergency, including Muckross House, County Kerry, mentioned in Chapter One. An attempt had been made in 1940 to dispose of the building and about 20 acres of adjoining land, but no suitable offers were received.[32] It appears from this that officials in the Department of Lands were not simply jumping to decisions over demolishing these properties. When it came to them, the Department had attempted to sell it, although admittedly with very little acreage adjoining it to make it viable. However, the thrust of this division's work was the development of forestry and, therefore, they had no desire to acquire land for forestry and then to have to sell off a huge parcel of it to make the country house an attractive or viable purchase. Only when the sale of this house was unsuccessful – and after consulting with the Department of Local Government and Public Health, who did not propose any use for it – was a decision made by the Department of Lands to pull it down.[33]

Leask was again influential in deciding on the OPW's actions in this case. On 8 May 1945, he explained to Division C that, as far as he could ascertain, Jenkinstown was 'not a "Georgian" (18th century) house but modern, not older than the early part of last century ... I greatly doubt if it contains any features worth recording but it would be well to be quite definite on this before replying to the Department of Lands or taking any steps about record work.'[34] He recommended that, if there was nothing known about the house at OPW headquarters, then the assistant architect might visit it when he was next in Kilkenny.[35] The assistant architect did inspect Jenkinstown House, but only from the outside, since the day he visited it was locked. As a result of his report, and unsurprisingly, the NMAC wrote to the Department of Lands (Forestry Division) on 15 June to inform them that they did not intend to take steps to even make a survey of Jenkinstown House.[36]

In the same year, J. Darby of the Department of Lands informed the NMAC that the department had under consideration the question of the demolition of a mansion house known as Beaufield House on state forest lands near Clonegal, County Wexford.[37] When the opportunity to inspect or record Beaufield House was offered to the OPW, Leask was again the one who wrote to Division C on the subject. He said that as a result of local enquiries 'addressed to a qualified observer I have ascertained that the only objects of architectural interest in the house are some mantelpieces. These might be acquired and preserved locally by interested persons'.[38] He then suitably replied on behalf of the NMAC.[39] This is revealing as it appears that neither the OPW nor the NMAC's staff considered some of these houses worth inspecting, even when the Department of Lands informed them they were available if they wanted simply to make a record of them. It may have been disheartening to inspect them if they had not the legislative powers to protect these houses, but surely it would have been worthwhile to make a record of them for perpetuity.

In another case, in March 1954, Land Commission officials wrote to the OPW to say that they had Mote Park House for sale, on a Land Commission-owned estate in Roscommon, with 'a suitable area of accommodation land if required'.[40] The Land Commission's staff favourably described the mansion as 'an imposing structure, in an excellent state of repair and would appear to be suitable for use as a hospital, sanatorium, school, etc.'[41] The Commission enquired if the OPW would be interested in the purchase of the property and declared that if they did not receive a reply in 21 days, they would assume they did not require the property and 'other arrangements for its disposal will be made'.[42] Ten days later, OPW officials replied briefly to say that the premises were not required by the Office, suggesting both in the actual reply and its brevity that no interest was shown by OPW staff in the property, despite the willingness of the Land Commission to let them know of it as well as the Commission's positive comments about its repair and possible use.[43] Three years later, the Land Commission contacted the OPW again to inform it that efforts that had been made to sell the building with certain accommodation lands as a residential holding – its first preference – had failed, so that it then proposed to sell the building for demolition. It is notable it was not in the Land Commission's remit or budget to decide to keep and preserve this house; the OPW was the only department that could do so, and, if it refused, the Commission had no choice but to sell the house or, if that proved impossible, demolish it. However, even after the OPW's previous brief response, the Land Commission did not demolish without thought. One of its officials took the initiative to write again to the OPW, stating:

> Before any decision is taken in the matter, the Land Commission will be glad to know whether the building is of any historical or architectural importance and if so whether you are interested in preserving the building, either as a complete structure or as a roofless shell and whether you would be prepared to take over the building and its site at a nominal sum.[44]

On 5 November a member of the OPW requested a report from the Inspector of National Monuments on the matter.[45] Having received no reply at all from the OPW, on 30 November the Land Commission wrote again requesting an early reply and reminding the office of its previous letters; it did so again in December.[46] As a result, the OPW sent three reminders to the Inspector between December and January 1958 asking for his report.[47] Nonetheless, the Land Commission was obliged to send a further letter to the OPW on 27 January asking that it deal with the matter urgently.[48] The OPW finally replied on 10 February explaining that their Inspector of National Monuments had not yet found it possible to inspect the property to assess whether it would be eligible for preservation as a national monument, but they hoped this would be arranged shortly and would write when it had been.[49] As has been noted when

Leask was in this role, he argued that the workload was too large and onerous for one inspector and this may explain the delay in dealing with this case. When the inspector finally carried out his report, he described the house as a 'large, but not very attractive stone mansion of mid nineteenth-century appearance'.[50] To his mind, it did not merit the effort of an interior inspection and he concluded: 'there does not appear to be anything worthy of consideration for state care'.[51] Subsequently, the OPW informed the Land Commission: 'we do not consider that the house ... is of sufficient interest to merit preservation by the state as a national monument'.[52] Following this, the Land Commission went ahead with arranging for the disposal of the property and on 6 September 1958 the *Irish Independent* ran an advertisement by the Land Commission announcing the sale by tender of Mote Park.[53] Two options were listed: the first was 'Mote Park house, steward's house, out-offices and 112 acres of accommodation lands'; the second was 'alternatively, Mote Park House and some of the buildings for demolition (in lots)'.[54] Mote Park House sold under this second option and was demolished in 1958.

OPW POLICY IN PRACTICE

While these cases illustrate that the OPW did not preserve country houses that were in danger of demolition throughout this period, the complex motivations behind these refusals must be examined. Apart from individual cases, Leask was influential in forming OPW opinion and action on this issue more generally until 1949. This also lends an important nuance to this finding as Leask was personally and professionally passionate about the nation's archaeological and built heritage, yet he had to work within the budgetary constraints and priorities of the OPW. In addition, as Carey notes, Leask did not have the ultimate decision on which monuments to accept into state care. The decision was discussed by the NMAC and then a recommendation was put forward to the Minister for Finance.[55] Only recommendations for acceptance were sent to the Minister so, in most of the instances examined here, the file never got that far, with the recommendation by the Inspector of National Monuments not to accept a country house as a national monuments closing the case.

As documented in the previous chapter, concern from members of the public at the increasing numbers of country houses being destroyed was particularly evident from the 1940s onward. In 1943 the Limerick City Executive wrote to the OPW. Their Executive 'had recently under discussion the destruction and demolition of old mansions throughout the country' and requested that 'all those old mansions that are not falling down should be preserved for the use of the nation'.[56] On receipt of this, Leask wrote to Division C explaining that the letter gave 'expression to a very general feeling that the gradual disappearance, for one cause or another, of large country mansions in Ireland is to be deplored and that steps should be taken to preserve such structures.'[57] He argued that there was no doubt that this feeling existed and that it was justified to some degree by the 'comparatively rapid destruction which has gone on during the last thirty years'.[58] The Casino in Marino, Clontarf, was the only eighteenth-century building at that time that was maintained as a museum in and of itself, but in Leask's opinion it was not impossible that other cases may arise in the future.[59]

However, while he admitted there had been an increasing destruction of country houses which justified this concern, he expressed doubt as to whether its advocates had taken into account the expense and other considerations that would be involved in any such scheme.[60] He contended that as the owners of such houses knew, the maintenance charges on large eighteenth-century houses were considerable and would be even more so in a building not regularly occupied. Furthermore, there would be the costs of care; for example, salaries of caretakers and upkeep of grounds and gardens, which he believed were not likely to be offset by income from visitors' fees in most cases.[61] This crucial consideration of expense also influenced Leask's second reason underpinning why most of these country houses could not be preserved; the scale of costs meant that only a house of exceptional merit would warrant the cost of its preservation. His argument was that 'while these charges might be quite justified in the case of an 18th century mansion of special architectural interest taken over and maintained as a national monument, this would hardly be so in the average case'.[62] He further opined that there was a third restriction on their powers to preserve them, as any such property would be subject to a limitation imposed by section five of the National Monuments Act, which prevented the use of such a monument as a dwelling, except by a caretaker and his family. This meant that under this Act, country houses could not be maintained as historic homes with their families intact, but could only be preserved uninhabited, as museum pieces.[63] He concluded that the reply to the Limerick Executive Council should state that the Commissioners had not the powers required to put such a comprehensive proposal into effect, and this letter was sent.[64] A study of the attitudes and actions of local authorities, county and city councils in relation to the country house in this period would add considerably to historiography on this subject, given that there are numerous examples of such bodies pushing the government for action on this issue, long before any national policies were introduced with regard to these houses. This suggests that they may have viewed the situation more sympathetically and recognised the local tourist potential of these houses more quickly than some in government departments who had to take a broad national approach to issues and were also, usually, based in Dublin.[65]

At this time, Leask took the opportunity to inform Division C that the *Irish Times* had recently enquired if he knew anything:

> Of the operations of a syndicate at present engaged, through an agent not named, in buying up or obtaining options on old mansions with the object of demolishing them and selling or exporting for sale such fittings as panelling, mantel-pieces, doors, etc. I was then and still am quite without any information on the subject other than that provided by the query ... it suggests that the danger to old mansions has greatly increased of late.[66]

This situation had arisen because the value of country houses had increased during the Emergency when they became attractive for their salvageable materials, as discussed in the previous chapter. In Leask's view, any action that would put a stop to 'such needless spoliation for purposes of private gain' was worthy of consideration, although he did not think that the National Monuments Act could be used, except perhaps in some exceptional circumstances.[67] Therefore, no action was taken by the OPW on these claims, nor was there any investigation as to the truth or scale of the issue.

In the same year, in a letter from the Irish Tourist Board, which was forwarded to the OPW by the Department of Industry and Commerce, the Chairman, J. P. O'Brien, wrote that he wanted to submit on behalf of the Board 'that the demolition of large mansions should be forbidden except under permit from the Department of Supplies'.[68] The Department of Supplies had come into existence in 1939 for the duration of the Second World War. The Board believed the houses should be preserved because they could be of use. O'Brien argued:

> My board's interest in the matter is to ensure that no such buildings will be demolished until they have been examined from the point of view of their suitability, either now or after the war, for use as emergency housing; sanatoria or convalescent homes; holiday camps or hotels, or for preservation as historic monuments.[69]

He stressed that a number of houses had already been demolished which, in the opinion of the Board, could have been adapted for tourist purposes after the war and would have been worth more to them than their demolition value.

It is evident that this was based on their possible usefulness as buildings, not as family homes or examples of a specific type of house and the history and style of architecture they represented. The Board suggested that it be made necessary to obtain a license from the Department of Supplies before one could demolish a building of £50 valuation or over. O'Brien thought that it should be possible to give interested organisations an opportunity to examine the house before issuing a license and, in the event that they found it suitable for some approved purpose, to arrange for their purchase of the property at a figure not less than the demolition value.[70]

With regard to this request, Leask suggested that the OPW could not say whether the Tourist Board's suggestion would be practicable as it was an issue for the Department of Supplies.[71] On 8 January 1944, staff in Division C drafted a reply to the Tourist Board which stressed their reasons for not taking action on this matter. These were mainly based on what they explained were the confines of their functions under the National Monuments Act.[72] They made clear that the Act 'does not permit of the taking over of a building occupied as a dwelling by a person other than a person employed as the caretaker thereof, or the family of that person'.[73] Furthermore, funds allocated for the preservation of national monuments were limited and only selected examples, therefore, of structures which came under the definition laid down in the Act, could be considered for preservation. They concluded: 'it will be appreciated from the foregoing that the prevention or control of the demolition or destruction of old mansions generally is not a matter in which the powers provided in the National Monuments Act could be invoked'.[74] A member of the OPW became worried that this draft letter might result in pressure being put on the OPW to issue preservation orders in unjustified cases. They recommended confining the reply to stating that it appeared the buildings referred to in the Irish Tourist Board's letter were 'of modern date and construction and would not, save in very exceptional circumstances, be suitable for preservation under the National Monuments Act'.[75]

On 4 April 1944, public pressure was once more brought to bear on the OPW when a resolution passed by Tipperary Urban District Council was sent to them.[76] This again suggests that local councils and authorities at ground level were concerned about this issue. The Council had unanimously resolved:

> That we protect against the facilities given to syndicates and others which enable them to purchase old places of historic interest for the purpose of demolishing same, thereby denuding the countryside of old land marks [*sic*] very dear to the local people and very often enshrouded in their connection with glorious episodes of our former history and

that we place on record our appreciation of Muintir na Tíre for rescuing Thomastown Castle from those, who for gain, would desecrate it and destroy the former home of a great Tipperary family who gave to Ireland the venerable, patriotic and well beloved Fr Theobald Mathew O. F. M. Cap. And that we call on the government of the country once and for all to enact legislation preventing the exploitation of those old sacred places so dear to all true Irishmen.[77]

It must be noted in this case that the association of the castle with Fr Mathew appears to have been the main motivation behind this resolution. Fr Theobald Mathew, known as 'the Apostle of Temperance', was a Capuchin priest who had worked in Ireland and beyond during the early nineteenth century promoting temperance and abstinence from alcohol. He is also remembered for the work he did to alleviate the suffering of the people of Cork during the cholera epidemic of the early nineteenth century and the Great Famine, and so he was both a national and religious figure. The concerns of members of Tipperary Urban District Council regarding syndicates were not unwarranted as country houses were being snapped up at the time for low prices before being demolished for their materials, which were valuable commodities. Leask had already been contacted by the *Irish Times* about such a possibility as documented earlier, but neither he nor the OPW decided that this claim warranted investigation or action.[78]

On 12 April, Leask wrote a note on the bottom of this letter to Division C to say that he did not see that the OPW could take any action on the resolution and that it would involve legislation of a very comprehensive character that would apply to structures outside the scope of the National Monuments Act.[79] Once again, the primary reason for inaction was that Leask, on behalf of the OPW, did not think they could carry out this work under the National Monuments Act. A draft reply was then drawn up which made clear that the OPW's interest in such matters was confined to the functions it carried out in accordance with the 1930 Act. It stated that OPW officials were prepared to investigate any specific case of a structure in danger of being demolished, but it had to be one that came within the definition of a national monument as contained in the Act. Thomastown Castle, it seems, was clearly not considered eligible and they elucidated on this by stating that the wording of the resolution 'suggested to them that the "old places" referred to were mansions or houses of comparatively modern date and construction, and these would not, save in very exceptional circumstances, be suitable for preservation under the act'.[80]

It is interesting here that the OPW officials said that they were willing to investigate any case that came within the definition of national monument: that is, a building whose preservation is 'a matter of national importance by reason of the historical, architectural, traditional, artistic, or archaeological interest attaching thereto'.[81] However, they were absolutely unwilling to investigate cases brought to their attention by groups who obviously felt that the buildings they were highlighting to the OPW were of historical import. A historic property dating back to the seventeenth century that had an association with a nationally important figure still had not justification enough to gain Thomastown Castle protection under this legislation. By this score, it is difficult to see how any monument qualified. Nonetheless, this reply was sent and the OPW considered no further action needed to be taken.[82] Thomastown Castle, which could have become a tourist attraction and local amenity in rural Tipperary, instead lies in ruin today, a brooding roofless shell in the local landscape. It appears that the OPW excluded large houses and mansions from the above definition, and hence excluded them from the protection of the National Monuments Act, because of their perceived 'modern' construction. Yet, ironically, the Act was not the Ancient Monuments Act, but the National Monuments Act, which specified no date limits. In spite of this, the date of construction, a metric undefined by this legislation, became a determining factor in decisions taken by the OPW.

The rising volume of individual cases of houses in danger did not go unnoticed by the NMAC and in 1945 H. G. Leask and Joseph Raftery, its joint honorary secretaries, wrote to the OPW that the Council:

> Having had before it the matter of the increasing demolition of country houses and mansions or proposals therefore (four cases having been reported by the Land Commission within recent months in addition to statements in the public press) views the position with alarm and has passed a resolution which we are directed to convey to the commissioners. The resolution is as follows: – 'That the council deeply deplores the destruction of monuments with cultural and historic associations and urgently advises the setting up of a committee representative of the Departments of State concerned, the Irish Tourist Board, the architectural associations and learned societies to consider the best means of taking action for the preservation of such monuments'.[83]

The Council realised that 'much which is valuable may pass away before such a body could be set up (or if set up, become operative) and is of opinion that steps should be taken to have records made of any features of architectural and artistic interest which the buildings referred to may possess'.[84] One suggestion offered was that an annual sum be provided for a survey of houses or monuments likely to be demolished.[85]

On the basis of this letter, Division C wrote to Leask, who had co-signed the letter, requesting his attention to the matter. First, he was requested to supply particulars of some of the press statements that had been mentioned in the letter and secondly to furnish an estimate of the annual sum that would be needed to cover expenses in giving effect to the Council's second resolution. This suggests, initially at least, that this division of the OPW was willing to look into this suggestion. Thirdly, the inspector's views generally were sought on the subject of both resolutions in so far as they would affect the functions of the commissioners.[86] In relation to their first query about press attention, the particular case Leask had in mind was Coole Park House, County Galway.[87] Coole, former home of Lady Gregory, co-founder of the Abbey Theatre, had been demolished in 1941 while in state ownership. He admitted: 'I do not know if the house was of architectural interest but it certainly was a case of destruction without record'.[88] He outlined that cases brought to their attention recently had been Jenkinstown, County Kilkenny; Beaufield, County Wexford (although neither of these had proved of interest); Castledaly, County Galway (which photographs showed to have some interest); and Hazelwood, County Sligo. To illustrate the scale of the problem, he wrote: 'it is of general interest to note as showing how destruction goes on – that of 256 houses of the 18th century listed in 1913 by the Georgian Society, 20, to my certain knowledge, and probably a greater number in actual fact, have gone.'[88] In his opinion, these figures drew attention to a problem:

> Which, if not immediately a matter for the board, is one that will become so if any 18th century house of major architectural and artistic importance comes up for consideration as a national monument. This is by no means an unlikely contingency. There can be no doubt that the 'big house' problem is a real one or that the lesser houses also are part of the national cultural development and that, as such, their disappearance is to be deplored.[90]

It is again interesting here that, despite the cases listed, including Castledaly and Hazelwood, the quote makes clear that Leask did not feel that any country house had yet come close to even being considered as a national monument but that it was not 'unlikely' that it could happen in the future. The issue raised by the NMAC was broadly considered to be full of difficulties and Leask's view was that the Commissioners' function in the present state of the matter could not be more than to transmit the Council's resolution to the departments concerned, presumably that of the Taoiseach, Finance, and Industry and Commerce.[91]

Leask was placed here in a most unusual position. He was behind the resolution addressed to the OPW from the NMAC as their Joint Honorary Secretary, and also the person advising the OPW as their Inspector of National Monuments, that nothing could be done by the OPW about the resolution. This also makes it very difficult to ascertain the role he played in this regard. His response to the second resolution was that:

> The recording of work which may be destroyed – particularly in the interim which is inevitable before any comprehensive scheme could be worked out – is a matter which may be considered as coming within the scope of the Architectural Survey which, though naturally concentrating on work of an earlier period (the vastly more numerous prehistoric, early and medieval remains) endeavours to include all old work of interest.[92]

He concluded that only the suggestion of recording could come within the Commissioners' functions.

Based on Leask's advice, an OPW departmental minute recorded that no action was required on their part in relation to the first resolution, but that a copy might be issued to the Departments of the Taoiseach, Lands, Industry and Commerce, and Finance for any action they might consider desirable.[93] Leask had considered that the second resolution might come under the scope of the archaeological survey, the first stage of which was expected to be completed in 1946 when the second field-work stage would begin. The minute noted:

> It is rather difficult to estimate the number of houses [of the type concerned by the proposal] or monuments likely to be destroyed in, say, a year, but on the assumption that the average would be as low as 3 it should not be outside the capabilities of the … staff to be engaged for the field-work of the archaeological survey to deal with them.[94]

The minute also noted that the Board's local architects could assist in some cases if the Board agreed. Nonetheless, it concluded that it was doubtful that the work envisaged could come under the scope of the 1930 National Monuments Act. It is not clear here why the OPW or the Inspector of National Monuments felt that country houses, excepting perhaps the most architecturally important, could not be preserved under the National Monuments Act. Perhaps it was a necessary interpretation given their limited budget and staff. However, if this were the case, surely more internal arguments would have been made that these houses should be preserved as national monuments, though no such sentiments appear in any of the files. A draft reply was composed on 5 December. In this, the OPW noted that the subject of the preservation of mansions had been raised with them on numerous occasions since October 1943. Their attitude had been that they were only concerned with the matter if any structure qualified for preservation under the National Monuments Act. The internal note recorded that, while some of the houses brought to their attention since 1934 may have been of limited interest on politico-social grounds, not one of them had been considered a national monument under the conditions of the Act by reason of 'historical, architectural, traditional, artistic or archaeological interest'.[95]

In addition, the OPW officials were not pleased with the proposal of the council and argued that, unless the mansions concerned were national monuments, the council was stretching its terms of reference in raising the matter with the Commissioners of Public Works. In the absence of the Commissioners, it is worth questioning to whom the NMAC could have brought their concerns about these old mansions. No 'body' was officially or specifically concerned with historic houses and so the OPW was the only organisation they could approach and the one that had the greatest possibility of being able to preserve them. Furthermore, Leask, when wearing his OPW hat, knew that they would not act on this resolution, so perhaps the aim was simply that the NMAC would record their concern about this issue or to have this concern brought to the attention of other government departments. The draft suggested a reply to the effect that, as the buildings referred to in their first resolution did not appear to be national monuments within that meaning of the Act, then the Commissioners had no function to perform in respect of them and that the setting up of a committee on the lines they suggested was not a matter for the Commissioners. The civil servant dealing with the case thought they might add that the Board was not convinced of the necessity for such a committee anyway. In regard to the second proposal, they did not think that a provision of the type suggested, that is, a budget to make a record of the buildings, was appropriate to their vote, but that they were prepared to continue on the basis they had been operating in recent years by arranging for the examination of any specific cases brought to their notice for possible treatment under the Act.[96] Once again, the OPW took little interest in pursuing or supporting an investigation into the question of the demolition or even the surveying of these mansions, as they were not obliged to do so by the legislation under which they operated.

RESPONSIBILITY AND RESOURCES

As previously mentioned, limited financial resources was another factor that influenced the OPW's reluctance to become involved in the preservation of country houses. This is evident in an internal OPW letter of 24 January 1958 to a Mr Cullinane about the present position of a number of monuments that had been recommended for preservation by the National Monuments Advisory

Council.[97] There were some 500 monuments or groups of monuments already in state care for preservation and, in 1956, the inspector had reported that some 200 of them were awaiting more or less urgent works. The civil servant wrote:

> The figures quoted would appear to indicate that unless the Department of Finance would be prepared to authorise a substantial increase in the field maintenance staff and allot increased funds for the national monuments service, it would be pointless for the commissioners to take on additional liabilities at this stage by way of accepting further monuments for state care, when they already have in their charge some hundreds which are awaiting urgent repair works.[98]

Essentially there were two principal factors here restricting the OPW's preservation of country houses, namely a lack of funds and a lack of staff. While it was admitted that some of the 500 or so monuments already in state care required little or no maintenance attention, such as earthworks, the majority required periodic attention by field staff to maintain them in a presentable condition. Most of them, scattered throughout the country, could not be maintained properly by two clerks of works. The fact that the acquisition of country houses would leave the OPW open to criticism over their maintenance was another reason its officers would not get involved in the issue. The OPW officer therefore replied:

> With the money and maintenance staff available it is considered that, numerically, saturation point has been reached. The service is subject to a fair share of publicity from time to time, mostly adverse, and the acceptance of further monuments which may have to remain unattended perhaps for years after being taken in charge, will leave the commissioners open to criticism which would be difficult to counter effectively. It is submitted that it would be preferable to leave monuments unattended and liable to destruction, rather than have them taken into state care and left lying derelict until they can be attended to at some indeterminate time after acceptance.[99]

It was considered, however, that a decision to refuse additional monuments outright might perhaps be too drastic and that there were very many monuments in the country eminently worthy of state care and which would probably be referred to the Commissioners for preservation at some future date. In fact, some 44 cases of buildings that had been recommended to them for preservation at this time were, in their opinion, more important and worthy of state care than several that were already in their charge.[100] Despite this, it was concluded that it was not unreasonable to submit that, in existing conditions, a decision be taken to reject outright any further monuments for preservation by the state. The alternative position was that only proposed monuments of 'outstanding merit' should be considered for preservation.[101]

Apart from their views on various cases brought to their attention, the strongest statement on the OPW's own general policy and attitude comes from a memorandum of 1 January 1946, written by the Chairman of the OPW, Joseph Connolly, for the subject of a board conference on old mansions and big houses. Even the motivation behind this memorandum is revealing, highlighting that the OPW was seemingly more concerned about answering adverse criticism on this issue than addressing the issue of the disappearance of country houses themselves. Never before had the chairman initiated a discussion of this issue, even when houses were being demolished. The first paragraph read:

> The whole question of preserving mansions and big houses which, owing to the changes in social conditions and land policy, are no longer required as residences, has been the subject of considerable comment. A great deal of the comment has been ill-informed with the inevitable misrepresentation and charges of neglect by this department.[102]

The Chairman criticised a school of thought that 'considers that any house in which anyone ever wrote a play or a poem should be preserved as a place of pilgrimage'.[103] The recent agitation over Coole was cited as an example. While Connolly, an ardent nationalist, acknowledged that perhaps the house at Coole should have been preserved for architectural or other reasons, the arguments that had been made were based not on these reasons, but on Lady Gregory's connection with the literary and theatre movement. Acceding that no one would deny Lady Gregory's claims to a place of honour in Anglo-Irish literature, he thought it would be stretching it somewhat to suggest that her home should be preserved as a national monument on that account.[104]

Nevertheless, Connolly emphasised that the most important reason underpinning the OPW's decisions not to preserve these mansions was excessive cost, writing:

> It is quite clear that the majority of the big houses must under modern conditions be demolished for the simple reason that the cost of future maintenance would in most cases be entirely prohibitive. The exceptions are I think where: – (1) The house can be used by the state. (2) The house can be used by a local authority. (3) The house can be used by a religious community. (4) Where the historical or architectural merits of the building are such as to justify the maintenance of the house as a national monument.[105]

None of these exceptions allowed for, or justified, the state's maintenance of these houses as private residences and all these suggestions were only possible when the houses were emptied of their owners. This was probably based on a concern around public justifiability, given that, with owners still living in these buildings, they were not so much historic houses as private homes. Furthermore, Connolly's conclusions do appear reasonable; that a country house could only be preserved if it were fit for use by any private or public body or could be preserved as a national monument. Arising out of this appraisal, the second reason behind the OPW's reluctance to take on these houses was lack of use for them. He explained: 'there are comparatively few of our people who can afford to maintain them in proper order as residences and of those few a very small number indeed would consider it worth their while to do so.'[106] His views from this are clear: the life of the house as a sustainable residence was over. If it could not be used or considered a national monument, then the country house must be sold or demolished, regardless of sentiment relating to its associations with figures or works.

Discussing their possible use for state purposes, he noted that such uses were limited to agricultural colleges or forestry centres, but whether the Department of Agriculture or the forestry branch of the Land Commission would want to add to their number of existing schools was a matter for those departments. Either way, the numbers they could use would not seriously affect the overall problem, which was of a considerable scale. Furthermore, the suggestion that these residences might be acquired by religious orders was a matter on which there was a definite difference of opinion amongst church authorities. Connolly was equally pessimistic about the possibility of the houses being acquired by local authorities, stating that, while in certain cases they might find it possible to use some of these houses either for local offices, vocational schools, or for the activities of the agricultural committee, he did not believe there would be many cases in which they would be found suitable.[107] The report carried out between 1943 and 1945 by the Department of Local Government and Public Health into possible use by government departments of these mansions, discussed in the previous chapter, would support the Chairman's opinion, since only 5 out of 325 houses examined were considered suitable for any public purpose.[108]

Nevertheless, the Chairman did argue:

> Whatever about the ultimate fate of these houses it would, of course, be desirable that either we or some Department of state should have full particulars of them before disposal or demolition occurs. In the cases of such residences as have been or may be taken over by the Land Commission it seems to me that it should be possible for their inspectors in the course of their inspections to prepare a survey plan and report on the house which could be passed either to the National Monuments Advisory Council or to the OPW's inspector who could advise on the ultimate fate of the building.[109]

In addition, regarding the disposal of country houses by private owners, he could not see that they had any right to intervene under existing circumstances, and thought that undoubtedly 'any house of special interest from the historical or architectural point of view would come under our direct notice or be brought to our attention by the National Monuments Advisory Council.'[110] It was not unreasonable to assert that a private home owner selling their house was a private transaction involving the constitutional right to property, and many owners, too may have felt their rights invaded if the state had intervened in such business. This is an important point. Connolly highlighted the fact that, primarily, these country houses were private properties and were treated as such by their owners in terms of their care, preservation, use or sale, yet public pressure over specific houses had begun to suggest and even assert that the government had a responsibility to preserve these homes as part of the national built heritage. This draws attention to another important reason why the OPW did not often step in to preserve country houses: they believed they had no right to intervene.

The subject of public justifiability for the OPW's decisions, which was obviously important to the Office, was then addressed. Connolly thought it would be desirable, if possible, to make it known to the public generally:

> The real reasons if any for the preservation of such houses and above all the extremely heavy expenditure involved if the houses are to be preserved and maintained. It is quite clear that the public, misled by irresponsible and dishonest attacks, has only the vaguest notions of what it is desirable to preserve and all that such preservation involves.[111]

This suggests that the Chairman believed there might not be any reason that would justify the preservation of country houses. He thought that the NMAC would be more helpful if they faced the problem 'realistically' and indicated the Office's opinion on what was the extent of the problem, and which houses should be considered for preservation and why. The purpose, it seems, was to convince the chairman of the OPW of why he should act.[112] Perhaps here we have a clue as to understanding Leask's behaviour in a professional capacity when he did not deem country houses worthy of preservation in contrast to his personal appreciation and work for them. Official policy positions of departments and state bodies are dictated by those in charge and this filters down through the whole organisation, so that it may have been Connolly, as Chairman of the OPW, whose views on the preservation of country houses were taken up by, imposed on, the staff of the whole Office.

THE CASE OF DUNSANDLE HOUSE

When Dunsandle House, County Galway, was reported to the OPW as being in danger of demolition in June 1954, the Office was hesitant to get involved. The circumstances faced by Dunsandle were typical of the situations in which many country houses found themselves. The discussion within the OPW on the preservation of Dunsandle illustrates the diverse opinions and the subjective nature of many of the decisions taken in such cases, given that the 1930 Act and the 1954 Amendment Act were broad in their scope and contained no limitations surrounding the dating of monuments.

The NMAC had recommended a preservation order for Dunsandle in 1954 and a member of the OPW's Division F staff supported this course, arguing: 'the house is one of the finest late 18th – early 19th century houses in the country and it contains fine plasterwork and fireplaces of the period. The three-part architectural composition of the house is a good example of the finest work of its time.'[113] As such, a draft preservation order was drawn up for Dunsandle under section 8 (1) of the National Monuments Act, 1930. This section read:

> Where it appears to the Minister for Finance on a report made by the Advisory Council or otherwise that a monument which in the minister's opinion is a national monument is in danger of being or is actually being destroyed, injured or removed, or is falling into decay through neglect, the minister may by order entrust the preservation of such a monument to the Commissioners of Public Works in Ireland.[114]

However, a local commissioner did not recommend the issue of a preservation order as the house was only 140 years old and did 'not appear to be of much historic interest', although he thought an old castle on the estate, possibly of Norman origin, might be.[115] The furnishings of Dunsandle were sold at an auction in July, while the Land Commission was negotiating for the purchase of the lands, excluding 100 acres and the house. The Commission was not interested in the house, given that it had no use for such a residence. The owner of the property, Major Bowes-Daly, who was then living in South Africa, intended to offer the house for sale together with 100 acres, and a member of the OPW believed that this indicated that he did not expect to have to sell for demolition. They argued, then, that to interfere by issuing a preservation order could reduce the owner's chances of a sale to a person who would live in the house, and so could defeat their objective.[116]

In July 1954, a civil servant in the OPW pressed for a reconsideration of the issue of the country house more generally. They argued:

In 1946 it appeared unlikely that many of the most architecturally distinguished houses had any future as residences ... but even by 1947 conditions had changed ... and since then the existence of fine 18[117] century houses in Ireland has attracted a number of wealthy people to take up residence here. About ten days ago I visited Russborough House, County Wicklow, and found that a great deal of money is being spent on it by its new owner.[117]

The civil servant emphasised that it was now the case that the state had the power to prevent houses of outstanding merit from being sold for demolition or without prior consent, since the National Monuments Act, as amended in 1954, provided for the issue of preservation orders for houses used as dwellings, which the 1930 Act had previously disallowed. The official wrote that in some cases this could mean that the market value of the houses would be reduced so as to make them a reasonable proposition for purchasers who wished to live in them. In all cases, in their opinion, preservation orders could be used to delay destruction and this could mean that some would be spared long enough for them to find a suitable owner. Despite this, the sympathetic civil servant highlighted:

As far as I know Ireland is the only country in Europe where no government action has been taken to preserve country houses in the face of changing social and economic conditions. Republican France is sufficiently far-sighted to spend very large sums on the preservation of royal palaces and the residences of the nobility. It is most unlikely that, in proportion to our resources, the problem here is anything to compare with the problem there; but no realistic assessment of the magnitude of the problem in Ireland can be made without a country-wide survey of country houses, which would be part of the Archaeological Survey. In any case the issue of preservation orders for houses in danger does not involve the expenditure of state funds and it appears to be the minimum action that should be taken to preserve some of the finest pieces of architecture in the country and, of the 18th century, some of the finest works in the British Isles.[118]

Returning to Dunsandle, another OPW official believed that a preservation order could result in loss to the owner and was also likely to result, sooner or later, in pressure on the Board to spend money on maintaining the building. Therefore 'the special importance of, and the danger to, the house would need to be established beyond doubt before the issue of a preservation order could be justified'.[119] Enquiries about Dunsandle did not confirm that the house was, at the time, in serious danger of demolition and so it was recommended that a preservation order should not be sought until it was seen whether the house would find a purchaser who would maintain it.[120] A departmental colleague also stressed that the issue of preservation orders frequently cost owners some loss of personal profits. In addition, there was no way that the Board could be pressed into contributing towards the maintenance of an occupied dwelling house. Since, in their view, the danger to a house could only be established when it was bought by a firm for demolition, they stated:

> The issue of a preservation order at that stage would be most inopportune since the buyer would have bought in good faith at a price based on the value of the house as scrap. If, however, it is made clear that the house may not be demolished, no such buyers will bid and it will not be possible to assess what they would have been prepared to offer.[121]

Cullinane, an official in the OPW had, in contrast, agreed to the NMAC's call for a preservation order to be issued. While he was aware that the proposal would create a precedent, he argued: 'the matter of country houses in Ireland should be brought under control so that, when a proper evaluation of the situation can be made, some coherent policy can be laid down. I would point out that a P. O. [preservation order] can be revoked and that Dunsandle would provide a good test.'[122] In the end, he was overruled by colleagues who did not think that the OPW should in any circumstances undertake guardianship in this case, and who thought it unwise of the Office to interfere prior to the result of the auction of Dunsandle on 11 August being known.[123]

The advertisement for Dunsandle in the *Irish Times* of July 1954 read: 'Magnificent gentleman's residence on 131 acres – freehold. Suitable for religious institution, etc.', and did not refer to its demolition value.[124] The house was described as 'one of the finest examples of Georgian architecture of its period in Ireland'.[125] It had central heating throughout and all modern conveniences, while all the downstairs rooms were described as having fine Adam and marble fireplaces and the large salon had 'magnificent Italian walls'.[126] Yet, at an auction of Dunsandle on 11 August 1954, there was little interest with only eight attendees.[127] The auctioneer asked for an opening bid of £12,000, but on receiving none had reduced that figure to £5,000. When there was still no bid, the property was withdrawn.[128] On 15 October the NMAC wrote to the OPW to say that they had been informed that the Commissioners had decided not to recommend issuing a preservation order for Dunsandle.[129] During their discussion 'the question of the preservation of representative historic houses generally was raised' and it was decided to place it on the agenda for their next meeting. They therefore wrote that it would be of considerable assistance to this discussion if the Commissioners' reasons for their decision on Dunsandle were made available.[130] The draft reply from the OPW declared abruptly that they were not satisfied that Dunsandle House was 'one which merits permanent conservation as a national monument. It is of little historical or archaeological significance'.[131] The last admission by the OPW is difficult to understand, even in the context of their limited resources.

In spite of this, the OPW was still under pressure to preserve Dunsandle and in December 1954 Galway County Council wrote to the OPW to inform their commissioners that a resolution was passed at a recent meeting of the local NMAC of County Galway: 'that the Commissioners for Public Works be requested to take immediate steps for the preservation of Dunsandle House which is a very important eighteenth-century Georgian house, the only one of its kind in County Galway. It is indeed believed to be the best example of Georgian architecture in the west of Ireland.'[132] The county manager had written to the Minister for Health to suggest that some religious order might take the house as a home for children with mental disabilities, but the minister had not thought that action necessary as such homes were being established in Sligo and Limerick. Furthermore, it was unlikely that the premises would, at any time, be required by the County Council for such purposes. He also understood that the NMAC was very anxious that a preservation order be made and requested the matter be attended to as quickly as possible.[133]

As seen in other examples, the interest taken by local authorities in this issue – perhaps because of the possible immediate amenity or tourist value of such houses to the locality – was often at odds with the stance taken at a national level by government bodies. No action on this case was taken by the OPW except to inform the Department of Finance of the representations received. Furthermore, it appears there were no other ready buyers for Dunsandle House as a residence as it was not until three years later, in September 1957, that the *Connacht Tribune* reported in a very discrete article that Dunsandle had been purchased by a Dublin demolition firm, Messrs. Roche Bros., for the sum of £2,000.[134] Once it had been purchased, work dismantling it began immediately. A few days later *The Irish Press* ran an advertisement for the sale of cut limestone blocks from the house together with window surrounds, sills, steps etc.[135] By December the demolition of much of the 250-year-old structure had already taken place as the *Connacht Tribune* ran an advertisement for an 'Important Demolition Sale' at Dunsandle.[136] Items for sale at the public auction included 80 windows, 40 doors, copper piping and eight stable doors. The walls of the mansion, built of cutstone blocks, were also offered for sale, as well as 'two handsome Entrance Doors' and a 'large Glasshouse with Furnace'.[137] As a result, only a few walls of Dunsandle now remain standing as stark ruins in the Galway countryside.

CONCLUSION

The period from 1930 to 1960 was one of the most dramatic in terms of the dereliction and demolition of the country house in Ireland. It was therefore the period during which the OPW began to come under pressure from the public, local authorities and those concerned with tourism in terms of how it could cease this destruction by preserving these houses. The OPW, however, was not enthusiastic about doing so. From an examination of the Office's correspondence and action, their reluctance can be attributed to a number of reasons. Firstly, the OPW stated repeatedly that the only powers it had were the ones given to it under the 1930 National Monuments Act and its staff did not think that a country house would qualify as being of sufficient historical, architectural, traditional, artistic, or archaeological interest to merit preservation under this legislation. While in some cases the OPW acknowledged the associations of houses with historical figures, this was not believed to make them worthy of preservation under the 1930 Act, and it appears that the OPW quite often stuck to the letter of the law to avoid becoming involved in the issue of their preservation. In any event, the 1930 Act would not have made the preservation of these houses as private residences possible with the owners occupying them.

Another reason that OPW officials thought the country house unsuitable for preservation under this Act was that they were too modern. Most of the structures that the office had previously preserved dated prior to the seventeenth century. Aware of the number of houses that were being abandoned, sold or demolished for their materials, and also conscious that they had no market value and were hugely expensive to maintain, the OPW did not want to set a precedent in this regard by taking on newer buildings and ending up in a position of responsibility for the many country houses in danger at this time. If they took one, they could not refuse others on any solid ground, and therefore stuck rigidly to their principles. Their disregard for more 'modern' sites as national monuments notably also applied to more 'vernacular' architecture. 'Ancient' monuments took precedence over all more 'modern' constructed buildings, not just those with a 'foreign' association. Round towers were preserved; the thatched cottages of the ordinary classes were, predominantly, not. It must be remembered that these were relatively 'new' buildings, as were historic houses, both often still in use as homes all over the country. It was therefore difficult for officials to imagine them as historical entities worth preserving at the time, particularly as the new state was anxious to assert itself as a modern nation, capable of holding its own among the industrialised nations of the world, and seeking to rid itself of its 'colonial', but also its more old-fashioned or backward, image.

In addition, the monuments that the OPW had previously preserved were primarily ruins and sites that took little more than a fence or sign to establish their position as national monuments; very achievable with limited budget and staff.[138] The OPW had emphasised in the case of Russborough that, if they took on these houses, it would significantly restrict the OPW's resources. It would also mean they would be unable to obtain many other monuments that they could preserve for the same cost as one country house.[139] A living house to be preserved as such would be a constant drain on their finances and OPW officials feared adverse publicity if they took on monuments they could not maintain. They thought it better for a country house to go to ruin privately so that blame would not be apportioned to their Office for its demise, given that they had reached 'saturation point' in terms of their care of national monuments. In addition, the contents of many country houses, including Dunsandle, had been sold prior to the sale of the house and it is questionable what value a country house would have had as a national monument with its many rooms devoid of the contents that describe and define its history. How could the OPW attract visitors to such a house? Certainly, it would be another expensive task for the OPW to try to refurnish a large empty house with period pieces authentic to the time.

The OPW's limited budget was undoubtedly a restricting factor during the period considered here. While it seems from the evidence that the OPW avoided taking on these buildings, this may have been because they were not in a position to do so financially and the National Monuments Act or their modern construction gave them sufficient excuse to refuse to do so. The OPW's budget was very low in relation to national monuments at this time as governments focused budgets on more pressing social issues, and both the limited budget and small field staff meant that the OPW was constrained in being able to take on these structures. The Department of Finance controlled the OPW's limited resources, which restricted them from acting, although there is no evidence in OPW files of their staff contacting, let alone pressurising, the Department of Finance for an increase in budget. In fact, when the NMAC had proposed amendments to the 1930 Act, as documented in the previous chapter, the OPW acknowledged that there was more important legislation for the government to be concerned with. This may also have been considered by the OPW in relation to the budgetary constraints of the government from 1930 to the 1960s and beyond.

One figure who appears particularly influential throughout this period was H. G. Leask, as he did not consider that country houses could be deemed national monuments by the OPW.[140] His view was of paramount importance as the sole full-time employee of the National Monuments Branch of the OPW for most of his 26-year term in office.[141] It is evident from his published works and his term as President of the Royal Society of Antiquaries of Ireland that his passion and knowledge were particularly focused on more ancient monuments.[142] However, he was also influential in the acquisition by the state of the guardianship and repair of the Casino at Marino in Dublin in 1932. While Carey has argued that Leask did not have a *carte blanche* to dictate which monuments should be accepted by the state, it appears, in most cases examined in this chapter, that his opinion was the one that was influential.[143] It also seems that Leask may not have felt like fighting a battle for resources and personnel to preserve these houses when it was a battle he was not going to win.

By way of illustration, he was a member of the NMAC and had been submitting proposals to the Commissioners of Public Works since the 1930s for an archaeological survey of Ireland to be carried out, so that the commissioners could accurately discern what should be prioritised for preservation. They continued to submit these proposals to the commissioners from the 1930s until the 1950s. Although some work was done, a comprehensive survey was not authorised during this period, with 'economies of scale and personnel being foremost in the minds of the established civil service administration of that time'.[144] Given the importance placed on this survey by the NMAC and the inability of the OPW to commit to it for many years, another battle for resources to record or preserve historic houses may have seemed too onerous a task for Leask.

Leask was followed in the role of Inspector of National Monuments by Percy le Clerc who was to be the last Inspector of National Monuments until c. 1970 when this charge passed to senior architects. However, there is another significant figure in this story who, though largely absent from the debates around individual houses, may yet have controlled the priorities and objectives, as well as cultural ethos, of the OPW; namely Joseph Connolly, Chairman of the Office. Certainly, nationalist Connolly was the man in charge, and Leask may have toed the line when it came to disregarding country houses as national monuments. Irrespective of whoever was the most influential, what is certain from all files is that the country house was not thought to be of sufficient historical or architectural importance to warrant the required level of expenditure for preservation during this period.

The changes of minister or government did not appear to affect the OPW, which as an office kept working without any noticeable difference in policy as new governments came to power, uninterested in making their mark in this area. During the period from 1930 to 1960, in all cases brought to the attention of the OPW detailed in this chapter, this body declined to designate country houses as national monuments worthy of preservation under the 1930 Act and often considered them unworthy of survey or record. On a number of occasions, reference was made to the possibility that exceptional examples, particularly of Georgian architecture, might qualify under these terms, but no country houses were preserved as national monuments. It is also arguable that the OPW had no public mandate to preserve the country house at this time. The government report of 1943–5, discussed in the previous chapter, had already concluded that these houses were not useful for government purposes and there was no tourism industry to support them. While there was increasing public concern in this period, this did not mean that the general public would have sustained these houses in any tourism capacity. Terence Dooley has contended that it was not really until the 1990s that

> Big houses became a major tourist attraction in Ireland, attractive to the indigenous population as well as to foreign tourists. For the three years from 1992 to 1994, the cumulative number of visitors to the fifty or so big houses opened to the public aver-aged around 1.48 million per year, almost twice as many as in 1975 … It was a long time after the big house had been stripped of its landed estates and political power that their symbolic nature was put to one side and their owners no longer regarded with the degree of enmity and suspicion that had been inherited from their ancestors.[145]

The late Egerton Shelswell-White has also described how, 'when things were really good at the end of the 1980s and the beginning of the 1990s', around 70,000–80,000 people a year visited Bantry House.[146] The OPW were really only given their mandate to acquire such houses in the 1990s, when they could also be hopeful that tourism would provide the income to maintain them. In 1992, for example, the OPW acquired Castletown House, County Kildare, which is currently open to the public. It should be remembered, though, that Castletown was originally saved by the private individual efforts of Desmond Guinness who, recognising the importance of the house, purchased Castletown in 1967, after which it became the headquarters of the Irish Georgian Society and was greatly restored through fundraising and, significantly, private initia-tive.[147] Possessing a mandate is one motivation, but having foresight on behalf of the nation and its citizens is another, and, owing to the OPW's refusal to consider country houses as national monuments throughout this period, numerous magnificent buildings were dismantled, demolished or laced with dynamite and destroyed. Many buildings that might have proved to be amenity centres or tourist attractions in locations all over Ireland today instead lie in ruin and, while it appears that the OPW simply did not have the resources to take them on, the loss of houses such as Coole Park and Dunsandle is a regret future generations must bear.

FOUR

POLITICAL CHANGE AND SILENT DECLINE, 1948–57

The period from 1948 to 1957 was one of the most changeable in Irish political history as an inter-party coalition government led by Fine Gael and a single-party Fianna Fáil government wrestled each other in and out of power. This resulted in a much-fractured period in terms of politics and policy, with neither administration in power long enough to make significant changes. The inter-party government was also the first of its kind and had to attempt to appease its varied membership when in power, so while this period was a quickly-changing one for governments, in terms of wider public policy, much remained static. With little time in power, the cabinets in this period had to prioritise the issues that they would deal with and, as such, private historic mansions hardly featured at all on their agenda. The little discussion on this subject that did take place came from the press or interest groups such as An Taisce or the NMAC. This chapter will examine governmental attitudes to the country house during this period, whether there were any changes in perceptions or if the country house even featured as a matter of political or public concern in such a politically fractious environment.

POLITICS AND ANGLO-IRISH RELATIONS

In February 1948, Éamon de Valera's 16-year reign as leader of a Fianna Fáil government came to an end and the first inter-party government under Fine Gael Taoiseach John A. Costello came to power. However, Fine Gael was only back in power as the largest group in a coalition that included the Labour Party, a splinter-group called National Labour, Clann na Talmhan, and Clann na Poblachta. Dermot Keogh has described this coalition as 'one of the most ideologically divided governments in the history of the state, united only by the unanimous wish to see Éamon de Valera and his party on the opposition benches and the desire to hold on to power for as long as possible. It very soon became faction-ridden.'[1]

They were pushed aside in June 1951 by de Valera's Fianna Fáil, although this was to be for an equally short period. Just three years later, Costello once again led an inter-party government into Dáil Éireann in June 1954, although, in line with the pattern of the previous administrations, this was only a brief tenure which ended in March 1957. While southern politics was thus dominated at this time by primarily middle-class parties and farming interests, the situation was very different in Northern Ireland and Britain. There, Olwen Purdue has argued that:

> The most remarkable manifestation of landed political survival was that three out of Northern Ireland's six Prime Ministers came from old landed families. While this was very far from the situation that existed in the Free State and later in the Republic of Ireland, it could also be perceived as an aberration from the prevailing pattern in British politics. Closer analysis shows, however, that the resurgence of landed political leadership in Northern Ireland actually mirrored a similar phenomenon in Britain … when war threatened British society in the 1940s … the country once more found itself with a Prime Minister from an old aristocratic family in the form of Winston Churchill, grandson of the seventh duke of Marlborough.[2]

Purdue has argued that the continued political and social importance of the northern gentry was a significant factor in the survival of the landed class in the North longer than in the south. It maintained their confidence as a group and encouraged them to retain their ancestral homes, 'therefore extending the life of big house society in Northern Ireland long after it had gone into serious decline elsewhere on the island.'[3]

One of the initial and most significant undertakings of the first inter-party government in the south was the decision to repeal the External Relations Act in the summer of 1948, making Ireland a state 'associated with, but not a member of, the Commonwealth'.[4] Costello made this move public on a trip to Canada. F. J. McEvoy has claimed that, while Fine Gael 'was the party traditionally most favourable to the Commonwealth [connection]', the government decided on the repeal 'under the influence of its more radical elements', particularly the other parties who were part of the government coalition and more left-wing than Fine Gael.[5] The Republic of Ireland was formally established on Easter Monday 1949 – the 32-year anniversary of the 1916 Rising. Nonetheless, Keogh has argued that the announcement was 'a hollow victory' as it led to renewed tension between Dublin and London and served to further institutionalise partition on the island.[6] The Ireland Act of 1949 declared that Éire ceased to be part of His Majesty's dominions from April 1949, but guaranteed that 'in no event will Northern Ireland or any part thereof cease to be a part of His Majesty's dominions and of the United Kingdom without the consent of the parliament of Northern Ireland'.[7]

The declaration itself was not a radical departure. McEvoy has shown how, in July 1945, de Valera stated that 'Ireland was, in fact, a republic "associated as a matter of our external policy with states of the British Commonwealth".'[8] In December 1936, under a Fianna Fáil government, legislation was enacted that removed all references to the Crown and Governor General from the Constitution, while further legislation introduced immediately thereafter recognised the Crown only for purposes of diplomatic representation and international agreements. These legal changes, commonly referred to as the External Relations Act, left Ireland 'a more or less undeclared republic with ambiguous links to the Commonwealth'.[9] This had been part of de Valera's project of continuing to create distance between Britain and Ireland, but it was Cosgrave's government that made the break official. The British response to the Ireland Act 1949 made 'provision for the changed circumstances following the declaration of the republic.'[10] The Act also contained a guarantee that no change would be made in the position of Northern Ireland without the consent of the parliament of Northern Ireland and '[t]he result was an immediate storm of protest and an abrupt end to the goodwill so recently exhibited.'[11] This period of change and instability in the Irish political establishment thus began with a hardening of relations with Britain.

Anti-British sentiment was also still being expressed by some of the more staunchly republican deputies in Dáil chambers. For example, in 1953, debate surrounded the utilisation of Dublin Castle and its architectural symbolism. Fine Gael TD for Galway South, Patrick Cawley, asked: 'was it not a pity that it [Dublin Castle] did not fall down long ago?'[12] Robert Briscoe, Fianna Fáil

TD for Dublin South-West, supported this suggestion, adding: 'I would be delighted to help the deputy to knock it down.'[13] While in another debate, Fine Gael TD for Meath and outspoken republican, Captain Giles, extended this argument, proclaiming: 'I want Dublin Castle blown sky-high and nothing put in its place. I want to see the houses of parliament here closed down and to have houses of parliament built in the country.'[14]

THE 'LANDED' CLASS

As these politics were playing out on the national stage, the landed gentry, who had been in decline since before the beginning of the century, were dwindling to an isolated minority in the new republic. Given their decreasing numbers, the fact that they no longer had any real part to play in the politics of the state, and their physical isolation in the remaining county houses, their demise was barely noticed by the bulk of the population. The *Irish Times*, when discussing the seventeenth edition of *Burke's Landed Gentry*, which was published in 1952, noted that half of the included gentry now owned no land at all.[15] This reflected the social revolution that had taken place in Ireland over the preceding 70 years. The paper reported that the landed gentry were 'dying hard', their most savage threat being death duties imposed by the government.[16] The status of the ascendancy class was again in doubt in 1955 when it was reported that a new edition of the *Landed Gentry of Ireland* was being prepared for publication. L. G. Pine, director of Burke's Peerage Limited, had declared that entitlement to entry was based on 'property and pedigree'.[17] While applicants were supposed to have property of 500 acres or more, they recognised 'that some people for economic reasons have had to sell their property, but, at the same time, have been in Ireland for centuries. It is felt that it would be unjustifiable to preclude such families from entry.'[18] This further reflected the drastically altered position of the 'landed' gentry. The foundations on which their identity as a class were built were, by the mid-1950s, either no longer valid, such as 'landed class', or irrelevant, as in the case of their 'ascendancy'. Any distinctions that remained were continually being eroded, particularly their position as country house owners.

The perception that country house owners were a social group that was dying out was popular throughout this period. Instead of being considered part of the rural communities in which they lived, they were now generally perceived as eccentrics who were rarely seen. Terence Dooley has argued that 'for those who remained, rural Ireland became a lonely, isolated place of residence.'[19] He maintains that 'their feelings of not belonging to mainstream Irish life were linked to the growth of a new nationalism that made them question their position and identity in Ireland.' He also admits that they 'became very much turned in upon themselves and subsequently often became regarded as eccentrics in local communities quite often simply because they spoke differently from locals or they dressed differently or they had different cultural tastes and values.'[20] Yet, this was not the only reason for their isolation and Brian Casey has suggested that, in earlier decades, the landlord class largely refused to admit or appreciate that their former tenants could play an important role in the sphere of politics. This sense of hubris also distanced them from their tenants.[21]

By the 1950s, owners were often being ridiculed or stereotyped in the national press. In an article in the *Irish Times* in 1952, the paper alleged:

> The Anglo-Irish are still there, still using words as intoxicants in their lively, irrespon-
> sible fashion – emerging at times, especially in horse show week, as a kind of social
> entity under the glittering chandeliers of cocktail bars in Dublin's fashionable hotels.
> But, as a political entity, they are either caught up in the life of the new state or, like
> the French aristocracy, financially impoverished and exiled in a dream world of their
> own invention.[22]

The *Irish Times*, always regarded as an establishment newspaper of the upper classes, was attempting to appeal to a wider readership here, or perhaps awaken their own readership to the realities of their position in modern Ireland at this time. The editor, Robert M. Smyllie, aimed to establish a more modern profile for the one-time ascendancy paper during his tenure.[23] In this, he was quite different to his predecessor, John Healy. As Mark O'Brien outlines:

> It was in terms of politics that the difference between the two men was most pronounced.
> Whereas Healy had been irrevocably opposed to the Free State pulling away from
> Britain and 'had fought every step of the way, using all the weapons, from cold logic
> to ridicule, in his stylistic armoury', Smyllie was of a more pragmatic disposition.[24]

While he was undoubtedly a monarchist and a supporter of commonwealth membership, Smyllie approached these issues from an Irish rather than an imperial angle: Healy criticised the country's move away from Britain because he believed it was bad for the commonwealth, whereas Smyllie criticised it because he believed that it was bad for Ireland. Compared to Healy, Smyllie had 'the contemporary outlook; he knew that "West-Britonism" as a policy or a point of view was dead'.[25]

With the press fuelling these stereotypes, the image of the remaining country house owners as eccentrics and oddities gained increasingly common credence at this time, cementing it in popular perception. In 1953, the *Irish Times* reported on an American journalist, Ernest O. Hauser, who had written of his rather clichéd impressions of Ireland in an article in the American magazine, *Saturday Evening Post*, further fuelling these caricatures. He spoke of the 'Englishmen' who decided to stay on in Ireland after independence and said that 'banking, insurance, and, to a lesser extent, big business, are considered an Anglo-Saxon preserve, and British accents are discernible both in the legal profession and in the higher brackets of the civil service.'[26] The *Irish Times* quoted him as saying:

> Still known as the ascendancy group, these thoroughly domesticated despots hold on to their exclusive rendezvous; Dublin's bumptious Kildare street club remains a redoubt of ascendancy strength. They print their own respected daily, the *Irish Times* and, forever arranging spring festivals and horse shows, they play a surprisingly vigorous role in the community.[27]

He had also maintained that 'up-country, in some particularly pleasant spots, Britannic gentry carry on as usual, subscribing to the *Tatler*, riding to the hounds, and bundling junior off to Eton.'[28]

This idea that the owners of historic houses were continuing to live the lifestyle of a century before was not an accurate portrayal. Those who remained were a small, isolated group, no longer involved in the exclusive social life of the city.[29] In 1954, the *Irish Times* portrayed the reality more honestly when they reported on the decline of the country house, stating that the power of the 'ruling class' was irretrievably broken.[30] Nevertheless, the stereotypes that had developed around the landlord class continued in popular perception and added to the mystique that surrounded them. In fact, L. P. Curtis has highlighted the remarkably 'enduring nature of these negative images both north and south of the border long after the old gentry had ceased to lord it over their largely Catholic tenantry.'[31] He maintained that

> Despite creeping insolvency, the decimation of the officer class on the Western Front, the voluntary or compulsory sale of estates, arson attacks on over 250 Big Houses and emigration, the former landlords remained an object of abuse or derision in the popular imagination. In this scenario of denigration, myth played a major role.[32]

Rather than providing the subject for political debate, as at the beginning of the Free State, now deprived of their power and status, they had become media fodder, or the perfect odd family around which to base a plotline. In fact, they lived on in drama and fiction throughout the century, longer and with greater presence than their actual contribution to Irish life would suggest.[33] Edith Somerville and Martin Ross' *The Big House of Inver* was one of the early depictions of the country house way of life in Ireland, while later, Lennox Robinson's 1926 play, *The Big House*, about a decaying and isolated country house family, was often performed on stage or on radio. In 1949, the revival of Brinsley McNamara's play, *The Grand House in the City*, twelve years after it had been last performed, reflected the reality of the demise of country house life at this time. Its central theme was the conflict between the 'effete, ineffectual survivor of the old landed gentry ... the loud, vulgar, land-grabber', and a journalist writing articles about ruined houses.[34]

In spite of such portrayals, behind the crumbling walls some owners tenaciously hung on. Desmond Sharp Bolster of Glenlohane and Springfort, Kanturk, remembered 'life being very hard for my father in the 1950s due to these rates and depressed prices, but he held on through thick and thin. Houses like ours have seen a lot of history, and history ebbs and flows. When you own these places, you've got to consider yourself a caretaker and try to weather the storm.'[35] In Sarah Connolly-Carew's memoirs of growing up in Castletown House, her chapter on family life in the 1950s suggests the way of life they were accustomed to living continued, even if there was a sense that the halcyon days were passing. She wrote: 'we didn't know it at the time but we lived in the last generation of the "Upstairs/Downstairs" life, with a full complement of staff to look after both the house and us.'[36] Furthermore, up until the 1950s and sometime thereafter, the *Irish Times* still ran occasional advertisements such as: 'cook seeks post with gentry',[37] although those seeking a position in service were becoming rare. In fact, after the world wars had brought people into factories and industry, owners had difficulty filling posts in domestic service, viewed now as an anachronistic mode of employment. Dooley has argued that, in the aftermath of the First World War, much had changed:

> There was to be no rejuvenation of the domestic service industry. With the spread of education and new ideas and alternative forms of employment, domestic service went into irreversible decline. Young women were no longer prepared to be perceived or treated as skivvies in an age when social equality was gaining more and more credence and any work deemed to be demeaning was considered unacceptable. As the twentieth century progressed, those who retained Big Houses in Ireland found themselves increasingly unable to replace servants as their old ones died.[38]

QUIET DECLINE

In reality, there were numerous national and international factors that contributed to the decline of the country house in Ireland, including those as seemingly unconnected as increasing levels of education among the populace and varying work patterns.

Voices bemoaning the demise of the landed class and the passing of the country house were not frequently heard in the Oireachtas. Governments in this period were changing quickly, had many more prominent issues than this to pursue, and had shorter terms in which to bring their electoral promises to fruition. Rather, it fell to newspapers, such as the sympathetic *Irish Times*, and also groups like An Taisce to chart their passing. As An Taisce was financially struggling at this time, with no government assistance or reliefs from rates or duties, they were largely incapable of action. Their main function in this period was to highlight the plight of historic houses in the media. They performed this well, maintaining an awareness of the issue at least occasionally in the national press, as houses continued to silently disappear from the landscape. One such house was Castle Freke, County Cork, which was dismantled in 1952 and left to ruin, just 39 years after Lord Carberry had celebrated his coming of age ball there in 1913. Shortly after this he had been compelled by financial difficulties to sell and abandon the house to its fate. Based on the figures estimated from Mark Bence-Jones' *A Guide to Irish Country Houses*, mentioned in Chapter Two, the period from 1950 to 1960 was the most destructive decade for the country house in the twentieth century.[39]

It is also worth remembering that, by the mid-twentieth century, many of these houses were aging, having been built in the eighteenth or nineteenth centuries. Without the proper funds to keep up restoration and repairs, they were beginning to need extensive maintenance work. As such, they became difficult to manage as family homes with rampant problems like damp and dry rot, as well as leaking roofs. Some did not have hot running water or other modern amenities that would have helped their claims of being adaptable as schools or hospitals. Dermot Edwards remembers his relative, Phyllis Godfrey, living at Kilcoleman Abbey, Milltown, County Kerry, from 1942–58, a period of huge decline when 'the house was falling down around her because of dry rot.'[40] The house was abandoned in 1958 due to the extent of the dry rot and fell into a ruinous state. It was demolished in 1977 by Kerry County Council. Similarly, at Castletown, County Kildare, Sarah Connolly-Carew remembered that, by the second half of the twentieth century, 'constant repairs to the house became overwhelming. The roof leaked in several places, and buckets stayed on permanent guard duty underneath each drip into the bedrooms. Everyone in the house became custodians of a number of allotted buckets to catch the leaks.'[41] The cost of repairs to Castletown had become so onerous that, by 1963, Sarah's father made the 'awful decision' to sell the house.[42] While in former years outlying land could be sold to cover costs of roof repairs or rewiring at Castletown, by the early 1960s, '300 acres of the farm land had already gone. There was only the house and 500 acres left of Speaker Connolly's great estates.'[43] This situation was replicated for other country houses, with little left by this time for owners to sell off to fund maintenance and repairs. In 1966, the contents of Castletown were sold over three days, following which the house itself and around 500 acres were sold for £166,000. The new owners did not occupy or maintain the great house and, as the land around Castletown became an important commuter belt, housing estates began to close in around it.

Connolly-Carew wrote succinctly of the factors that led to its sale. She acknowledged that when Speaker Conolly built Castletown, it was estimated that he received the rental income from 'a fifth of Ireland' in order to fund its grandeur and maintenance. Once these lands had been sold or compulsorily acquired under the Land Acts, 'the death knell was sounded for many of Ireland's great houses.'[44] She described how the Land Bonds issued as compensation became almost worthless in time. Castletown House and its family did not go down without a fight and there were moments of reinjected vigour. Sarah's father married an heiress, mirroring a similar pattern being replicated in England. This new money 'rejuvenated' the house for 30 years between the 1930s and 1960s, but it was not a permanent solution and these funds soon dried up. Similar to most country house families, a large drain on finances, too, came from the fact that owners usually had more than one such property to maintain. Sarah Connolly-Carew's mother's family also had a stately home in Scotland to keep going, Thirlestane Castle. She described how, when her grandmother, the Countess of Lauderdale, died in 1972, the Castle needed works to the value of £1 million to deal with extensive dry rot and structural repairs to its ancient towers. She acknowledged 'all houses need repairs, but historic houses only have a certain lifetime before they start to crumble and die if left without substantial financial support. It is our legacy to help preserve the best of them.'[45]

Connolly-Carew's summation of the difficulties in keeping Castletown afloat by the second half of the twentieth century represents, in this one example, the seemingly unending lists of challenges facing the country house in Ireland and in Britain. A great number were simply historical. The houses were built for different times and, in many ways, these houses were never going to be sustainable on income from the land once times changed in terms of society, social classes and land ownership from the late nineteenth and early twentieth century onwards – as they did in many countries internationally. For example, Castletown was built on, and depended on, a vast amount of land – an unsustainable position for one house or family in any equitable society. Sarah Connolly-Carew also mentioned the efforts of some landlords to re-inject wealth into their houses by marrying a new wealthy elite, usually from America, who were anxious to gain historic titles. This practice went on to an even greater extent in England. Aside from the fact that such unions primarily for financial gain could result in great unhappiness for both parties, it was only ever going to be a short-term solution. The burden of other properties, such as Thirlestane Castle for the Connolly-Carews, was also very onerous. When money was scarce, the Irish property was often the first to go, particularly for families who saw England as their political and social focal point or more of a natural home.

A NATIONAL TRUST

In 1952, the *Irish Independent* ran a series of articles on the preservation of monuments in Ireland, the second of which focused on An Taisce and the difficulties it faced. The paper reported that, according to many authorities, the preservation of monuments in Ireland suffered from weaknesses in the National Monuments Act: the primary limitation being the inability of the OPW to acquire houses in which there were occupants. The County Councils could not spend money on ancient monuments but could not sell them, while the OPW would not spend money unless they had obtained guardianship of the monuments.[46] A member of An Taisce told the paper: 'the real trouble is not so much a lack of money, but the fact that the whole position is in a bit of a mess. The Board of Works is hopelessly inadequate to deal with the work. There is only one man in charge of all this work with two or three gangers.'[47] Another difficulty for the Trust was the demand by the government for rates and taxes on properties offered to them, a point brought up by T. H. Mason at the annual meeting of An Taisce the previous year. When speaking of properties offered to them by owners unable to maintain them, he had said that 'unless the Trust found some means of providing or avoiding the large amounts required for rates and income tax, the Trust could not undertake the responsibility.'[48]

Therefore, the biggest obstacle to preservation for An Taisce was actually money owed to government and local government themselves. In reality, without any financial assistance from the state, it is hard to see how An Taisce would have been in a position to maintain any historic mansion gifted to it, even without the burden of rates. Mason compared the position of An Taisce to the situation in England, where, in 1945, the government had given the National Trust £60,000 because in England and Scotland:

> The National Trusts were regarded as charities, so that property and legacies bequeathed to them were exempted from death duties and, by an act of 1937, they enjoyed immunity from many other taxes in a manner which did not exist here. Local authorities were also given power to contribute towards the purchase of Trust properties, and to contribute annually to their upkeep.[49]

Peter Mandler has shown how, by 1947, the English government had fallen into the ownership of a small but increasing number of country houses, both through endowing the National Trust and providing funding in its own right. This was made possible because 'under the influence of their own scholars at the national museums and the ancient monuments service, ministers could now be heard advocating the educational value of great houses intact with their collections (but not with their owners).'[50] Such public value justified the public spend. Once again, this idea of country houses being valuable or useful without their owners is something that also carried weight in England and would later be important to the re-imagining of the country house as Irish heritage, and importantly, the heritage of all. Similarly, in England at this time, while 'most country houses were still destined for alternative use', when 'reconceptualised as national museums, a sample of the very best country houses was now deemed a worthy target of public expenditure.'[51] With assistance from the Historic Buildings Council, 'the number of houses held by the Trust grew from 42 in 1950 to 75 in 1960 and their physical state improved markedly.'[52] It is also true that Britain had a long history of domestic interest in visiting these stately homes, which a Trust in Ireland could not rely on as this tradition simply did not exist.

Despite its limitations, An Taisce did take on the task of voicing concern about these properties and the need to preserve them, even when predominantly unable to act. As the law stood, An Taisce had to pay full rates and income tax on bequests or any property that they acquired. However penal the tax system, it can be seen from this that rates were not just antagonistically levelled at original owners: no organisation, no matter how 'national' its outlook, was exempt. Despite the arguments claiming that the rates and taxes due on a property rendered An Taisce unable to act, or meant that owners were unable to keep their properties, there was still no change in government policy. It was left to newspapers or public committees to discuss individual cases or attempt to raise funds necessary to save properties.

The need to change this situation was emphasised in an article in the *Irish Times* in January 1957. It reported that An Taisce was shortly to make representations to the government in an effort to ensure that historic buildings in the country were preserved. A spokesman for the Trust had said: 'until we get new legislation to put the trust in as favourable a position as the British National Trust, we can make very little advance.'[53] The paper emphasised that houses 'of the greatest historic value' were being destroyed in Ireland because of the high rates payable on them.[54] In contrast, the paper highlighted that property acquired by the British National Trust was allowed to be occupied and the public had access on certain days.[55] The article went on to say that, while Castle Coole, near Enniskillen in Northern Ireland, had been acquired by the British Trust for £50,000, in the Republic, Henry Grattan's house at Tinnehinch, County Wicklow, had been demolished, as documented in the previous chapter. It further highlighted that, some years previously, Lady Gregory's house had been destroyed and the spokesperson for the Trust 'considered that the ancestral residence of a person so outstanding in the cultural history of the country as Lady Gregory, should not have been allowed to be pulled down.'[56]

GOVERNMENT ACTION AND INACTION

The inter-party government under Costello did take some steps to improve the situation of tourism, arts and heritage in Ireland. Keogh has written of how 'Costello felt very strongly about the need to assist culture and the arts. [Minister for External Affairs Seán] MacBride appointed members to the first Cultural Relations Committee, which had been planned by the previous government.'[57] Dr Thomas Bodkin, a former director of the National Gallery of Ireland and at the time Director of the Barber Institute in Birmingham, who had first submitted a report on culture and the arts to the Irish government in 1922, was commissioned again in 1948 to investigate the state of the arts in the 26 counties. Although this was a wide-ranging report, Bodkin did address the issue of historic houses and was not optimistic that they could support themselves without a particular use. His report described how the recently founded

National Trust was aimed at supplementing the activities of the OPW in relation to monuments and sites. The first council of the Trust had been elected in 1949 and, in emulation of the National Trust in England, aimed at being self-supporting, although Bodkin noted that, even if it operated extensively, it was not likely to achieve that ambition. He also explained that the English Trust derived considerable income from several hundred farms that it controlled and 'from fees paid by tourists for admission to historic houses, often lavishly furnished, and to famous gardens.'[58] The report additionally noted that the English Trust had been incorporated by an Act of Parliament. Furthermore, although the state allowed it generous tax exemptions and it administered more than 142,000 acres of land, it was 'only just solvent at present'.[59] In contrast, Bodkin believed that 'such historic houses in Ireland as may eventually come under the control of the Irish National Trust are not likely, either by virtue of their architectural interest or as repositories of beautiful objects, to attract great numbers of tourists.'[60] This was the opinion of an individual concerned with the preservation of arts and architecture and hence one of the most sensitive in this regard, yet even he acknowledged that it was doubtful whether there was sufficient, if any, market in Ireland. The sustainability of these houses as tourist attractions in Ireland remains a pertinent issue today, particularly for those not in state care.

Bodkin's report was influential in a positive way and motivated Costello to introduce the 1951 Arts Act.[61] The Act established the Arts Council, An Chomhairle Ealaíon, which was to be charged with stimulating public interest in the arts and improving artistic standards. This government also enacted the first changes to the 1930 National Monuments Act, with a 1954 Amendment Act. Although this act did not make many modifications, it was at least an attempt to remedy some of the difficulties with the original legislation. The amended act allowed for the issuing of temporary preservation orders to last six months for properties considered important, thus attempting to place protections on buildings that had sometimes been destroyed in the interim period of delay when a full preservation order was waiting to be issued. The Act also extended the term for those on the NMAC.[62] However, the work of this government was halted suddenly when it fell because of the mother-and-child scheme issue. While the election that followed had an indecisive outcome, Fianna Fáil scraped back into power in 1951.[63]

When Fianna Fáil assumed power in the three-year period between the inter-party government's terms, the country house did not feature on their agenda. Although the second coalition government again attempted to make some improvements in terms of heritage protections more generally, when they returned to power in 1954, their short term in office and pressing demands once more demoted the importance of this issue – not least of all because the 1950s were a decade marked by staggering levels of emigration. By one estimate, 40,000 Irish people left the country during the decade.[64] Another more recent estimate puts this figure at 400,000 – it is likely that the figure is at the higher end of the scale.[65] In 1957, unemployment figures reached a record 78,000 people 'and the country was on the brink of destitution'.[66] It fell to the NMAC to attempt to keep this issue on the government's agenda. On 4 July 1955, they wrote to the OPW about the preservation of houses of historic and architectural interest. Their letter stated: 'the question of preserving such monuments is involved and needed careful deliberation, in consequence of which a special sub-committee was appointed to deal with the whole matter'.[67] This sub-committee produced a report on the issue which was forwarded to the OPW to enquire if they had any observations to offer.[68]

Their report on lands and buildings of architectural and historic interest ineligible for preservation under the National Monuments Act began by explaining that the National Monuments Acts of 1930 and 1954 enabled the state to provide funds for the preservation of buildings of architectural and historic interest. Houses occupied as dwellings and churches in use were specifically excluded and, in practice, buildings fully used for other purposes had not been regarded for preservation either. Furthermore, 'although the acts allow for buying buildings for preservation as national monuments it has not been the policy to do so. This means that until a building becomes disused and of no significant commercial value (this usually means until it has become more or less ruinous) no action is normally taken by the state to preserve it.'[69] Here the NMAC revealed how the 1930 National Monuments Act, while quite broad in its scope, was implemented in a very limited fashion by the OPW. As discussed in the previous chapter, the OPW had primarily preserved ancient monuments under this Act, not least of all because these required less finances and personnel to maintain them. The advisory council's committee admitted that, in the case of medieval buildings, where most of their perishable materials were already lost, the preservation of their stonework was sufficient. This did not apply to more modern buildings, particularly from the seventeenth century and later, where 'the internal architectural effect depends to a very large extent on features and decorations made of perishable materials.'[70] This was an important consideration in terms of the preservation of country houses and contributed, and still contributes substantially, to their maintenance costs. In the case of these buildings, 'the stone or brick shell represent only a fraction of the architectural effect and the shell itself usually becomes structurally unstable when deprived of the support and protection of perishable structural features such as the floors and roofs.'[71] Therefore they maintained that such buildings could only be adequately preserved more or less complete, adding:

> It is also desirable, for good maintenance and for economy, that they should be put to some suitable use. Ideally they should remain used for their original purpose, so that their contents, which contribute greatly to the internal effect, will be appropriate; this cannot always be ensured, but it is felt that a mitigation of economic pressure will save many buildings of merit from destruction and enable some of them to be preserved in their original use and in their original setting.[72]

The most extensive category of buildings under consideration by the sub-committee was houses in the country, where their only practical use was residential. The committee argued that when these houses were owned and used by state and semi-state bodies or local authorities, the main difficulty appeared to be 'the lack of competent professional advice which leads to thoughtless alterations, structural neglect and in some cases unnecessary demolition because those in authority have not been made aware that the architectural qualities of some of these buildings amply justify special treatment.'[73] Examples of this were country town market houses, court houses and government or local authority offices located in Georgian houses. Maintenance was entrusted in some cases to engineers and was usually unsatisfactory, yet even under the supervision of architects they were 'not immune from thoughtless mutilation'.[74] The language of this sentence alone conveys the anger of the committee at examples of such action, which had obviously taken place in state ownership. They did admit that full and complete maintenance of every property might not be possible and thought that in towns it might be desirable to preserve even the facades of buildings which, although of no great architectural interest in themselves, formed part of a street, crescent, or square, and so had qualities transcending that of the individual building.

The NMAC sub-committee was primarily concerned with three main categories of buildings in this report: houses for which no alternative use could be found, but their maintenance as a dwelling was uneconomic; old buildings used by public bodies; and buildings that formed part of a large-scale architectural composition. In relation to the first category, the council recommended that the owners of such properties should be encouraged 'to maintain houses of merit, and their essential setting, by reducing the economic pressure that has led in the past to the destruction of some of the finest houses.'[75] It was suggested that this could be achieved by three means: a remission of rates and income tax in whole or in part on the house and its setting; remission of income tax in whole or in part on certified necessary expenditure on the maintenance of the house and its setting; and a remission of death duties on the value of the house and its setting. In return for these concessions, it was proposed that

> Owners would be required to admit the public to the principal parts of the house and grounds on certain specified days; owners would be encouraged to charge an agreed entrance fee to be set against the costs they would incur in supervising visitors; owners would be prohibited from carrying out any alterations without permission and repairs would have to be carried out by them when necessary and in an approved manner.[76]

Such proposals were well thought-out and ahead of their time in terms of the proposed exchange of tax breaks for a level of public access: something that would not be introduced by Irish governments until the 1980s. It was also made clear that if owners wanted to stay in these houses and benefit from remissions or aid from the state, then there would have to be a justifiable public benefit from doing so. The concept of owners of historic houses being merely caretakers or custodians for a certain period of time, before passing on the house to the next generation, was an idea that began to be cultivated by owners themselves in later decades. This concept could be used to their benefit in order to portray themselves as caretakers of heritage houses, and therefore worthy of state aid, but it must also have exerted some pressure on those owners who came to a point where they had to sell a house that had been in their family for centuries. No one wanted to be the person under whose stewardship the house was lost to the family. Justin Green of Ballyvolane House, County Cork, has described how he sees himself in this light, 'dedicated to maintaining the integrity of the house and keeping it in good order until it is passed on.'[77] Lord Henry Mountcharles has been vocal about the struggle it takes to maintain such an inheritance in order to pass it on to the next generation, stating:

> When you have an unwieldy inheritance, which I did – the Slane Castle estate is a heavy thing to deal with, it absorbs vast sums of money – you just have to get on with it ... I say to my children now and again that Dad isn't going to be able to pull rabbits out of hats all the time. So we have to have sustainable forms of business ... to walk the sometimes thin line between what is my family home, what is part of my family's heritage.[78]

It is worth noting, however, that through ingenuity, a variety of business exploits and sheer determination, Lord Mountcharles has managed to preserve Slane and maintain it in family ownership to this day.

To establish the system of concessions for owners suggested by the sub-committee legislation would be needed, and it was foreseen that such a bill should incorporate a schedule of houses and lands to which it would apply. This list could be voluntary, although there was a suggestion that provision would also have to be made for compulsory inclusion of a country house.[79] In the case of an owner willing to have his house included, but unwilling to admit the public at all or to the extent required, the committee generously thought that such individuals could also receive some reasonable portion of the concessions. Estimates had shown that the number of houses likely to qualify for such a scheme came to about 100, so that initial inspections and subsequent supervision and administration were not likely to constitute an insuperable problem.[80]

The second category suggested for preservation were old buildings used by public bodies, including houses that had been converted for use as offices, schools and monasteries.[81] In the council's view, since these buildings were controlled by responsible bodies the only action necessary would be to make the owners aware of the importance of the buildings and to induce them to treat them with respect. Therefore, this was not so much a financial problem as an administrative one, although it would still require more specialist architectural advice than was available at that time. The third category was buildings forming part of a large-scale architectural composition, which had to be entrusted to the care of town planning authorities, although it was still considered useful to list what were considered the best examples so as to draw attention to them.[82]

The report estimated that a rough annual cost of the scheme would be £14,500 on remission of rates, £24,000 on remission of income tax, and £1,500 on death duties, giving a total cost of £40,000.[83] This was a considered and applicable report which, if acted on, could have changed the entire position of the country house in Ireland and led to the preservation of many more houses than remain standing today. The council was not pushing for financial aid in grants and donations from government, but rather only concessions for historic-property owners in terms of remission of taxes and rates which, if their calculations were correct, would have reduced government receipts by £40,000. In addition, there was public gain for this loss to the Exchequer in terms of the public access stipulation, although it was doubtful that there was much public interest in visiting country houses at this time. In any case, the OPW was characteristically unwilling to get involved in any such scheme. It appears that the Office did not even offer any observations on the detailed and considered report and took no action on it.[84] This represented an undeserved slight on a balanced and realistic report that the NMAC had gone to great lengths to prepare and which could have turned the tide for the destruction of the country house in Ireland. While the governments in this period – both inter-party and Fianna Fáil – were attempting to secure their seats in power and address the more high-profile issues that would win their election on polling day, they avoided becoming embroiled in the still contentious financial vacuum that was the big-house problem.

THE CASE OF KILLARNEY HOUSE

Government attempts to avoid becoming embroiled in the big-house issue were often complicated when cases arrived on their desks for decision; in particular, offers of gifts to the state that required definitive 'yes' or 'no' answers. While this period did not see much pressure being put on the government to preserve individual houses – remarkably so given that it was the most destructive period for the country house – a prominent case that did arise during the inter-party's second term was that of Killarney House and the Kenmare estate in Killarney, County Kerry. This case is interesting because, while there was a country house at the centre of the landed estate, through various rebuildings, it was the estate land in this case that garnered all the attention and concern when it was put up for sale. The house, on the other hand, was ignored in debates, not least of all because it was not one of the grander-style historic houses. Killarney House had originally been a stable block of the first Kenmare House and was converted by the fifth Earl of Kenmare into the family home in 1915 after fire gutted the second Kenmare House. Killarney House eventually fell into ruin, while its estate became part of the state's portfolio of national parks.

The Kenmare estate was put up for sale in 1956 by its owner, Beatrice Grosvenor, niece of the last Earl of Kenmare. The seventh Earl had died in February 1952 and, with his death, the title had become extinct. Grosvenor claimed that the cost of death duties had driven her to sell the estate.[85] The financial difficulties of the estate were not new and, in 1930, the fifth Earl had tried to sell the estate to the government, but the offer was declined. Interestingly, most of the attention surrounding this sale in 1956 was because of the lands of this estate, particularly given their position beside the national park incorporating Muckross House, Killarney, which the government had acquired in 1932. This highlights again that public concern in appeals for the preservation of country houses was often for the amenity value of the demesne rather than the house itself. On 12 June 1956, the *Irish Times* reported that the directors of the Killarney Tourist Development Company Ltd. announced that because of 'its importance to the people of Killarney and the nation, it was prepared to undertake the purchase of the Kenmare Estate' if they could raise the funds.[86] It noted, further, that Dublin City Council, at its meeting the previous night, had passed a resolution 'exhorting the government to take the necessary steps to prevent the Kenmare Estate from being disposed of by any foreign agency and to examine the possibility of having the estate acquired by the National Trust', which belies at least some nativist prejudice.[87] The paper revealed that 'the greater part of the death duties – the payment of which has forced the trustees of the estate to put it on the public market – is due to the Irish government.'[88] One prominent Killarney man pointed out that the government was crying out for the development of the tourist industry and, at the same time, was crippling the industry with taxation.[89] This is a notable situation, since the exaction of death duties by the state was forcing the sale of this property, which itself incited local groups to pressure the state to acquire the property. This would have meant that the state would be single-handedly financially burdened with its maintenance.

On 16 June 1956, Felix E. Hackett, President of An Taisce, wrote a letter to the *Irish Independent* voicing his grave concern about the possible exploitation of the Kenmare estate. He believed that it should instead, with the Bourn Vincent Memorial Park, form 'one great area of scenic beauty which requires to be under some such state control as is provided by the National Park and Access to the Countryside Act 1949' in Britain.[90] This Act was intended 'to make provision for national parks and the establishment of a National Parks Commission'.[91] Hackett also lamented that there was not a provision available for this emergency amongst the Acts of the Oireachtas that was similar to the provision that set up the Ulster Land Fund in the Finance Act of 1948 of Northern Ireland.[92] This Act gave the Ministry of Finance power to accept property in satisfaction or in part satisfaction of any estate duty, settlement estate duty, succession duty, or legal duty. He noted that this legislation in Northern Ireland had allowed for the purchase of properties, such as Castle Coole and Florencecourt in County Fermanagh. Since no such legislation existed in Ireland, he recommended a special act that would allow the government to purchase the property on behalf of the nation.[93]

Under increasing pressure, in July 1956 the OPW summarised the situation in an internal memorandum.[94] Muckross House – which was vacant at this time – and its surrounding land and buildings, already in their possession, cost in estate expenditure almost double their income, despite the offsetting of gate receipts. The public had free access to the estate and the park included many of the features of interest in Killarney, including Muckross Abbey. With no information as to the administration costs, or standards of maintenance on the Kenmare Estate, the OPW concluded:

> In relation to the notice of motion quoted in the memorandum for the government dated 21 June, 1956, by An Taoiseach, viz. 'to request the government to take all possible steps, if necessary by legislation, to acquire the Kenmare Estate as a National Trust' the Commissioners of Public Works having regard to experience in the administration and cost of the Bourn Vincent Memorial Park, are of opinion that the acquisition of the Kenmare property by the state should be avoided if possible.[95]

The OPW was concerned that the expenditure and scale of the undertaking was too great to recommend and adamantly resisted acquiring the estate.

Despite this, public pressure continued, and the *Irish Times* of 7 August 1956 reported: 'the formation of a Trust, on the lines of the National Trust in Britain, and the launching of an appeal for a national subscription to cover the purchase price of the Kenmare Estate are urged in the latest edition of *The Irish Hotelier*, official organ of the Irish Hotels Federation and of the Hotel and Restaurant Association.'[96] They went on to discuss that it seemed that in An Taisce 'we already have in embryo the Trust we envisage.'[97] Just three days later, the same paper reported that it understood the negotiations for the sale of the Kenmare Estate were almost complete.[98] The report highlighted again that 'the payment of death duties on the estate has been given as the reason for the projected sale, and it is understood that the biggest portion of this duty is payable to the Irish government, which has announced its concern that national interests should not be prejudiced by the sale'.[99]

The main concern, however, came from the public, particularly local groups. On 11 August 1956, the *Kerryman* reported on prospective buyers for the estate, including the Killarney Tourist Development Company who 'hope to be able to make their purchase offer soon', as they had thus far raised a purchase fund of £10,000.[100] John Boland, a former MP for South Kerry, now living in London, sent a telegram to the effect that he would form a local committee in London to aid the Killarney fund. Killarney Sinn Féin Cumann sought the acquisition for very different reasons. They wanted 'the entire Kenmare estate taken over by the government and divided among the landless people in the area who would be willing to work it' and argued that 'the descendants of those who were evicted from the estate be given back their holdings and compensated for any loss incurred since the eviction.'[101] This demonstrates that, in the 1950s, bitter historical memories associated with such estates had not entirely disappeared, at least not from the rhetoric used by some more nationalist organisations. The committee of the fund to purchase the estate had quite an alternative sugges- tion. They were of the opinion that the money raised should be used to estab- lish a factory that would employ about 200 people, in order to give the working people of Killarney a chance to stem the flow of emigration, while the house could be converted into an agricultural college.[102]

In 1972 the state did purchase part of the lands of the Kenmare Estate as an extension to Killarney National Park, but Killarney House was bought by an American syndicate and then sold on to John McShain, an Irish- American philanthropist, who eventually sold it to the state for a nominal sum. Disappointingly, the house was allowed to fall into decay in state care and it was not until 2011 that the government announced it would spend €7 million on its restoration as a centre for biodiversity and a visitor centre for the park on the Kenmare Estate.[103] Killarney House was finally opened to the public in July 2017 after a €10 million restoration project. It will become an interpretive centre for Killarney's national parks and lakes.

CONCLUSION

The preservation of the country house and the financial positions of their owners were not major concerns for members of governments during the period 1948–57; instead, governments were focused on trying to establish a secure tenure in power and to tackle issues that affected the entire popula- tion, particularly the soaring levels of emigration. While Fianna Fáil's brief three-year tenure under de Valera saw the country house problem ignored, the inter-party government's two terms under Costello were more pro-active in relation to the arts and heritage more generally, commissioning the 1949 Report into the State of the Arts in Ireland, establishing the Arts Council and, in 1954, amending the National Monuments Act. Despite such movements forward, it still fell to bodies specifically concerned with the preservation of built heritage, in particular An Taisce and the NMAC, to keep the issue of the country house alive in the media and to press the government for changes in policies or for reductions in rates and taxes on historic houses.

The report on possible schemes to maintain and preserve historic houses by the NMAC sub-committee was comprehensive and, for the first time, explic- itly suggested tying concessions for historic-house owners to a public gain drawn from access to view houses. This report did not simply seek government funding to preserve houses, but was detailed, practical and considered. It sought remission of taxes and rates to make it easier for houses to survive in original ownership and therefore not become burdens on the state. It even suggested that, in towns and cities, preserving the facades of buildings alone would be worthwhile, suggesting the pragmatic approach adopted by the NMAC in this regard. Ultimately, despite the practical nature of the report which understood the limited economic position in which the governments of the day were oper- ating, it is hard to know if the government ever even saw this report. It was sent to the OPW for observations, though none ever seem to have been returned and this report may have been conveniently forgotten and left to gather dust. It is notable that, years later, when concessions were given to historic-house owners, it was on this model that it was done, with public access being a condi- tion of eligibility for exemptions. If this report had been acted on in the 1950s, it is certain that many more country houses would have survived and could potentially now be tourism draws, centres of employment or amenities in their local areas. Instead, this period was the most destructive for the country house in Ireland and this demise hardly featured on any government agenda.

During this period of political change, governments were silent on the question of proposals for the preservation of the country house, or indeed any scheme that would make survival more likely. Then again, any action by governments that would have made the sustainability of living in what were still seen as old mansions easier would have been hugely unpopular at a time when the country was struggling with economic stagnation, massive unemploy- ment and emigration. These short-lived governments were careful to avoid the potentially inflammatory issue and had other more immediate and populist concerns to prioritise during short terms in office. As a result, the substantial decline of the country house in this period went either unnoticed or ignored, while, for the remaining owners of such houses, their increasing minority status and isolation from the communities in which they lived – the latter often by choice – meant that they became caricatured in popular perception as a class of eccentrics.[104] This pointed increasingly to the fact that if the country house were ever to appeal more popularly, its cause would have to be separated from its original owners in perceptions and in reality, as had happened in England.

FIVE

THE IRISH LAND COMMISSION, 1940–65

I have lived in important places, times
When great events were decided, who owned
That half a rood of rock, a no-man's land
Surrounded by our pitchfork-armed claims.
I heard the Duffys shouting 'Damn your soul!'
And old McCabe stripped to the waist, seen
Step the plot defying blue cast-steel -
'Here is the march along these iron stones'
—Patrick Kavanagh, 'Epic'[1]

Under the 1881 Land Law (Ireland) Act the Irish Land Commission was created as a rent-fixing commission. It further developed into a body that mediated and controlled tenant purchase under the 1885 Ashbourne Act. The Land Commission continued its work under the 1903 Wyndham Land Act and, post-independence, under the 1923, 1931 and 1933 Land Acts enacted by independent governments. In this regard, it was one of the most important public bodies in the newly-independent state. It was responsible for effecting land division policy as decided by governments and as legislated for in the Land Acts. These began as land purchase acts before the work of the commission expanded to include compulsory acquisition and division of land among former tenants as well as landless men. In 1965, the last land act was signed into law and so the once vital Land Commission became largely obsolete and was later wound down. Its work had a lasting legacy on the ownership of land in the Republic. Its division of land in local areas often pitted neighbour against neighbour, while the business of granting land from large estates in the east and midlands to those from uneconomic land holdings in the west was wrought with contention. The sensitive nature of this issue even now is attested to by the fact that most of the Land Commission's files are not open to researchers or the general public as are other governmental files. This is undoubtedly, in part, in anticipation of the resurrection of age-old feelings and divisions in communities where 'blow-ins' were unwelcome and boundary disputes, such as that immortalised in Patrick Kavanagh's poem at the start of this chapter, led to lasting bitterness. The lack of Land Commission files open to researchers also means that this chapter must rely on correspondence that the Land Commission carried out with other departments, or the public statements that Ministers for Lands made in the Oireachtas, to try to piece together its attitudes towards country houses.

The scale of the complex work undertaken by the Commission saw 5,686 estates comprising almost 847,000 acres compulsorily acquired for £45.3 million and a further 4,346 comprising over 510,000 acres voluntarily sold for £26.5 million between 1923 and 1978.[2] In charge of this work until 1933 were four Land Commissioners, namely: Kevin O'Shiel, Sam Waddell, who was also Chief Inspector, M. J. Heavey, and, lastly, Michael Deegan, who filled the dual role of Commissioner and Secretary.[3] After 1933, the number of commissioners was raised to six and the two new positions were filled by Eamon Mansfield and Dan Browne.[4] This was to deal with the extra work taken on by the commission under the 1933 Land Act introduced by a Fianna Fáil government who committed more aggressively to increase land division to 100,000 acres a year.[5] This chapter examines the attitudes and policy of the Irish Land Commission towards country houses situated on demesnes and landed estates that it was charged with acquiring or dividing. It aims to enquire what the Commission's actions were in relation to such houses, how it disposed of them, and what motivated its policy and decisions.

ERSKINE CHILDERS AS MINISTER FOR LANDS

Erskine Childers became Minister for Lands in March 1957. While his tenure was short – he left in 1959 – it is important to address here that his time as Minister was significant and different to both his predecessors and his successors.[6] Patrick Sammon, who worked for decades in the Land Commission, has written of how, when instituted as Minister, Childers 'immediately proceeded to issue queries on all aspects of the work ... We were dealing with a new Minister who from the beginning gave the firm impression that he was going to do a root and branch examination into the Land Commission and all his queries merited and got priority treatment.'[7] Indicative of such proactive interest in the working of the Land Commission, and with Childers' ideas for improvement, in 1958 the Office of the Minister for Lands in the Department of Lands compiled a memorandum for government on his request, pressing government departments to formulate a policy that would make the survival of mansions and large houses more feasible. This document, coming as it did during a decade that was the most destructive for the country house in Ireland, and compiled under an exceptionally sympathetic Minister for Lands, is a significant source that captured a moment in time in the story of the country house in Ireland. Numbers were most severely declining and yet the tide was on the cusp of turning in terms of concern for their destruction. This document, and the responses from government departments, reflect the contemporary views on how the country house had been dealt with in the past and also pointed to how these departments thought it should be dealt with in the future.

The motivation behind this memorandum came from Childers himself. Such an initiative does not appear to have been undertaken by any other Minister for Lands or other departments during this time. Most government departments, already struggling with tight budgets, did not want to take responsibility for the financially expensive and emotionally fraught issue of the preservation of country houses. For the most part, the Land Commission worked as an independent body under the auspices of the Department of Lands in its various manifestations. Its work had to continue without interruptions with each passing government. As a result, the minister was predominantly little more than a figure-head of the department, although, in other instances, individual ministers such as Childers took a more hands-on approach. Sammon has written of how the post of Minister for Lands: 'did not rank as one of the more arduous or prestigious of ministerial posts ... Without reflecting on any incumbent, it can be asserted that all ministers must have enjoyed generous spans for their constituency business. Land policy arose as an issue quite infrequently.'[8] Dooley has also illustrated how, during evidence given to the Commission on Banking in 1935, Land Commissioner Michael Deegan informed the Banking Commission that Land Commissioners made their own rules and regulations.[9] Aside from answering parliamentary questions (on a very regular basis in the case of the Land Commission), annually steering the estimates for the Land

Commission through the two Houses of the Oireachtas, and responding to ministerial duties in relation to legislation and policy, the Land Commission worked as an exceptionally independent body. Nonetheless, even here, Sammon noted that Childers was 'unique in his extremely detailed enquiring role'.[10]

Childers was particularly proactive in relation to the preservation of country houses. The fact that Childers had himself been brought up in a country house at Glendalough, County Wicklow, that he was a Protestant, and that he had been schooled in England presumably also made him a more sympathetic ally of country house owners. It appears to have been an issue with which he was especially concerned and anxious to take the initiative in addressing while in office, even before he was Minister for Lands. The same is not true for other ministers. For example, Tomás Ó Deirg, Fianna Fáil TD for Carlow-Kilkenny and Minister for Lands from 1951–4, does not appear to have had any desire to change the policy of the Land Commission or interfere in their work. During his tenure, the fate of French Park, County Roscommon, was discussed: a case that highlights his complacency on the issue and Childers's initiative, even when in a different position. Childers, then Minister for Posts and Telegraphs, wrote to Ó Deirg on the issue, as Childers had been informed that the Land Commission had bought the house for demolition. Childers argued that, while the house was 'not quite in the first grade of Georgian residences, I am informed, [that it] is worth preserving'.[11] In Childers's opinion, far more social venues were needed for organisations such as Macra na Feirme, An Óige, and parish councils, and he believed: 'we have now reached a stage when we should do something to avoid the destruction of any more reasonably good Georgian houses. My information may be wrong about the Land Commission. The matter is of real importance. Is there nothing we can do in this case?'[12] Ó Deirg's reply clarified that the Commission was not in possession of the property, nor had it any proceedings for its acquisition. In any case, he wrote: 'I am told that where sizeable houses come on their hands, the Land Commission acquaint other government depart-ments of the fact, so that the question of their utilisation for public purposes may be considered.'[13] He suggested that it was therefore only when no department expressed an interest in using or preserving such houses that the Commission sold them for use or demolition. This is also supported by Sammon's claim that the Land Commission's standard practice was to offer for sale a country house with 'an appropriate area around it' when such residences were too extensive for even the largest of over-standard migrants (those who required more land or bigger holdings than were normally given). He explained how, through such a policy, 'many splendid properties offered for sale by the Land Commission were purchased by religious orders'.[14] In one particular case, he recalled that the film director John Huston had acquired St Cleran's from the Commission, a period dwelling house in Craughwell, County Galway, and was assumed to have spent generously on its modernisation and refurbishment.[15] Returning to the case of French Park, Ó Deirg's use of the term 'I am told' suggests that, while he was in the position of Minister for Lands, he did not meddle with the work of the Land Commission, and that the extent of any one minister's influence appears to have depended mostly on the personal interest the particular minister took in the matter.[16]

MEMORANDUM ON THE PRESERVATION OF MANSIONS AND LARGE HOUSES

Childers appears to have had a passionate and personal concern regarding the preservation of the country house, even when he was not in a position to intervene. In light of this, when he took up the position as Minister for Lands in March 1957, a memorandum on the preservation of mansions and large houses was compiled by his office. Under his direction, this memorandum from the Office of the Minister for Lands actually pressurised relevant government departments to formulate a policy on the preservation of country houses at a time when their rate of destruction was higher than any time previously, even though this was not in the Department of Lands' remit.[17] This is an invaluable document for revealing the Land Commission's actions in relation to country houses it acquired during this time. It also clearly shows the attitudes of other government departments towards the country house and the importance they placed on this issue, as well as their willingness or reluctance to act to make preservation more feasible.

On 5 August 1958, E. Ó Dálaigh, Secretary of the Department of Lands, wrote to the Secretary General of the Department of Finance, T. K. Whitaker,[18] on the direction of the Minister for Lands, Erskine Childers, and enclosed for his observation a draft memorandum for the government on the preservation of mansions and large houses. Copies were also included for distribution to the OPW and the General Valuation Office.[19] Ó Dálaigh explained that 'in acquiring land the Land Commission acquire a number of mansions and large houses in good repair which are unsuitable for their uses. Some of these with accommodation land are sold to persons or institutions for occupation. Some prove unsaleable and have to be demolished.'[20] In what can be seen as an effort by the Minister for Lands to keep the department's actions in line with practice in other countries on this challenging issue, Ó Dálaigh remarked how 'other countries try to encourage the preservation of their mansions and large houses and the Minister for Lands considers that similar encouragement should be considered here'.[21] The personal influence of the minister is evident, as this comparison and concern with keeping in line with the policy of other countries is very similar to arguments he made just four years previously, to the then Minister for Lands, Tomás Ó Deirg, with regard to the proposed demolition of French Park. Childers had similarly argued that: 'all over Europe legislation is being passed enabling Governments or bodies sponsored by the Government to acquire old houses and to turn them to useful purpose'.[22] In this regard, Childers can be viewed as exceptionally proactive. The memorandum discussed different means by which the preservation of these historic houses would be more feasible, namely under the following broad categories: use, taxation, rates and the establishment of a governmental committee on the issue. This was despite the fact that these options were outside the remit of the Land Commission or Department of Lands. The memorandum and responses will be discussed further on.

UTILISATION OF COUNTRY HOUSES

In relation to the utilisation of country houses, the Office of the Minister for Lands' summary of the memorandum noted that country houses could still be put to use as private residences, as they had proved very attractive to foreign capital in times of British and European economic unrest. It advised that 'it would be well to retain them for such contingency'.[23] Tax relief or rating concessions were suggested as a help in this regard. Writing in a particularly sympathetic manner about the contribution of these houses to society, the department stated:

> Large properties give employment, promote advances in agriculture, more particularly in specialised matters such as pedigree breeding and afford example in good husbandry … Some of these properties might with comparatively little adaptation save the erection of new buildings for institutional use for agricultural education, homes, hospitals, residential schools, etc. or as country type houses to stimulate tourism.[24]

In contrast, a Department of Local Government report of 1943–5, discussed in Chapter Two, had found these houses overwhelmingly unsuitable for other uses.[25] The memorandum described how the Commission often had to take over buildings situated on acquired lands and that these comprised 'large structures of the mansion type; residences of medium size; or, as in a good many cases, reasonably sized dwelling houses'.[26] The Department of Lands recognised that their state of repair, which varied considerably, determined their fate. Therefore, while some smaller dwellings that were in reasonable repair were reconstructed and allotted with holdings for division, 'if their condition is poor, they are demolished by the Land Commission and the salvaged materials sold or retained for use of improvement works; or such premises may be sold for demolition and removal of salvaged materials by the purchaser. Some cases of clearance are for the purpose of replacement by new houses on allotments to migrants'.[27] In other cases, the department explained that there were buildings that, although perhaps in a reasonable state of repair, were unsuitable for allotment owing to their size, for example. In such circumstances:

> Government departments and local authorities are consulted as to whether they require them. If they do not efforts are made to dispose of them, together with a certain amount of accommodation land, to suitable purchasers, usually by auction. If that method of disposal fails, the question of demolition has at least to be considered, because rates on the properties must be met and no income by way of rent is forth-coming; in any event, it is not a function of the Land Commission to retain such buildings on their hands indefinitely.[28]

The Land Commission's policy outlined above was then to try to find uses for such houses, and the Commission only considered demolition when no other option was available and they had not the powers to keep the buildings. First, though, sale by public auction was the norm. If the auction proved abortive or was considered undesirable, then sale would be by tender. Sales of property under the Land Acts were not subject to stamp duty. The department clarified that in cases where a house was offered for sale for residential purposes, enough land (usually between 20 and 120 acres) was provided with it in order to make it a saleable proposition. Thus, it appears that the Land Commission attempted to sell such houses as residences with at least some land, although not enough to make such houses sustainable on income from land alone. The days when this was possible were long gone and the purchasers who sought such properties were not interested in using the house as the centrepiece of a large demesne.

In addition, the department believed that mansions and large houses in good condition in the possession of the Land Commission or other departments or bodies could be put to use, even when sale was impossible, thereby avoiding the necessity to demolish. The memorandum stated that, in 1954, the Minister for

Health had reported that there was a need for more residential schools for those with intellectual disabilities. However, in reply to an enquiry by the Minister for Lands about the possible use by the Department of Health of mansions on lands acquired by the Land Commission more recently, the Minister for Health, Seán MacEntee, had informed him that, as a result of the slowing down of the hospital building programme, it was unlikely his department would be undertaking any expansion for some time. The minister also mentioned that a number of the smaller institutions hitherto used for tuberculosis treatment were becoming redundant and, before acquiring new premises, his department would have to endeavour to find new uses for existing premises.[29]

The Office of the Minister for Lands then outlined the motivation behind this memorandum, stating, 'the Minister for Lands is aware that it is not the practice outside this country to demolish properties of the mansion type which are in good condition. He feels that the utilisation of large houses in good condition is a national problem which requires decision at Government level.'[30] The minister proposed that an inter-departmental committee be formed, comprising representatives from his own department, the Department of Finance, the General Valuation Office, the OPW, the Department of Industry and Commerce for Bord Fáilte, and the Departments of Health, Education and Local Government. Such a committee could examine the problem generally, but also, aim in particular:

(a) to ascertain future requirements of state and state sponsored bodies and local authorities over the next ten years in regard to large premises intended for various purposes such as institutions, homes, hospitals, educational, agricultural and/or residential establishments, etc., or in respect of tourist amenities;

(b) to ascertain and collate particulars of comparative costs of building new premises as compared with renovating or altering existing buildings in reasonable condition;

(c) to obtain from local authorities full lists of empty habitable residences;

(d) to ascertain from house agents particulars of properties in the rural districts for sale and unsaleable.[31]

An appendix was attached to the memorandum (and is included at the end of this work). Table A listed country houses in the possession of the Land Commission.[32] Four of the large houses that were part of this table were considered to be of use for a migrant or to be offered for sale with land. However, the memorandum reported that an auction of Mote Park House, County Roscommon, with 112 acres had proved abortive. It was to be offered for sale, firstly with accommodation lands or, alternatively, the buildings only for demolition, although this was a last resort. Both Dalystown House, County Galway, and Franckfort Castle,

County Offaly – the latter dating from the twelfth century approximately – were identified as the only two large houses suitable only for demolition. Demolition appears to have been an option for houses mainly when their condition was deemed too bad to make them eligible for use or sale. Franckfort's condition was described as being very bad. In the category 'medium houses', only one (unnamed) house on the Bennett estate, County Offaly, was similarly deemed 'suitable only for demolition', presumably owing to its poor repair.[33] The second list in this table provided a record of properties that the department thought likely to come into the hands of the Commission in the near future. Two large houses were included. The first, Oakley Park, County Offaly, was thought to be 'suitable only for demolition' due to its 'very poor condition'.[34] Similarly, Kill House in Offaly was said to have been in 'bad repair'.[35]

Table B tabulated the results of auctions and sales by tender of Land Commission houses over approximately the previous four years. Three large houses and one small/medium house were listed as having been sold by auction. The second group listed those sold by tender, including private treaty after abortive auction. These included two large houses and three small/ medium houses. In the third category, 'Abortive auction or tender', two large houses were listed: Mote Park House and Shanbally Castle.[36] As the auction of Mote Park had been aborted, the house was to be offered for sale by tender with accommodation lands or else buildings for demolition.[37] In the case of this house, all options for sale as a viable residence had failed and the third and only other option was to sell the buildings for demolition, indicating how small the market was for these houses in the mid-twentieth century.

The second property on this list was Shanbally Castle. Sammon remembers that while he was in the Secretariat, 'the Land Commission was under fire from the press because of the demolition of Shanbally Castle in County Tipperary, in the course of land division operations. There were Dáil questions and the Minister was in a vulnerable position. Over time, the criticisms and allegations of vandalism slowly abated.'[38] Shanbally Castle was described as late Georgian, of imitation Tudor design, and 150 years old. Table B illustrates that the Land Commission did not simply demolish the castle when they got their hands on it. Rather, it was first offered for sale by tender in November 1956 with 173 acres, no doubt intended as an incentive to buy the property as a residence, but not as a self-sustaining one. The sale was abortive, and it was as a last resort that the buildings were sold for demolition in August 1957. It is easy to remonstrate against such decisions in hindsight, but no other body or organisation stepped forward at the time to preserve the property and the preservation of such properties was not in the Land Commission's remit. They had also stated that before demolishing a property they always first informed government departments and enquired whether they had any use for it. Assuming this was also done in this case, no government department, including the OPW, offered to take on this property and maintain it. Therefore, the Land Commission had very little option but to sell to the only market there was and face the post-demolition backlash from politicians and press.

The memorandum's third table, C, is a record of the premises that had been acquired by the Land Commission and were estimated to have been demolished during the previous four years. These included Pallas House, County Wexford, Lissard House, County Longford, and Leamlara House and Castleharrison, both situated in Cork. Each is described as being in 'very poor repair' or suitable only for demolition.[39] Shanbally Castle is listed again here. From this table it can be seen that five large houses in the possession of the Land Commission were demolished in the period 1954–8: a relatively low number, even despite the short period. Only four small/medium houses were demolished in the same time frame.[40] The low number listed in this document as having been demolished by the Land Commission is in stark contrast to the fact that this period was one of the most destructive periods for the country house. The inference is that the Land Commission does not appear to have been responsible for the majority of the demolition of country houses that took place. During this time, the Land Commission had acquired in the course of its land division work a total of 36 houses, nine of which were demolished, only a quarter of the total acquired.[41] This illustrates that three-quarters of the houses acquired by the Land Commission in this time frame were either put to use or sold on. Those demolished appear to be only the houses that were in poor repair or could not be sold. This is also less than half the number of houses that were roughly estimated to have been demolished between 1950 and 1960, using descriptions given in Mark Bence-Jones's *A Guide To Irish Country Houses*, when the minimum figure for houses demolished in this decade was approximated at around 23, although the total is probably much greater.[42] This suggests that possibly more than half of the houses that disappeared during this period were destroyed by private buyers or owners themselves, leaving them to ruin or selling them for demolition. In the main, houses acquired by the Commission during this time were primarily located in Leinster – a total of 16 – while the numbers from Munster and Connaught were similar at ten and nine respectively. There was only one house listed for Ulster: Fern Hill, in County Donegal. Leinster was presumably the province where most houses were acquired, as this was where the Commission was most active in dividing large estates among economically disadvantaged migrants from the west, particularly Connaught.[43]

By September, the Minister for Lands was growing anxious for a response to the memorandum from the Department of Finance, who were charged with compiling the responses from all departments concerned.[44] The department could not reply as they had not yet received the responses of the OPW. On 7 October 1958, the Department of Finance wrote to the OPW requesting their observations as soon as possible.[45] Yet, by 21 November no response had been received and, following another request from the Land Commission to speed up the reply, the OPW was contacted again. This illustrates that it was the Minister for Lands who was pressing for policy and suggestions on this issue, while the OPW appears to have been reticent, or at least the slowest of all government bodies concerned to respond.[46] The Commissioners of Public Works eventually sent their reply to the Department of Finance after a lengthy delay of four months.

The Secretary of the Commissioners of Public Works laid out their views. The commissioners asserted that the proposal to establish an inter-departmental committee to examine the problem was a matter of policy and they offered no views on it, leaving such matters to ministers.[47] While they had no objections to being on such a committee, they pointed out that, because of other commitments, the amount of assistance that their architects could give would be limited. They argued:

> With regard to the question of renovating and altering the buildings in question to meet the needs of modern institutions, schools etc., we have to state that in our opinion few, if any, of those buildings, which were of course designed as private residences, would economically lend themselves in lay-out to adaptation for the purposes mentioned, while defects arising from age, faulty initial construction, dry rot, etc. are liable to be encountered in very many cases and would almost certainly prove very costly to remedy. Furthermore, maintenance costs would be very high. In general, having regard to our experiences, particularly at Shelton Abbey, County Wicklow, and Johnstown Castle, County Wexford, we would be averse to the acquisition of such properties with a view to their adaptation for any of the purposes with which we are likely to be concerned, and we consider that the erection of new purpose designed buildings would be much more economical and satisfactory.[48]

In this, the Commissioners of Public Works practically echoed the views given a number of years earlier by the Minister for Lands, Fianna Fáil TD for Cork North, Seán Moylan, when he declared that these mansions were predominantly unsuitable for adaptation and therefore would be demolished.[49] The writer of a letter to the editor of the *Irish Times* during debates over Hazelwood House, County Sligo, which has been examined in Chapter One, (possibly Moylan again), also maintained that new buildings were preferable for housing institutions as they would be more suitable and serviceable.[50] The Commissioners of Public Works concluded that the houses would be useless for the purposes proposed and that they would be opposed to their acquisition for 'any' of the suggested uses. Based on their experience with Shelton Abbey and Johnstown Castle, they wanted nothing to do with the proposals. This comprehensive judgment of the long-term value of such properties, based on only two properties, is questionable, given that both are still being used by the state today. Despite this, the commissioners implicitly recommended demolition when they stated that they considered the erection of new buildings more economical and satisfactory. The Commissioners of Public Works also discouraged the suggested compilation of lists of empty, habitable and unsaleable houses by inquiries directed to the local authorities and house agents on the grounds that such enquiries could 'give rise to undesirable publicity and perhaps misunderstandings'.[51] Instead, they suggested that it might be possible to procure such information through the local officers of the departments on any proposed committee.[52]

In contrast, a draft letter prepared in the Department of Finance for the Minister's signature argued that 'where additional accommodation is required by government departments it would be generally desirable to make use of old abandoned mansions for the purpose.'[53] This contrast is notable, given that the commissioners responsible for the preservation of national monuments were against investigating uses for these houses, while the Department of Finance recommended their use. It may have been the case that the commissioners knew from their particular expertise and experience that these houses were unsuited to other uses; although the Department of Finance was also the department who would have been most concerned with frugality above sentimentality, if these houses were unsuitable.

TAXATION OF COUNTRY HOUSES

The memorandum from the Office of the Minister for Lands also addressed the issue of taxation and its effect on the viability of the country house. It stated:

> In relation to the national economy the following comments occur in regard to the possibility of furthering the disposal of medium-sized properties:

(a) Whilst the inflation of property values which was a feature of the post-war years has largely ceased, it might recur to a similar, or even greater, extent in the event of, say, a further disturbance throughout Europe or the accession to office of a Labour Government in England;

(b) A revival of home confidence might stimulate demand or interest in acquiring such properties;

(c) So also might alteration in future taxation policy by the Government in regard to estate duties; or concession in regard to rating abatements, even for a period of years, after the properties have been acquired by their new owners. Such abatement would cost local authorities nothing for as things stand the homes will be demolished, whereas if preserved they will continue to yield some rate revenue.[54]

In relation to the sustainability of private houses, where the Department of Lands definitively did not have a duty of care, it was observed: 'it is possible that some owners of large residences are not aware of the possibility of having valuation revised on the plea of reduced letting value. Publication of this possibility might save some of these houses.'[55] The department expressed the view that the question of taxation necessitated urgent study. In addition, attention was drawn to the fact that 2.7 persons were employed on every estate of 200 acres and upwards and on average one person on estates from 100 to 200 acres as agricultural workers. This figure was not inclusive of employees such as gardeners, domestic help, and so on. The department thus emphasised a view that was not very current in the popular rhetoric of the day: that some owners not only provided good employment but exercised good husbandry methods and developed pedigree stock. The Minister for Finance, Dr James Ryan, had also indicated his desire to attract persons from outside the state with a view to their residing in the rural districts of this country and so the Department of Lands thought it worthy of consideration whether such persons should be accorded tax concessions and incentives for certain types of specialist production.[56]

On 2 September 1958, the Revenue Commissioners responded to the Department of Lands' suggestions in relation to taxation. This office observed that the draft memorandum, while mentioning tax relief, made no specific recommendation, particularly for the type of tax concessions they had in mind for 'foreigners' with unearned incomes who purchased large properties in the country.[57] It had also stated that alteration in future taxation policy with regard to death duties might stimulate demand or interest in acquiring medium-sized properties. The Revenue Commissioners maintained that the question of death duties did not arise in relation to most of the proposals for disposal of these types of property, that is, buildings earmarked as teacher training or agricultural training centres. They concluded: 'in the case of private ownership it is suggested that, in view of the restricted market for such properties, their market value would scarcely be so considerable that any reduction in death duties could be said to constitute an incentive towards the acquisition of properties.'[58]

On the issue of granting taxation concessions and abatements for country houses, the Commissioners of Public Works' objection was that while the question of granting tax and rating concessions in the case of any of the properties mentioned was a matter of policy, with a view to attracting purchasers from outside the state, it seemed that if such a proposal were made, a strong case could be put forward for the application of similar concessions to other properties. However, a Department of Finance official wrote in a note on this: 'but what harm would it be to inquire into the matter?'. This indicates that some civil servants in the Department of Finance – the department that would be most affected by any such financial concessions – viewed the suggestion favourably.[59] This contrasted with the commissioners who argued for precisely the opposite, although, one would have thought they, should have felt that a special case should be made for historic properties such as country houses with regard to taxation.

The reply from the Commissioners of Public Works then went on to deal with the matter of the preservation of the mansions for their own merits, noting that the draft memorandum did not contain any specific reference to the question of the preservation of mansions and large houses for architectural or historical reasons. They recollected that one of the two resolutions passed by the NMAC at a meeting in 1945 called for 'the setting up of a committee representative of the departments of state concerned, the Irish Tourist Board, and the architectural associations and learned societies to consider the best means of taking action for the preservation of such monuments.'[60] They had sent a minute to the Department of Finance in July 1946 that had stated that, as far as the resolution was concerned, their interest in the question of the demolition of country houses and mansions was confined to the functions that they carried out in accordance with the National Monuments Act. They had written:

> It seemed clear that country houses and mansions of the type to which attention had been drawn from time to time would not qualify for treatment under the act, save in exceptional cases which would probably be brought to our notice specifically and that accordingly we had no special views as to the desirability or otherwise of setting up a committee such as was visualised in the resolution.[61]

In the meantime, they had conducted inspections of several buildings brought to their notice in one way or another, as being likely to be demolished and, where

1. Jenkinstown House, County Kilkenny by Robert French c. 1865–1914.
Demolished. Courtesy of the National Library of Ireland.

2. Mote Park, Ballymurray, County Roscommon. Originally home to the Crofton family. Sold for demolition in the 1950s by the Irish Land Commission. Courtesy of the National Library of Ireland.

3. Erskine Childers, Minister for Lands, 1957–9. Courtesy of the National Library of Ireland.

4. Shanbally Castle, Clogheen, County Tipperary by Robert French
c. 1865–1914. Sold for demolition in August 1957. Courtesy of the
National Library of Ireland.

5. Slane Castle, County Meath. The castle is in family ownership to this day. Courtesy of the Centre for the Study of Historic Irish Houses and Estates.

6. Bishopscourt, Straffan, County Kildare, 20 August 1967. In private ownership. Courtesy of the National Library of Ireland.

7. Glenstal Abbey, Murroe, County Limerick. Photograph by Independent Newspapers (Firm), 31 May 1930. The abbey subsequently became a Benedictine Abbey and boarding school for boys. Courtesy of the National Library of Ireland.

8. Shelton Abbey, County Wicklow. Shelton Abbey is currently owned by the Irish Prison Service. Courtesy of the Centre for the Study of Historic Irish Houses and Estates.

9. Directors of Muckross House, 14 February 1964. L–R: Dr Frank Hilliard, Fr J. Sheahan, Beatrice Grosvenor, Seán O'Connor, Arthur Fairley, Fr Conleth and Edmund (Ned) Myers. Courtesy of the Trustees of Muckross House.

10. Muckross House, Killarney, County Kerry. Currently open to the public and operated as a museum. Courtesy of the the Trustees of Muckross House.

11. Carton House, Maynooth, County Kildare. In use as a hotel and golf course. Courtesy of the Centre for the Study of Historic Irish Houses and Estates.

12. Avondale House, Rathdrum, County Wicklow. Purchased by the state in 1904, it is currently operated as a museum and forest park. Courtesy of the Centre for the Study of Historic Irish Houses and Estates.

13. Castletown House, Celbridge, County Kildare. Transferred into state ownership in 1994 and is now operated by the OPW. Courtesy of Lori Strang, WikiCommons.

14. Johnstown Castle, County Wexford. Presented as a gift to the nation in 1945. It is currently owned by Teagasc. Courtesy of the Centre for the Study of Historic Irish Houses and Estates.

15. Farmleigh, Phoenix Park, Dublin. Purchased by the state in 1999. Photograph by David Davidson, spring 2018. Courtesy of the OPW, Farmleigh.

16. Russborough House, County Wicklow. Currently owned by the Alfred Beit Foundation and open to the public. Courtesy of the Centre for the Study of Historic Irish Houses and Estates.

17. Bantry House, County Cork. Bantry remains in the ownership of the original family to this day and is open to the public. Courtesy of the Centre for the Study of Historic Irish Houses and Estates.

18. Derrynane House, Waterville, County Kerry by Robert French c. 1865–1914. Former home of Daniel O'Connell. Courtesy of the National Library of Ireland.

19. Killarney House (Kenmare House), County Kerry. Sold to the state for a nominal sum in 1978, it was assumed into full state ownership in 1998. Courtesy of the National Library of Ireland.

20. Hazelwood House, County Sligo. Advertised for demolition in 1946, Hazelwood was subsequently bought by the Department of Health and an Italian business group, SNIA, among others. Courtesy of the National Library of Ireland.

21. Hazelwood House, County Sligo. Hazelwood remains in private ownership today but is currently boarded up and unused. Courtesy of Emer Crooke.

22. Moore Hall, County Mayo. Burned down in 1923. Courtesy of the Centre for the Study of Historic Irish Houses and Estates.

considered necessary, had drawings and photographs made. Nevertheless, the commissioners added: 'none of the premises inspected was accepted for preservation by the state as a national monument.'[62] As such, they believed that making a record of exceptional buildings that were to be destroyed was enough, that such mansions could not be utilised for any substantial purposes, and that the subject was not of pressing public concern. The Commissioners of Public Works wrote:

> The problem is obviously a very vexed one and has from time to time been the subject of a good deal of comment, much of which has been ill-informed. We doubt if the general body of the public have any real interest in the matter and in our opinion the preservation by the state of any of the buildings in question as could not economically be utilised for some specific purpose would involve disproportionate expenditure of public moneys. There may be a case for the preservation of a few such buildings as show places or as places of general, etc., interest, but this might perhaps be best done by a body other than one of the government departments.[63]

In this matter their principal architect had pointed out that, while the British Ministry of Works was not empowered to take over houses that were still inhabited or not yet ruined, the preservation of outstanding country houses was undertaken by the National Trust. By this time, it owned over 500 places of scenic, historic or architectural interest. They understood that the Trust had statutory powers to hold such properties in permanent trust and received no government subsidy; however, in reality it did. The Commissioners of Public Works suggested that a study of the Trust's activities be part of any inter-departmental inquiry into the question of the preservation and that the views of An Taisce might be useful.[64] The commissioners' views here are extraordinary and, of all the department and state bodies consulted, they are the most overwhelmingly negative about any proposals to investigate the preservation of these houses or the possibility of easing the financial burden for their owners, even though the latter suggestion would not have impinged upon the work of the commissioners or their budget at all.

A civil servant in the Department of Finance, identified only as J. W., offered his views in a draft letter on the issue of taxation, which had been raised by the Department of Lands' memorandum. His draft letter explained that, in the absence of detail, the Minister for Finance, Dr James Ryan, had no particular views on tax concessions and incentives for certain types of specialist production undertaken by persons with unearned incomes coming to live in the country. J. W. did point out, though: 'it would be well to remember that when a small number of persons from Great Britain settled here after the war, there was such an outcry about it that the Oireachtas imposed a penal rate of stamp duty on house and land acquisitions by non-nationals.'[65] This Finance official believed that, in light of current economic thought, particularly as enunciated in the 'Programme for Economic Development', 'it is questionable if that xenophobic attitude was correct.'[66] This shows how, even in a short space of time, attitudes were changing. Similarly, in another internal Department of Finance note on the subject from a J. M. (presumably J. Mooney, who was involved in other correspondence on this issue) to a Mr Hogan, it was suggested that stamp duty relief for purchases by non-nationals might be called for.[67] This note concluded with a proposal that, if this suggestion were favoured, and before any approach to the government, a conference should be held in the Department of Lands and attended by representatives of the departments concerned in order to explore the matter and settle the terms of reference of the committee of inquiry. This positive proposal was to be forwarded to the Department of Lands.[68]

RATES

One of the most significant views on the issue of rates brought up by the Department of Lands' memorandum was that of the Commissioner of Valuation. On 21 October, the observations of the Commissioner of Valuation were received by the Department of Finance.[69] Given that his office was responsible for the setting of rates, his views on this topic were the most significant and also the most influential in terms of whether the status quo on this subject would change. Firstly, he outlined the valuation of the houses, excluding those only fit for demolition, which had been listed in Table A. Using that year's estimates, he calculated the rates on these houses: the maximum being between £150 and £3200 per annum in the case of two of the largest houses. He added that 'normal annual maintenance expenses would amount to at least twice the rates and to more than ten times the rates where valuations are low. Adequate domestic staff for these houses would probably cost at least twice the maintenance expenses'.[70] It is worth noting that rates were given as the reason throughout this period for sale and demolition by owners and also as a reason preventing the take-over of such properties by An Óige or the National Trust, as has been documented in previous chapters. In spite of this, the Commissioner of Valuation, a figure in one of the best positions to assess the relative value and effect of rates, stated that they were only a portion of the monies that would be spent on maintenance of the house alone, perhaps ten times less in some cases. The commissioner explained that if 13 of the 18 houses listed in Table A were completely de-rated, the occupier would gain less than £2 a week. In none of the cases would complete de-rating save the occupier £4 per week, that is, less than the cost of a maidservant. Therefore, in the commissioner's opinion, complete de-rating would be much too small a subvention to couple effectively with guarantees as to the use and proper maintenance of any property. Rating abatements for occupants of mansions would not be worth considering if they amounted to less than complete de-rating.

The commissioner expanded upon the wider implications of such a scheme which he regarded as controversial, commenting:

> There are more occupied than unoccupied mansions and large houses. An increase in rate poundages would inevitably follow the legislators' unwillingness to offer to future occupiers of currently unoccupied mansions a relief which was to be withheld from, say, religious communities caring for mental defectives or epileptics in similar mansions. How could the legislator defend derating of the native, not to mention the foreign, occupier of a mansion to the cottier, the widow or the father who gets no relief from a burden which normally represents a higher proportion of net income the lower the income group to which the ratepayer belongs?[71]

No evidence was found in any other government file examined that the work of the Valuation Office and the Land Commission intertwined like this, pointing again to the fact that this 1958 memorandum was exceptional in its pan-departmental approach to the question of the preservation of the country house, including the issue of buildings' possible use and the subject of taxation and rating.

The Commissioner of Valuation concluded that rates were relatively insignificant in the economics of running a mansion. In his view, their irrelevance jettisoned the suggestion that owners could be made aware of the possibility of having their house valuation revised on the plea of reduced letting value. He believed that the spread of valuations of the properties on the commission's hands indicated the danger of making any generalisation about valuations, since, if the mansions were fully occupied, revision could result in more increases than decreases in valuation. He anticipated that advertising appeals for revision of valuation would have an undoubtedly provocative effect on thousands whose valuations had been increased in recent years. The commissioner also indicated that opportunities for reductions in valuation were actually known to those who advised the occupants. In addition, he explained that the Valuation Office did not agree that the properties might increase in value with a growing housing trade or another disturbance in Europe, arguing: 'state departments are particularly unsuited to speculation in property. The maintenance expenses involved in holding mansions for a rise in value would tend to be much higher in the case of the state department than in the case of the private speculator.'[72] Instead, he maintained that if a reasonable opportunity for speculation did exist, the commission should be able to sell such properties to a private speculator. In any case, the commissioner believed that what attracted the rich foreigner was general freedom from taxation or low rates of tax, which were applicable to all residents.

The Valuation Office then outlined the Commissioner of Valuation's criteria for whether these mansions should be preserved or disposed of, highlighting:

> Architectural interest, historical associations etc. are factors which influence the decision as to whether a premises is worthy of preservation as a national monument. The taxpayer can fairly demand that if an old mansion is not the subject of a preservation order by the Commissioners of Public Works as a national monument it should be treated as an ordinary surplus property and disposed of as early as possible – the saving in maintenance expenses and the loss in value due to vacancy being the prime considerations.[73]

In conclusion, the Commissioner of Valuation did not see a necessity for setting up an inter-departmental committee.[74] This was a significant conclusion given that one of the main suggestions that necessitated the need for a committee to be set up by the Department of Lands was the question of the reduction of rates in order to make the position of the country house more viable. Owner after owner throughout this period stated that rates, coupled with taxation, were unequivocally threatening or indeed causing the sale or destruction of the country house. However, since the person in charge of this area of valuation, the commissioner, definitively stated that a reduction in rates would be of negligible value and did not need to be discussed further, this disposed of the Department of Lands' proposal to pursue this suggestion.

The Department of Finance official J. W. also addressed the issue of rates in his draft reply to the Department of Lands. He wrote that it was the opinion of the Department of Finance that these houses could be used in two ways: occupied for private purposes, or for public or institutional purposes. The question was whether either course were feasible or practicable.[75] Discussing the first use as private homes, J. W. noted that they were clearly not popular. Equally, he acknowledged their viability problems as private residences since they were built for the landed gentry 'when their share of the national income was much higher than it is today and when they could afford to get the two things necessary for keeping their houses comfortable and in good repair, namely, cheap servants and cheap fuel.' He went on to say that the landed gentry had since been 'virtually wiped out' by the Land Commission's work and high taxation, while it was also no longer possible to get servants and fuel cheaply. With regard to the suggested proposal of rating concessions, he did not believe that it would have any meaningful effect on the survival of country houses into the future because, in his opinion, 'remission of most, if not all, of the rates on a large mansion would still leave servants and fuel too dear for the man who finds one-fifth, one-quarter or even one-third of his income taken from him in taxation.'[76]

Tellingly, he went on: 'it is hard to see the Oireachtas agreeing to any change in this.'[77] This is significant as normally it was the Department of Finance that controlled decisions on these country houses, since it controlled the purse strings. Here, this departmental official was suggesting that these proposals would not so much be received badly by the Department of Finance's staff but by the wider political body through whom any such proposed budgetary changes would have to pass. The sentence about the Oireachtas was crossed out in the end and replaced with a statement that did not specifically assign blame. This read: 'it is hard to see the position in this regard being altered for many years to come, so the melancholy fact must be faced that the day of the Big House is almost over as far as occupation by the private individual is concerned'.[78] It seems that civil servants in the Department of Finance were realistic that, however laudable the scheme was, it would never receive wide-spread political support and that was the reality in which they were working.

On 10 February 1959, another civil servant in the Department of Finance, J. M. (mentioned previously), wrote internally to a colleague in the department, Mr Hogan, outlining a different view. J. M. thought that the attitude displayed by the Revenue Commissioners, the OPW and particularly the Valuation Office was: 'rather unsympathetic, uncooperative and perhaps unrealistic. *Prima facie*, the present system of valuation and rating, etc., encourages the destruction of large old buildings and old buildings in general'.[79] Despite the fact that the Commissioner of Valuation asserted in his letter that rates would have no effect, here a Department of Finance official stated clearly that the current policy of rates and taxation encouraged the destruction of the country house. J. M. expressed unequivocally that 'it has been a common experience in the Irish countryside to see old buildings in fair condition being deliberately pulled down or de-roofed to escape valuation and rating. This is done even where the valuation is insignificant in amount.'[80] He believed that, as a result of this, 'unlike other countries, we have practically no real buildings, apart from ruins, left in the country.'[81] His view was that 'the factor that determines the fate of the building is not so much the amount for the rates but the obligation to pay any rates at all on a building that is not fully suitable for the owner's purposes.'[82] In his opinion, farmers particularly regarded rates as a levy for which they got no return and he thought that the Commissioner of Valuation did not appreciate this fully.[83] The Land Commission, in some cases, allocated a country house situated on acquired lands to the allottee. In most cases, these allottees were farmers who did not have uses for these houses or the resources to maintain them, as this finance official highlighted.

ESTABLISHMENT OF A GOVERNMENTAL COMMITTEE

A draft letter from the Department of Finance advocated replying to the Department of Lands that the Minister for Finance considered that no useful purpose would be served by setting up an inter-departmental committee to deliberate any of its proposals. The draft letter suggested that the Minister for Lands should not pursue the matter.[84] In contrast, J. M. in the Department of Finance, who appears to have been a particularly concerned civil servant in this regard, argued that 'a more sympathetic and non-committal attitude is called for. An investigation by an inter-departmental committee as advocated by the Department of Lands should do no harm and might yield fruitful results, i.e., give a line for practical policy.'[85] In his view, the terms of reference of the proposed committee should include specific direction to enquire into the system of valuation, rating, taxation and the law that affected properties of the kind concerned, and the feasibility of modifications that could be calculated to encourage their preservation. He argued: 'if grants and reliefs from rates on new buildings are warranted to stimulate building, it is arguable that some kind of corresponding assistance and reliefs for a limited category of old buildings of historical interest might be justified to encourage their continued use and preservation. Indeed, in theory at any rate, they might be more justified'.[86]

These arguments were taken no further, however, as another Department of Finance official, identified as L. Ó. N., overrode J. M.'s proposals. This civil servant requested it be stated, instead, that based on the information that was presently available, the department doubted whether there was a problem that would require the attention of an inter-departmental committee on the lines suggested. It was therefore thought premature to approach the government on the issue until the *prima facie* considerations of policy had been further examined. It was suggested that if the Minister for Lands desired to pursue the question before formulating a submission to government, the Department of Lands might arrange a conference of representatives from the interested departments.[87] L. Ó. N. was obviously in a more senior position in the department than J. M. and able to pull rank to dictate the response; the exact opposite of that which Mooney had proposed. The revised reply was sent to the Department of Lands on 16 February, with copies forwarded to the other departments involved.[88] In reality, it was a reply that promised nothing and was a rebuke to both the Minister and the Department of Lands to do more homework before approaching the issue again or proposing to broach the topic with the government. It also shows that the power of the Department of Finance was so dominant that it could stop proposals, even from other ministers and government departments, from ever being considered by cabinet.

PROPOSALS COME TO NAUGHT

Despite the efforts of the Department of Lands, spearheaded by Childers, to inspire a cross-departmental approach to halt the destruction of the country house in Ireland, in the end they were shot down by senior civil servants in positions of power in central government and its financial arms. The practical and tempered suggestions of the memorandum came to nothing and its proposals were confined to historical record. In July 1959, Childers left the position of Minister for Lands, and when Michael Moran succeeded him it does not appear that this proposal was pursued further. This suggests that the drive to construct a policy came from Childers, and appears to have left with him.

It is also possible that pursuit of Childers' initiatives after his departure was thwarted by top-ranking officials in the Land Commission itself, who may have been only too happy to let this extra work drop when Childers was not demanding it – work that they were not obliged to perform under their remit. Sammon has shown how such behaviour was not uncommon. In one case, the Secretary of the Land Commission did not let Childers see a draft speech containing new ideas for the Land Commission to adopt and instead was 'fed' an 'orthodox draft speech'.[89] Once more, it is clear that the junior civil servant who drafted the speech was open to suggesting and pursuing new ideas. It was the senior officer, at the head of the Commission, who again ensured that such ideas never arrived on the Minister's desk. Speaking of the impact that Childers had in the Department of Lands, Sammon wrote that, in the end: 'no great decisions of any real worth were taken by the Minister', although he admits that the fact that 'he had grandiose ideas when he arrived in the Land Commission cannot be questioned'.[90] Sammon believed that Childer's inglorious legacy at the department was actually orchestrated by senior officials within the Commission who 'had an inkling that Erskine Childers was not long for the Land Commission' and so fed to him 'the stale old diet that was dished up, year after year, on the estimate for lands', rather than exploring new proposals for how they could improve the work of their department.[91] As such, Childers was hoodwinked by the very staff who were supposed to serve him. Their decision to withhold information and ideas from him because of their presumption regarding the length of his tenure shows that, by this time, many in the senior ranks of the civil service were bloated with arrogance and a sense of their own importance. Having been in departments for decades, some clearly felt that they knew better than the ministers who were democratically elected to govern, anathema to the ideals behind a true civil or public service. Sammon concluded that

> In his efforts to reform and improve the performance and the work of the Land Commission, Erskine Childers found his way blocked by both politicians and by his top advisors … In the wider sphere of his hopes to introduce a more modern and effective land settlement policy, Erskine was spancelled firmly by the Secretary and AS [Assistant Secretary]. On his record, he must fall into the broad category of Ministers who allowed themselves to be won round to the status quo by hide-bound top civil servants. All his ideas and hopes of transforming the Land Commission failed to come through to the stage of action. Erskine Childers was, accordingly, a disappointment in the Land Commission.[92]

In contrast, the 1958 memorandum sent on his initiative is illustrative of his desire to be an involved and pro-active minister. It is also an invaluable resource that reveals the Department of Lands' and the Land Commission's policy toward country houses. The department and the Land Commission appear to have worked very closely on this document. The Land Commission was the nerve-centre for the implementation of legislation and policy on lands, while the department looked after the formulation of policy or legislative considerations. The department therefore predominantly took a hands-off approach to the implementation of policy on lands and relied on the expertise and experience of the Land Commission. The memorandum reveals privately to other government departments the policy that the Land Commission adopted in relation to country houses that came into their possession, at least from 1954–8. As this was never intended to be a public document, it presumably represents an honest appraisal of the issue from the Land Commission, Department of Lands, and all the other offices involved. The policy of the Land Commission with regard to country houses appears to have been a practical one, borne out by the comments of various ministers, and it was also a policy that was not questioned in this document. Rather, the memorandum's aim was to attempt to address the issue of the preservation of historic houses more generally. As such it was mostly concerned with recommendations on rates and taxation to make the ownership of such properties easier for owners and organisations, the possible utilisation of these houses by government departments, and also the proposal that this issue merited an inter-departmental committee to seek ways to halt the destruction of the country house. Notably, no one who was consulted suggested that it was in the remit of the Department of Lands to preserve these houses.

The 1958 memorandum is an enlightening document for revealing not only the Land Commission's policy, but also the reluctance of every government department contacted to give *any* concessions to the suggestions proposed. Most emphatic in their opposition were the OPW's commissioners – a conclusion that could have been foreseen from the findings of Chapter Three – as well as the General Valuation Office and Revenue Commissioners. In fact, some enlightened civil servants in the Department of Finance were among the most sympathetic, perhaps owing to the change in attitude that was coming about after the publication of the *First Programme for Economic Expansion* under T. K. Whitaker.

In the end, the suggestions proposed by the memorandum came to nothing. An initiative motivated by the personal interest of the Minister was not welcomed by the Commissioners of Public Works, the Revenue Commissioners or the Valuation Office for many different reasons. In Chapter Three, it was evident that the commissioners were reluctant to take on any of these houses for fear of setting a precedent. The Valuation Office and Revenue Commissioners were also reluctant to agree to any concessions for the owners of such mansions when it would not be given to ordinary house owners or organisations, and they, too, feared the public response. Significantly, however, the Commissioner of Valuation also practically asserted that if such houses were not national monuments eligible for state preservation, then they were not the state's concern and should be sold on immediately, as this was in the best interests of the taxpayer. In essence, these offices and departments felt they could not justify concessions for these country houses. Probably owing to a combination of their limited budgets and staff, a reluctance to become responsible for this difficult and emotionally-loaded issue, and a realisation that the preservation of the country house was not then justifiable under public expenditure, these departments were overwhelmingly negative in their response to the proposed state intervention. The single-most important factor limiting action on this issue was that these houses were not deemed national monuments by the Commissioners of Public Works, which became one of the primary reasons for their large-scale destruction post-independence.

CRITICISM OF THE LAND COMMISSION

The Land Commission and the Department of Lands at times attracted criticism over the handling of country houses that they acquired during their land division work, such as in the case of Shanbally Castle, demolished in 1957. Another case that drew adverse criticism to the Department of Lands' policy in relation to country houses was that of Dromore Castle, when Tomás Ó Deirg was Minister for Lands. On 26 October 1953, the *Irish Independent* reported that the Limerick castle 'must be demolished at the insistence of the Department of Lands as a condition of the purchase of the premises with one hundred acres of woodland by the forestry division of the department.'[93] According to the paper, the castle had been built by the third Earl of Limerick in 1878 at a cost of £40,000. It had been purchased by Morgan McMahon, owner of a Limerick sawmills, in 1937 and was occupied by him until 1948 but had been vacant since. The owners were reported to have obtained permission to demolish the castle, allowing the sale to the Department of Lands to go ahead.[94]

In a letter dated 30 October 1953, written by S. Mac Piarais of the Forestry Division of the Department of Lands to Mr Doyle, Mac Piarais explained that Dromore Castle had been unoccupied for many years, during which time the owners, Messrs McMahon, had advertised the property for sale on a number of occasions.[95] In March 1953, during negotiations for purchase, Messrs McMahon requested that the department 'make alternative offers for (1) the estate complete with buildings, and (2) the estate with the buildings demolished, in case it should be to their own advantage to sell the buildings before disposing of the estate for forestry purposes.'[96] The department was not at this stage prepared to make an offer for the estate complete with buildings, but complied with the firm's request for an offer on the basis of the prior demolition of the buildings, thereby intimating that they would require the demolition of the buildings and the removal of the materials to be concluded before completion of a sale. Messrs McMahon had obtained the County Council's permission to demolish the castle and it was their intention to accept the department's offer – apparently the only viable one. The department required only such demolition work as would leave the walls in a safe condition and so that the owners would have no further rights to the property after the sale. Mac Piarais clarified the department's reasoning by explaining:

> From the department's viewpoint, the acquisition of this estate for forestry purposes is highly desirable but the castle would have no value as such to the department. The forestry division would necessarily have had to view with reluctance the purchase of the estate at a price inflated by the inclusion of a castle for which, if the unsuccessful advertisement on Messrs McMahon's part is any indication, no market could be found but for which Messrs McMahon would reasonably have expected an appreciable price. The exclusion of the castle at their request was, therefore, fully acceptable from the department's viewpoint.[97]

While, at first, the insistence of the Department of Lands that the castle be demolished may appear to advocate the destruction of an historic building, as the Forestry Division pointed out, the castle could not be sold, had no market value and would be of no use to them, although it would inflate the price at which they could purchase the whole estate.

Regardless, such cases fuelled negative perceptions of the Department of Lands and the Land Commission's policy as indifferent to, or antagonistic toward, the survival of country houses on acquired lands. Dooley has shown how such perceptions were evident, for example, in the *Sligo Champion*'s coverage of the case of Hazelwood House, discussed in Chapter Three. He explained that, given the stipulation to demolish the house and level the site in the advertisement for the sale of Hazelwood, the editor of the *Sligo Champion*, one of the few to oppose the move, condemned what he perceived to be the Land Commission's policy of acquiring houses simply to demolish them and sarcastically proclaimed: 'In Ireland the value of such a house is measured by the contents of lead in the roof.'[98] Desmond Guinness, who established the Irish Georgian Society in 1958, was just as critical of Land Commission policy, arguing:

> When it came into possession of what is loosely termed nowadays as an 'historic property' the consequences were dire. The buildings were emptied and left shuttered up for years while the dreamers decided how to carve up the place. A favourite ploy was to run the statutory concentration camp fence ten feet or so from the front steps. The trees were cut, the garden went wild and no longer gave any employment. In terms of national investment it was a waste. The house would be advertised for sale, through

the means of a five line advertisement on the back page of a local paper, to ensure that no one except the demolition men could possibly be misguided enough to buy it.[99]

Furthermore, Dooley has explained that the surviving landed families who managed to retain their historic houses also condemned the fact that 'where the commission acquired lands and accompanying houses, all too often it simply demolished the house with no consideration for its architectural or heritage value.'[100]

While this may have been true in many cases, it appears that the Land Commission had a very pragmatic approach, at least by the 1950s, in relation to country houses acquired on lands for division, as was demonstrated in the 1958 memorandum. This is supported by the claims of other Ministers for Lands on this subject, although these too must be viewed with some scepticism as political speeches. When Fianna Fáil TD for Cork North, Seán Moylan, was Minister for Lands from June 1944 to February 1948, he maintained that 'residences on lands acquired by the Land Commission for division which are not suitable for disposal to allottees may be demolished in order to provide material for building smaller houses for allottees or may be sold by public auction.'[101] While Moylan also displayed his share of particularly unsympathetic views on the survival of these houses, the predominantly practical approach of the Commission was even elucidated by this minister who did not appear to view the preservation of such houses kindly. In fact, Moylan believed that the majority of country houses were 'not structurally sound, have no artistic value and no historic interest' and he argued: 'the sooner they go down the better – they are no use'.[102]

Fianna Fáil Minister for Lands from 1959–68, Michael Moran, also expounded the ostensible practical policy of the Land Commission when he stated in 1964 that there was no policy of deliberately breaking-up demesnes as such. Nevertheless, he maintained that the Land Commission had a duty to help uneconomic holders, and, for this purpose, they needed good land. He admitted that in this work 'they have very little use for castles or great mansions'.[103]

Even so, Moran maintained that the Land Commission recognised that a castle 'must have a fair share of land around it if it is to survive at all.'[104] He re-emphasised this policy in the Seanad in 1965 when he specified that the general policy of the Land Commission was to apportion a considerably larger amount of land than 25 acres with such houses in order to enable people to sell this type of residence. In his opinion, 'it is a good thing from a public policy point of view that these places should be preserved.'[105] He admitted that, in many cases, the owners of such properties gave good employment and that it took a substantial income to be able to afford to take over such properties and the costs involved in keeping them.[106] Moran explained that, 'as a matter of policy', the Land Commission tried to keep the country house intact. The policy when they took over an estate for division which came with a 'big mansion' was to allocate what they considered to be sufficient amenity land to make them attractive to a purchaser. He argued that if they did not do it, then the Land Commission would have the house for its scrap value, something that served no purpose of the Land Commission. That was why he emphasised that

> It is good business for the Land Commission to allocate a sufficient amount of land to these places and, particularly to ones of historic interest, to ensure that they will be kept going as living concerns ... That has been their practice and their policy to enable such a person to get rid of the place economically, and to ensure that the place would be preserved if it were of any interest at all'.[107]

Moran explained that if the Land Commission acquired a very large house, like Oak Park, County Carlow, and it received a demand from the Agricultural Institute for facilities, the Commission automatically gave the house to the public body as this was in the public interest. In fact, where there was any question of the public interest, he was adamant that any state department, including the Land Commission, automatically took that into account and he stressed that the department was very conscious of preserving any worthwhile property.[108] It could be argued that this was political rhetoric; however, the fact that the same policy was repeated by different ministers over a long time-span, and that it is similarly explained in private government files from the Land Commission in relation to the Dromore Castle case, for example, or the 1958 memorandum, suggests that this was the reality of the Land Commission's policy and attitudinal disposition towards these country houses. The Land Commission was not antagonistic to the survival of the country house in Ireland and had no deliberate or callous policy of destruction. The nature of their work and the limitations of their brief, however, meant that rapid land division, rather than historical preservation, was pursued at all costs.

CONCLUSION

The nature of the land division carried out by the Land Commission over the twentieth century meant that most country houses were no longer sustainable and, as such, the Land Commission was unquestionably responsible for many country houses that were abandoned, left to decay or sold off for other uses or demolition. In fact, Land Commission acquisition and redistribution policy as legislated for by the land acts presented by independent governments made the decline of the country house inevitable. Nonetheless, as has been illustrated in this chapter, when the Commission itself acquired country houses with land, demolition by the Commission itself appears to have taken place in a minority of cases – at least during the short number of years for which Land Commission statistics are available – and was not the Commission's first preference or a matter of policy. In spite of this, prevailing public perceptions and historiography have criticised the Commission for their role in the destruction of the country house in Ireland. In 1992, the *Irish Times* reported that as a body it: 'had its own objectives and they did not include the conservation of colonial history. Too often, the buildings that came into its hands met the fate ... [of] Coole Park ... this was demolished and the stones carted off by the County Council. The Land Commission fiat did not, luckily, extend to national monuments.'[109] Again, the importance of the decision of the Commissioners of Public Works not to classify any country house as a national monument in this period is highlighted. Had they done so, the Land Commission would not have been able to demolish a single house designated as such on lands that they acquired. Magnificent structures like the fairytale Shanbally Castle might have survived until today.

The Minister for Lands had a unique role. The Commission appears to have continued with its established policy if the minister was not interested or individually motivated to change it. Yet, in the case of a minister such as Fianna Fáil's Erskine Childers, his very different ideas on the preservation of these houses motivated the Land Commission to propose policy changes as part of the 1958 memorandum. Childers, in particular, took such an interest that he attempted to push the government to formulate a policy on preserving the country house, even suggesting the abolition of rates and taxes for owners still in possession – not even on the Land Commission's books. As discussed, however, no department wanted to become responsible for this issue as they did not believe that these houses merited protection. It is clear that until the OPW was willing to class these country houses as national monuments, no state department could justify the expenditure of public funds or concessions to owners of these properties alone when there was no legitimate reason for doing so above an ordinary house or householder.

In addition, while some demolitions appear on paper, and in hindsight, to be callous decisions, the Land Commission did not ostensibly demolish because of antagonistic attitudes. Evidence suggests the Land Commission's perspective was simply pragmatic in accordance with the work with which they were tasked. They were working under the policy brief given to them by the Department of Lands and individual governments' programmes. Country houses were left with a small amount of land to make them saleable as residences, although not enough to make them economically viable on land alone. Houses that were left with some of their demesne fared better in terms of their survival into the future, as they could be sold on as private country homes, luxury hotels or impressive golf courses later in the decade. The era of Big House landlords was over, as it was all over Europe, and the Land Commission was given the task of ensuring that such large tracts of land were broken up among migrants, uneconomic landholders and the landless – this was government policy, not Land Commission policy. It is true, however, that this policy was very black and white and looked at the division of land as its primary and only real aim in independent Ireland. The preservation of country houses was never really considered as the by-product of this process and, when it was, it was often viewed unsympathetically, as was seen with Moylan.

Other unintended, destructive consequences were also not given much thought or appraisal, such as the felling of large native woodlands. It is also worth remembering that dramatic destruction, such as was the case with Shanbally Castle, is more visible and draws more public outcry, as befitting the striking nature of demolition, while those houses that were sold on, reused, or gradually decayed in the hands of owners, new and old, are not often noticed. It needs to be emphasised that this chapter is specifically concerned with the *attitudinal* disposition of the Land Commission toward the country house and its survival. As such, the evidence available illustrates that the Commission did not have overtly antagonistic attitudes towards country houses. Rather, if one can take the limited sample data on the years 1954–8 as even somewhat indic-ative of their overall policy, it appears that the Commission attempted to find uses that would allow for the survival of the historic houses that it acquired. That is not to say that the work of the Land Commission, particularly after the 1923 Act, in compulsorily acquiring landed estates surrounding these houses, was not detrimental to their survival.

As times changed and priorities shifted, in February 1977 the Department of Lands became the Department of Fisheries, having largely down-scaled its work after the last land act and, in 1992, the Irish Land Commission (Dissolution) Act provided for the dissolution of the Land Commission.[110] This chapter does not argue that the Land Commission was not responsible for the actual sale or demolition of country houses, but it does argue that blame for this, which has been laid at the Commission's feet, should be also be laid at the feet of other government departments, most particularly the Commissioners of Public Works. Unlike the Land Commission, the Commissioners were in a position to save some of these houses under the National Monuments Act, even just by conserving them as they were, or by issuing preservation orders to prevent their demolition. The Land Commission had no power whatsoever to preserve or retain these houses and, when it turned to government departments in this period to ask if they had use for them, the answer was unfailingly no.

SIX

A CLIMATE OF CHANGE, 1957–73

In March 1957, Fianna Fáil returned to power for 16 years, though their years of unbroken government from 1957 to 1973 saw three different Taoisigh. The first was Éamon de Valera, who resumed the position for the last time from March 1957 until June 1959 when he resigned to become President of Ireland. Seán Lemass took over after de Valera's departure and was Taoiseach until November 1966 when he resigned from government. His successor was Jack Lynch who saw out the last term of Fianna Fáil domination, which ended in March 1973. This chapter will examine attitudes towards the country house over this extended period, which saw relative stability in government but radical changes in society. It will assess to what extent wider international and national shifts in economics and society affected a change in attitudes toward, and perceptions of, the country house in Ireland. This broad economic and political context will be outlined first because it formed the basis for changing attitudes and also situates the fate of the country house in the overall national story.

ECONOMIC AND POLITICAL CHANGE

After the insular, protectionist attitude that had been adopted by de Valera for many years, his successor, Seán Lemass, began to argue, along with civil servants and economists, that Ireland needed to move away from this policy and engage more with the European community if it were to develop. In fact, this period is conventionally viewed as one of the turning points in re-evaluating this position. The 1958 publication of the Department of Finance document *Economic Development* along with the new Fianna Fáil government's *First Programme for Economic Expansion* 'is generally heralded as marking the policy shift from protectionism to outward orientation'. Accepted wisdom therefore credits T. K. Whitaker and Seán Lemass with effecting the policy shift.[1] However, Frank Barry has argued that while this document was influential, it was not an overnight publication that heralded a new dawn for Ireland. It was five years later that the dismantling of the protectionist tariff barriers was initiated, for example, whereas two years before Whitaker's influential document, tax relief for export expansion was introduced by John A. Costello, then Taoiseach and leader of the second inter-party government.[2] This tax relief represented the beginning of Ireland's low corporation tax regime that has been so essential to foreign investment in Ireland and remains influential today.[3]

Barry maintained that proposals for some form of tax relief, which had been circulating since the Second World War, were a bone of contention between the Department of Industry and Commerce, who were pushing for it, and the Department of Finance and the Revenue Commissioners, who strongly resisted it. The inter-party government, particularly Costello, was anxious to address the issue and 'in a major policy speech delivered to an inter-party meeting on 5 October 1956 ... Costello overruled the long-standing revenue and finance position and announced that EPTR [Export Profits Tax Relief] would be introduced.'[4] As such, Barry argued that Costello and the inter-party government pioneered moves towards increasing incentives for foreign businesses to establish in Ireland and for opening up the Irish market. Such initiatives also included the establishment of the Capital Investment Advisory Committee, the Industrial Development Authority, and the extension of the industrial grants scheme. These were comparatively radical moves that welcomed foreign influence in a way that had not been encouraged since the beginning of the Free State. This would have an effect on how the country house was viewed domestically. In 1953, Fine Gael produced their own document on the issue, entitled *Blueprint for Prosperity*.[5] In Barry's opinion, despite de Valera and others still railing against foreign involvement in Irish resources, at least in rhetorical flourishes, Costello's speech and the inter-party's position actually forced Lemass to change his tactics. He began to argue that the inter-party government should have introduced more generous concessions and, when Lemass came to power, both he and his Fianna Fáil government had to maintain this attitudinal position. As such, many of the limitations imposed by the Control of Manufactures Acts 'were rescinded with the passage of the Industrial Development (Encouragement of External Investment) Act of 1958', while the Acts themselves were 'repealed completely by an Act of 1964 that provided that they would cease to operate in 1968'.[6] Barry emphasised that the drive toward a more open economy and outward-looking nation, shaking off insular, xenophobic shackles that had remained since the War of Independence, was actually the result of a long process, not an overnight shift.[7] Dermot Keogh has similarly written of how Lemass became Taoiseach at a time when the Irish economy was already strengthening.[8] The substantive intellectual battle over the move away from protectionism to an open economy had already been won. Keogh explained that while

> It would be unfair to say that this was a little like reinventing the wheel … the Secretary of the Department of Finance, Whitaker, and Lemass and [Minister for Finance, Dr James] Ryan had gradually and painstakingly nursed politicians away from the false, womb-like security which economic protectionism had allegedly afforded Irish industry.[9]

This was to affect national attitudes that had tended towards xenophobia and move them to a new appreciation for foreign influence.

The year Lemass took over as Taoiseach and leader of Fianna Fáil, 1957, is often considered the turning point for when Ireland changed politically and socially from being insularly focused to being a progressively outward-looking nation. In contrast, Barry's arguments postulate instead that Lemass ploughed on from where the coalition government had already prepared the ground. Similarly, for the country house, changes in attitudes came about slowly over long time periods and owing to many factors, although they became most apparent at this time. Alvin Jackson also questions this perceived 'faultline in Irish history, marked by the return of the Fianna Fáil Government in 1957', writing that 'the geological strata on either side of the apparent divide are evidently related: the economic policies which Lemass and the new Minister of Finance, Dr James Ryan, pursued had been foreshadowed by a variety of initiatives or ideas launched by earlier administrations.'[10] Jackson elaborated that,

while Lemass is the figure most associated with the rapid economic growth and
the political and social change of the early 1960s, it was in fact the coalition
Minister for Finance, Gerard Sweetman, who had been the significant patron
of T. K. Whitaker. Sweetman appointed Whitaker as Secretary at the age of
just 40 in 1956. Jackson also argues that Ryan was influential in encouraging
Whitaker to pursue his ideas, and it was Ryan who sponsored Whitaker's paper
on Economic Development (originally 'Has Ireland a Future?') in December
1957 before a Fianna Fáil cabinet. It was not until 1958 that the full plan was
published.[11] Jackson argued that it would be unfair to detach the progress of
the 1960s both from wider global movements and also the initiatives taken by
governments as early as 1940, but particularly by Costello's second inter-party
government. In fact, in his view, Lemass and Whitaker both built on these
earlier achievements and also came to power at a particularly fortunate time
of international economic upswing, although he admits that the *Programme for
Economic Expansion* meant that Ireland could capitalise on this international
phenomenon.[12] This, again, shows the importance of civil servants such as
Whitaker in being able to develop thorough policies over long periods of time,
given their relative permanency in posts compared to politicians.

When these economic policies came to fruition, they acted as a catalyst for
a change in attitude for the governance of the country. John A. Murphy has
described it as 'a new departure also in the more fundamental sense of moving
radically away from the old Sinn Féin philosophy of self-sufficiency and industrial protection, which, the programme warned, "can no longer be relied upon
as an automatic weapon of defence."'[13] The effects of this economic policy
married with other external modernising factors to make the early 1960s a time
of buoyant and rapid change in the Irish economy and outlook. Murphy has
shown how the standard of living in Ireland rose, and, while there were still
serious social disparities in areas such as housing, education and healthcare,
there were signs of improvement with new factories opening, more foreign
goods being available for purchase, and an increase in the number of cars.[14]
While not all changes were positive, Murphy argued that 'after a long period
of conservatism, repressiveness and censorship, there began in the 1960s a new
frankness of discussion, a spirit of positive self-criticism, a liberalisation of religious thinking with the pontificate of John XXIII, an increase in intellectual
maturity, and a rejection of paternalism.'[15] However, in his view, 'the single
most powerful agent of change in the moulding of new attitudes was the introduction of a national television service' as it opened the population up to new
cultural influences like never before.[16] The introduction of a national television

service, Teilifís Éireann, in 1961 was a significant catalyst for improvement. The investment of British, European and American business in the country and their ownership of resources was now actively encouraged. All these developments meant that Ireland became an altogether less xenophobic place from the late 1950s.

This both allowed and necessitated a change in arguments surrounding the country house, in rhetoric at least. Now with Britain as allies in terms of accession to the EEC, and a feeling that the country was becoming more cosmopolitan and modern, arguments voicing concern for the preservation and sustainability of country houses became more frequent. The reduction in rates, in order to make it easier for houses to survive, was discussed in the Oireachtas at this time. The increasingly outward-looking nation and the temporal remove from the struggle for independence made the preservation of country houses a less flammable issue and not one that could be seen as unpatriotic to be involved in. Such concerns were most often vocalised in the Seanad, where they could be expressed with less publicity. For example, a 1966 debate on a Local Government (Reduction of Valuation) bill raised the issue of making it easier for private country houses to survive by reducing rates. On the subject, Fine Gael Senator Charles McDonald, who came from a Laois farming background and was on the agricultural panel in the Seanad, argued:

> The rating system is mainly responsible for the regrettable demolition of many of our Big Houses on estates and farms throughout the country … I know they are of little use … but most of these Big Houses are in fair state of repair and they are being demolished solely because the people cannot afford any more to pay the rates on them … Even though these residences or mansions were built in a period which we do not particularly like in our history, if they are in good repair people should be encouraged to keep them because surely they could be put to better use than just destroying them.[17]

Such views were certainly not universal, and another Senator, Labour's Timothy McAuliffe, a former school teacher, stated:

> Most of the people are demolishing these Big Houses, and I am not too sorry to see quite a number of them demolished, because we tried on a few occasions to make other use of them and found that we could not … they were totally out of date as regards converting them into any useful purpose. I have no regrets that these big old mansions … are going. Nobody wants them no matter how much land they have, because everywhere in the country there is the question of domestic help and you will not get anyone to come into huge barracks of houses and work in them.[18]

Nevertheless, arguments for rate reductions continued to be raised and, in a 1969 Seanad debate, the removal of rates from historic houses was again proposed. Fine Gael Senator Michael O'Higgins maintained that there were 'throughout our land fine mansions and substantial buildings that have been deroofed solely in order to avoid the payment of rates … I have seen buildings deroofed which it would have been well worthwhile preserving even for their architectural value.'[19] Charles McDonald, the Senator quoted earlier, clearly had a special interest in the preservation of these mansions, particularly those allotted to new owners, which he may have been interested in given his background in farming. Again, in a 1970 Seanad debate, he reiterated:

> In some of these old large mansions the only effective way of having the rates reduced is to take the roof off the building. Surely this is not in the national interest? … Most of these mansions have been reallocated by the Land Commission and to a great extent they are not occupied by the very wealthy owners for whom they were built. In order to preserve some of these very fine buildings in this category of ownership we should do something to alleviate the burden.[20]

This argument proposing that rates were the primary cause behind the ruin of many houses was one that was refuted by the Commissioner of Valuation in the previous chapter.[21] In contrast, though, the Department of Finance thought that, while it may not have been the cause of abandonment by the original owners, it was certainly influential for ordinary farmers who received houses on land from the Land Commission.[22] However, such cases may have been infrequent. Patrick J. Sammon has claimed that the Land Commission did not allocate houses that would be too big for ordinary migrants and instead tried to sell such mansions.[23]

NATIONAL AND EUROPEAN HERITAGE

By the 1960s, the government realised that appropriating country houses into the canon of Irish heritage could be economically valuable to the state owing to their growing tourism appeal. Therefore, from the 1970s onward, there were increasing arguments hailing them as buildings of great artistic merit and interest and as part of the national heritage. Terence Dooley has elucidated on the importance of this classification in the Irish context. He stated:

> Heritage can be used to exclude as well as include, and in the early years of independence ascendancy cultural artefacts were not presented as an acceptable part of 'a narrative of national achievement'[24]… So, there remained for decades the widely

held perception that the architectural grandeur of the eighteenth and early nineteenth centuries symbolised the dominant elitism of landlords built to the impoverishment of the Irish people. Historical associations overrode architectural significance.[25]

This attitude had been gradually changing – much influenced during this period by an increasing awareness of Ireland's place in Europe and catalysed by attempts to join the EEC, of which successive Irish governments were eager to become part. There were many economic benefits to be gained from membership, not least the large grants available through Europe, particularly to the farming sector and the large subsidy programmes for which they would be eligible under the Common Agricultural Policy. Yet, when Ireland first began to sound out the possibility of their membership, the dominant developed economies of the EEC were not sure that Ireland was suitable for membership, given its agriculture-based economy, its policy of protectionism, its dependence on the British market, and the poverty, unemployment, and emigration that were still crippling the country.[26] Additionally, the Irish government's decision to remain neutral during the Second World War was not popular. As a result, Ireland's first application to join the EEC in July 1961 was rejected after just a few weeks.[27] Enda Delaney has argued that, despite this, and while 'Ireland would have to wait a decade for entry … this did not stop its focus gradually turning from the Anglo-Irish and the global to the European in the enforced interim.'[28] In addition, after the introduction of the measures and economic plans detailed earlier, in attempts both to improve the economy and prove to Europe that Ireland was willing to embrace a broader policy in its relations with other countries, the Fianna Fáil government continued to press for EEC membership.

In 1972, the Treaty of Accession was signed. This was put to the Irish people in a referendum the same year, passed by 83 per cent,[29] and it came into force on 1 January 1973. Its overwhelming acceptance by the Irish people, and its enthusiastic espousal by the government, marked a substantial shift in policy. It was a radical departure from an Ireland that, in the decades following independence and particularly during the years of Fianna Fáil dominance, had taken such a hard-line nationalist and protectionist viewpoint to outside interests. Accession meant a softening of this blinkered nationalist view, in which any opinions deemed anti-nationalist were unwelcome. This was replaced by a situation where, from this time onward, tentative arguments for the preservation of country houses, for example, could be voiced without an automatic subtext that 'foreign' or 'British' architecture was being protected.[30]

As early as 1961, the European heritage aspect of these buildings began to be stressed. In a 1961 Seanad debate, Professor William Stanford argued: 'we have had tourists coming over purely to see the Georgian houses and the gardens of Ireland. I hope we will do all we can ... to preserve their amenities.'[31] Senator Denis Burke was even stronger in his beliefs, stating that, although there might be disagreement with the history behind the building of country houses, they were now something that could be objects of pride. He maintained, 'our Georgian houses are part of our heritage. Some of these houses are wonderful examples of architecture, decoration and stucco work. Great European artists and architects worked on many of them. We should now use them as tourist potential because they have become our heritage.'[32] These calls for their preservation were often based on a realisation of their possible economic value to the country. To make their preservation justifiable, and to make it possible for them to be promoted as part of Irish heritage to tourists, basic attitudes and the rhetoric surrounding these houses had to change. Pushed by such considerations as tourism potential and pressure from Europe to preserve the built heritage, country houses were re-imagined and re-presented as Irish heritage. They were reclaimed as a rightful part of Irish history and were set outside the usual negative stranglehold of Anglo-Irish relations. Instead, the British origins of such houses were often ignored and, instead, either their Irish or European influences were brought to the fore and highlighted.[33] Claiming the country house as part of the Irish national heritage in the 1960s and 1970s was possible only possible because the concept of national heritage and the nation itself are malleable categories, the boundaries of which can be set by those in control of their definition to suit the needs of a particular time.[34]

Justifying their inclusion were arguments that stressed that such buildings must be preserved as examples of a turbulent period of national history, or as symbols of an unpleasant past, thereby encouraging their preservation without necessarily celebrating them or their presence. For example, in 1962, Fine Gael TD James Dillon discussed the acquisition by the National Library of the Gormanstown register, a book that registered the title deeds of the Lords of Gormanstown. He stated:

> If the papers had not been found and finally deposited with the National Library that side of the story might have perished altogether, the story of a landlord ... these old family documents constitute a very vital and essential part of the social history of our people ... We should not be such fools as to suffer these treasures to perish simply because we associate them with a source of which we have bitter memories.[35]

Lord Henry Mountcharles has also maintained: 'I'm not going to deny what tradition I'm from. Part of the journey that we have to make as a nation is to embrace all aspects of our history'.[36] Fine Gael TD for Dublin South-Central, Maurice E. Dockrell, expressed similar sentiments in 1963, arguing:

> We have all sorts of lovely monuments in Ireland, some of which may be associated with various sad periods of our history. That, however, does not mean necessarily they were always associated with sad periods. Still less does it mean that the men who built and designed these beautiful buildings were not in themselves Irish architects or Irish craftsmen or Irish workmen. Therefore it is very good to see that we are proud of these things of the past, proud of what Irishmen, and, I am sure, Irishwomen too, did in building them and maintaining them and that we are going to hand on the beautiful and interesting things of the past.[37]

Dooley has similarly argued that champions of the country house in Ireland realised by the 1960s that the clue to unlocking political and public mindsets on this issue was to re-imagine the country house as part of the national patrimony.[38] The way was opened for country houses to be given state grants and allowances in later years and be promoted as an Irish tourist attraction. Also influential in this re-imagining of the country house was the pressure on the state to preserve such architectural heritage by the EEC, thereafter the European Union (EU). In 1976, Ireland was the only EEC member without an official national-buildings record.[39] The state was also subject to the United Nations Educational, Scientific and Cultural Organization (UNESCO) Convention Concerning the Protection of the World Cultural and National Heritage, signed in Granada in 1985, but which the Irish Government were almost ten years late in ratifying in 1994.

An article in the *Connacht Tribune* in 1977 portrays the country house as an example of Irish craftsmanship, and so we can deduce that this part of Irish national history was gaining widespread currency. It reported that the survival of the country house appeared 'fairly secure', but that the same was not true for the 'grand house' – the very large country houses, which, the paper argued, had the best architecture but had clearly outlived their function and were justly stripped of their lands. The article still deemed the disappearance of a country house as 'lamentable and a tragedy', as was the loss of contents, giving Malahide Castle and Clonbrock, Co. Galway, as examples. It reported that during the last 50 years the state had been offered 'many houses', 'that it has generally refused', including Russborough in 1929 and Malahide in 1973, and concluded:

> It would seem that as far as heritage is concerned the best solution to the houses question is state ownership … but the state are none too eager to accept houses, even when given as gifts. But it is encouraging that in March the Taoiseach accepted Barretstown Castle and in the same month the Board of Works accepted responsibility for the upkeep of Muckross House, Co. Kerry.[40]

The state already kept one Georgian 'folly' as a national monument, the paper reported, referring to the Casino at Marino, and continued, 'perhaps this is the heralding in of a bright new future for these great monuments to Irish crafts-manship – remember that these houses were physically erected by Irishmen – let us hope so.'[41] In the Dáil in 1978, Fine Gael TD for Donegal, James White, announced that 'it is a national crime to have some of the stately homes of the past fall into ruins.'[42]

This change in attitude related strongly to the shift in Ireland's perception of itself in relation to Britain and Europe. Brian Girvin and Gary Murphy have concluded that Ireland's attempts to become integrated into the international economy through accession to the EEC had two significant consequences of long-term importance:

> In the short-run it made Ireland very dependent on Britain, because without the United Kingdom's good will Ireland could and would not have gained entry. But it also shifted policy outwards in a more fundamental fashion than had previously been the case. Policy makers now recognised that Europe was the object of policy and this was quickly internalised. In this respect Ireland had been more pro-European than Britain because in the 1960s it had limited options ...[43]

The internalisation of the fact that a good relationship with Britain was of posi-tive benefit to Ireland, and the shift in focus from Britain to Europe, influenced a softening of attitudes towards the country house. The focus shift to Europe meant that to hold antagonistic attitudes towards these houses because they were owned by those who were often still considered foreign was now looked on as a rather archaic and xenophobic view. Politicians and the media were anxious to distance themselves from this view by championing the cause of the country house.

Such attempts to reconstitute the meaning of historical architecture from the period of British rule can also be seen in debates surrounding the utilisation of Dublin Castle. This illustrates that it was not deemed necessary to blot out such architectural heritage. It reveals that an emerging sense of such buildings' architectural, artistic, or historical importance, removed from bitter memories, was taking place more generally rather than just in relation to the country house. In a 1963 Dáil debate, there was a deliberation over whether Dublin Castle should be restored. Fianna Fáil TD for Sligo-Leitrim, James Gallagher, argued:

> These buildings are national monuments and their restoration and maintenance is necessary. They can be looked on with pride. These centres of alien rule must be preserved as a monument to the wonderful effects of the people who fought for and

obtained our freedom. Instead of putting a torch to these buildings as was done in the past, we should restore them as memorials to our martyrs.[44]

This bears the marks of the post-colonial archetype where, although some monuments are destroyed to erase the memory of the colonial regime, others are appropriated by the former colonised people themselves, in order not merely to erase but to take control. This can be seen in the cases of Dublin Castle or Leinster House in Dublin. The structure can then be transformed into a symbol of 'native' victory and freedom, as is illustrated in the rhetoric surrounding the construction of these houses, portrayed as though they were almost completely the work of Irish labour, craft and design.

Discussing such colonial transitions, Luke Gibbons has supported Thomas McEvilley's overview of the four stages of cultural formation as an accurate model that identifies first, an idyllic pre-colonial period, which subsequently becomes the subject of nationalist nostalgia; second, the 'ordeal' of conquest, alienation and oppression; third, a nationalist movement that vilifies the coloniser and attempts to reclaim some kind of original identity; and fourth, the stage ushered in by generations born after the departure of the colonising forces and which is therefore less concerned with opposition to the colonial legacy.[45] The third stage of this model was in evidence in the Irish case in the years following independence, when the coloniser and all associated with it was denigrated. Indications of this transition can be seen from the late 1950s and 1960s when the temporal remove, to the latter stage, meant that not all politicians had necessarily been directly involved in the struggle, nor did every political debate descend into arguments over the conflict. This allowed for a new attitude toward the 'remnants' of the colonial regime, including the country house.

This phenomenon can be seen in its nascent form as early as the 1940s when, as has been shown, arguments began to surface suggesting that country houses could be put to some national use. By the 1950s and 1960s, the preservation of these buildings could even be reasoned for on the basis of their own merits, simply in terms of architecture or historic interest. At this time, the Historic Irish Tourist Houses Association (HITHA) was formed, with owners realising that the increasing tourism potential of their houses and the growing acceptance of them by the domestic population could also be of economic benefit. In 1970, the *Irish Times* reported that Bord Fáilte had initially been wary of the scheme, but was now giving grants to the association.[46] This was presumably influenced by the fact that Bord Fáilte's 1970 figures showed that numbers visiting Irish country houses and gardens had been increasing and they realised the potential for them as draws for domestic and international visitors.[47] This manifested itself in greater investments aimed at the expansion of the fledgling tourist market in Ireland. Dermot Keogh has shown how, if the policy of an open market economy were to develop, then Ireland had to modernise its economy and find new markets with which to trade. To that end, 'there had been imaginative developments in tourism and travel, including the success of Aer Lingus and, in particular, its transatlantic route.'[48]

Dooley has also emphasised that the government did not invest in preservation 'until around the 1970s when the tourist industry realised the potential of country houses, but even then it was primarily those such as Muckross, Killarney House or Glenveagh in Donegal that came with attractive gardens and large parklands.'[49] The tourism potential of the country house itself was highlighted in a letter to the *Irish Times* in 1971. The correspondent wrote:

> One cannot help regretting the demolition and decay of Coole. What other nation would allow the cradle of its modern literature to be so neglected? But something can yet be salvaged. Fortunately, much of Coole Park is still the property of the nation. It must be preserved if we claim to be a civilised people. But even for material reasons, it is worth restoring as a valuable tourist attraction.[50]

This representation of the house as a useful economic asset to localities and the country was crucial in its increasing acceptance as a part of heritage worthy of preservation. Owners, too, realised – and had to realise in most cases due to financial difficulties – the tourism potential of their houses. Ireland's Blue Book, an association of country houses, historic hotels and restaurants, was formed in 1974 as an umbrella organisation for the many historic house owners who were now keeping their properties viable by turning them into authentic country house accommodation, with families who once were served now offering to serve within the walls of the same house. In contrast, while the country house in Ireland was only beginning to open its doors to tourism in the 1970s and later, in England the concern at this time was whether the tourist industry alone, which had been developing since the beginning of the century, was sufficient to sustain the country house. Peter Mandler has argued that the motivation in 1972 behind commissioning an independent study of the economic position of the country house by the British Tourist Authority's Historic Houses Committee (BTAHHC) was owners' concern about growing dependence on tourism. The BTAHHC wished to explore the case for further tax exemptions, illustrating that tourism revenue alone was not sufficient to ensure a viable future for these houses.[51]

TOURISM POTENTIAL AND COUNTRY HOUSES IN STATE CARE

Irish governments were slow to realise the tourism potential of country houses in their ownership, although this was also influenced by the fact that a significant domestic tourism interest was not evident for these houses until the 1970s at the earliest. Some houses that the government had acquired were put to use, such as Johnstown Castle, County Wexford, and Shelton Abbey, County Wicklow, mentioned previously, as an agricultural centre and an open prison respectively. The historic Georgian buildings the government had acquired in Dublin were also being put to use as offices for government departments or, in the case of Leinster House, as the seat of Parliament. They were not so imaginative in finding uses for other buildings in their care. The Royal Hospital Kilmainham in Dublin remained vacant in state ownership for many years. So too did Muckross House, which was acquired in 1932, as has been documented in Chapter Two.

In 1962, Seán Lemass, then Taoiseach, sought to address the situation of the latter property, concerned about the fact that Muckross had been unused in possession of the state for 30 years. He wrote to Donough O'Malley, Parliamentary Secretary to the Minister for Finance: 'I am sure that you agree that we should try to reach an early decision on the future use of Muckross House'.[52] Lemass explained that a suggestion had been made by the Institute of Public Administration to make Muckross House a conference centre and, when required, an overflow for the Great Southern Hotel.[53] In his opinion, this suggestion had much to recommend it and the Department of Finance had said it would take relatively little expenditure.[54] On 2 May, O'Malley replied to Lemass listing some provisional estimates for such a scheme.[55] He added:

> I have always thought it a pity that such a fine house as Muckross should be unoccupied. I know that other suggestions for using it have been made but since none of them seems likely to reach maturity I favour the broad idea of adopting the building for use as a residential conference centre. If you so wished we could see whether a presidential suite could be worked into the design for the use of the President, or other distinguished persons.[56]

On 16 May 1962, Erskine Childers, Minister for Transport and Power, wrote to Lemass discouraging this proposal. He explained: 'I have recently been considering the position of Muckross House because I feel it is a pity to see such a splendid building being put to no use. As you know because of our history there is far too little to see in Ireland. Most of the abbeys and castles are in ruins.

We need more presentation of the Irish image.'[57] It has already been seen in Chapter Five that Childers was vocal in enquiring as to the possible preservation of French Park, County Roscommon, and pressing for a government policy on the preservation of these houses when Minister for Lands in the late 1950s. This intervention over Muckross House runs parallel with the fact that, at this time, he was the Minister responsible for pushing the government to approve the demolition of Georgian houses in Fitzwilliam Street by the Electricity Supply Board (ESB) in order to build a new office block. It suggests that there was much more pressure being brought to bear on him and the government than may have previously been thought, given his views on the value of such architecture in every other case.

Childers's proposal was to use Muckross as a museum of Irish heritage and he believed it would be the ideal location as it was in a national park in a renowned tourist area and would provide an added attraction to the gardens, as well as meeting the need for a heritage museum.[58] In his opinion, this proposal would be more in keeping with the intentions of the donor than would the Institute for Public Administration (IPA) project.[59] At the same time, the IPA's Centre for Administrative Studies elaborated on their proposal that 'to meet the problem of an effective overall programme of courses, it is proposed that the state should give to the Institute as a centre for this activity Muckross House, Killarney.'[60] It noted that, apart from modernisation of facilities, a new bedroom block would need to be erected, thus enabling the house to act as a 'supplement to hotel accommodation in Killarney', the limits of which in the summer hampered the tourist trade as a whole.[61] They hoped that their suggestion would be considered a suitable proposal 'for this so long idle piece of state property'.[62]

Despite all these suggestions, no definitive decision was taken at this time. It was local concern over the utilisation of the house that motivated a public meeting in Killarney in December 1963 to debate the issue. At the meeting, Frank Hilliard suggested that the house should be used as a folk museum and the idea was enthusiastically received.[63] As a result, a sub-committee of the Killarney Tourist Industry Coordinating Committee was established to explore the feasibility of the matter. Following discussions with Minister for Finance, Dr James Ryan, the Committee was granted Muckross House for an initial trial period of five months and the house was first opened to the public in June 1964 on the efforts of private local initiative, not state intervention. In that first short season, 19,500 visitors passed through its doors.[64] Having demonstrated that it could successfully manage the house, the Committee was granted a further ten-year lease, on condition that the Committee became a limited company, and in May 1965, the Trustees of Muckross House (Killarney) Ltd., was incorporated.[65] The success of their scheme was evident, and the interest in seeing inside these houses was demonstrated. In October 1964, the *Irish Press* reported that almost 20,000 people from over 40 countries had visited Muckross House since it had been opened in June of that year, illustrating to the government that these houses could now be viably used as tourist attractions, and were therefore economic assets, in themselves.[66]

In spite of this, the Fianna Fáil government was unsure of this potential in relation to another house in County Kerry, which for many years they had been pressed to preserve. Earlier in this period, a trust had acquired Derrynane House, Caherdaniel, County Kerry, in order to preserve it as a memorial to its former owner, 'The Liberator', Daniel O'Connell. They soon ran into financial difficulty and frequently sought governmental aid. For example, in October 1949, Sylvester O'Brien of the Derrynane Trust explained that to pay for even a portion of the restoration work, the Trust were already short and had no prospect of getting the money by public subscription. National enthusiasm for such projects appeared to be waning. The Trust concluded that if it must fall, it would only be because they were powerless to prevent it: 'the public is apathetic, yet it will be a shame if this generation does not save Derrynane'.[67] O'Brien conceded that, without government assistance, he did not know how the Trust could save it.[68] In September 1959, M. A. Purcell, Secretary of Bord Fáilte, wrote to the Assistant Secretary of the Department of the Taoiseach, Dr N. Ó Nualláin, noting that representations for financial assistance had first been made to the Board as far back as 1952. At that time, the Department of Industry and Commerce had informed them that, if the Board were unable to give assistance, the Minister for Finance was prepared to make available an Exchequer contribution. A state grant of £5,000 was given.[69] The association of the house with O'Connell must have been the motivating factor here as it was not normal practice for the Department of Finance to grant special contributions towards the upkeep of country houses and it does not appear to have been done for any other house examined in this book. In fact, Derrynane was not one of the larger or most spectacular examples of historic houses in the country and therefore, from an architectural heritage point of view, it was less worthy of grants in aid than some other houses that were destroyed in the 1950s. Purcell, Secretary of Bord Fáilte also acknowledged this as he wrote:

> The board has not felt that Derrynane House is of real significance as a tourist attraction, while appreciating that its preservation is desirable for wider national reasons. In addition, the bord's [*sic*] policy, for a number of reasons, is to avoid involvement in

annual outgoings and to concentrate on capital grants and make arrangements with other bodies, e.g. local authorities, for maintenance expenses.[70]

Therefore, the initiation of an annual grant for an indefinite period would be a new departure from this policy and he added: 'from a tourism point of view it is questionable whether the Derrynane case merits exceptional treatment'.[71]

The Secretary of Bord Fáilte conceded that, owing to the Taoiseach's interest in the building, the Board was anxious to contribute. If a realistic scheme could be worked out with the Trust to estimate the costs of making Derrynane House a worthwhile and exploitable tourist attraction, the Board would be happy to do what it could within the limits of its funds.[72] In this respect, it was pointed out that the Board's budget for the year for all national monuments work was only £5,000. In October, the Trust sought an annual grant of the same figure, £5,000, to maintain this one property, Derrynane, highlighting again the exceptional outlay expended on Derrynane in contrast to most country houses in this period.[73] Given the large costs involved and the reluctance of the state to keep giving large grants to private trusts, the Trust eventually advertised the property for sale.[74] In 1963, after no buyers came forward, the government took over the house from the Trust, possibly due to the interest Lemass, and particularly de Valera, appeared to take in the property. On 21 August 1967, *The Irish Press* reported that de Valera had declared Derrynane House open as a public monument. Following restoration, Derrynane National Historic Park was later officially opened by President Cearbhall Ó Dálaigh – on the bicentenary of O'Connell's birth in 1975 – and continues to be administered by the OPW to this day.[75]

Interestingly, *The Irish Press* concentrated their report on the state acquisition of Derrynane with justifications for why O'Connell would have owned a country house.[76] They emphasised that 'the architecture and construction were a matter for local labour and the house was in no way pretentious, although it had to accommodate Dónal [Daniel's great uncle], his wife, twenty-two children and innumerable followers.'[77] The paper believed that when O'Connell inherited, 'his public position forced him to turn the locally imposing 80-year-old mansion into something grander, something that would not produce a smirk or a sneer on the faces of the international figures.'[78] It is notable that, in 1964, the newspaper felt it had to justify O'Connell's ownership of a country house, indicating that it would not do the cause to preserve Derrynane any favours to be seen as a campaign to preserve a country house of the ascendancy class. This suggests that there was still a portion of the public who had not yet bought into the reconstitution of the country house as Irish heritage.

GOVERNMENT PRIORITIES

In Ireland, as in Britain, there were many more demanding social issues that took priority over the country house 'problem' during this period. Dooley has stressed the importance of this wider context within which the government addressed the country house issue. He argued that the Irish government was:

> Forced for decades after independence to wear a financial straitjacket. There could be no expenditure on the preservation of country houses when so many other social issues had to be addressed … Social priority was most clearly articulated in the Dáil chambers in 1970 by Kevin Boland, then Fianna Fáil Minister for local government, in his now infamous 'belted earls speech'.[79] Much quoted as an attack on the Irish Georgian Society and its supporters, this speech is best understood in the context of its time.[80]

Dooley was right to assert the importance of context in this regard, as this speech is often seen simply as criticism directed toward the Irish Georgian Society (IGS). However, as Dooley stresses, in this address, Fianna Fáil TD for Dublin County and Minister for Local Government, Kevin Boland, unequivocally emphasised the validity the place of urban and rural Georgian architecture had within the canon of national heritage and also elucidated on his own personal appreciation for its merits. He argued that it was desirable to preserve as much as was possible of the Georgian buildings in Dublin city, as well as throughout the country and acknowledged fully they were part of the national heritage. He stressed, however, that they were 'part' only and therefore he would give such preservation efforts whatever assistance he could 'so long as it does not entail any diversion of scarce capital resources from what I consider the more important matters of housing and sanitary services.'[81]

Unyielding in this belief, Boland proclaimed, albeit rather derogatorily to those involved in the IGS and the protests over the demolition of Georgian houses in Dublin, that

> I make no apology whatever for saying that the physical needs of the people must get priority over the aesthetic needs of Lord and Lady Guinness and Deputies Dr FitzGerald, Dr Browne, Desmond and all the other deputy doctors … desirable as is the preservation of old buildings of architectural merit, while I am Minister for Local Government and while the needs of the people for housing, water and sewerage services remain unfulfilled, not one penny of the capital allocation that it is possible to make available to my department will be spent on such preservation, desirable as it is. That is not to say that every possible effort should not be made to conserve as much as is feasible of this part of our national heritage for as long as possible.[82]

CHANGING ATTITUDES

The 1960s was a decade of radical changes on many fronts. The introduction of free secondary school education for all and the development of the leisure and tourism industries were both catalysts and results of these changes.[83] In addition, the numbers emigrating dropped in the 1960s from the exceptionally high levels of the 1940s and 1950s.[84] Brian Girvin and Gary Murphy, editors of a volume largely celebrating Lemass' impact, were of the view that 'Lemass largely reforged Ireland after he came to office in 1959.'[85] They argued that de Valera had been a constant constraint until he retired as Taoiseach and leader of Fianna Fáil in 1959. As such, 'the years between 1945 and 1959 were to all intents and purposes lost years for Ireland. During this time the crisis got worse and the introduction of new policies was postponed. Indeed, it was the depth of the crisis that provided Lemass with his opportunity in 1959 when he succeeded de Valera.'[86]

John Horgan agreed with this claim as to the uniqueness of Lemass' period in office and added that 'the main foci of policy formulation in the late 1960s and early 1970s ... were effectively environmental: the Northern crisis after 1969, and the economic crises of the mid-1970s.'[87] The Troubles in the North are an important and neglected factor in the relationship of those living in southern Ireland to the country house and their inhabitants. The Troubles were in many ways a double-edged sword for the country house. For certain owners, particularly near border counties, the Troubles once again highlighted that, to some, they would always be seen as a foreign presence. Lord Henry Mountcharles of Slane Castle, County Meath, described how, during this time, he was preparing to hold the first concert at Slane Castle, which has now become synonymous with such events. This coincided with the time of hunger strikes in the North and the death of Bobby Sands. He has described how 'it was an extremely difficult time ... Here was this Anglo-Irish guy trying to put on a concert in his estate when there were black flags [in support of the hunger strikers] flying in the village of Slane and graffiti written on our gates – "Brits out" and worse – that my children would see on their way to school.'[88] Despite such perceptions, Lord Mountcharles is clear in his own mind about his nationality: 'we're Irish – I was born in Dublin. We come from a family that fought on both sides of the Battle of the Boyne, but to many I was just a west Brit.'[89]

On the other hand, when the Troubles in the North began to intensify in the late 1960s and early 1970s, and as the violence and death rates increased, many living in the south also sought to distance themselves from such views, shocked by the violence in the North. The effects of this attitudinal change can be seen in the decrease in popularity of Easter Rising commemorations from the 1970s onwards. To be a nationalist now meant an entirely different thing and many in the south swung to the other side, anxious to assert their distance from such radical and violent extremism. The country house in the 26 counties was to be an unwitting beneficiary of such a swing and, from the 1970s, arguments that these houses should not be preserved on historical and anti-British grounds became rare.

At the same time, the field of national architectural and art history, itself a growing area, started to celebrate the country house. From the 1970s, books were published that championed the cause for recognition of the importance of these houses. Their publication also illustrated the increasing public interest in this topic. Such works included Desmond Guinness and William Ryan, *Irish Houses and Castles*, which was published in 1971, Mark Bence-Jones' *Twilight of the Ascendancy* released in 1987, and his *A Guide to Irish County Houses* published a year later, while in the same year Desmond FitzGerald, David Griffin and Nicholas Robinson's *Vanishing Country Houses of Ireland* appeared. [90] Most of these books were written by a group of aesthetes who began to take up the cause of the preservation of the country house in Ireland, and were some of the first to do so. This passion was formalised with the formation of the IGS in 1958, established by Desmond Guinness and his wife Mariga. The aim of the society was to assist in the recognition of the value and the preservation of Georgian architecture, both through restoring buildings and giving grants to maintain others. The first major acquisition by the society was the purchase of Castletown in 1967, although by the time they took it over many of the original contents of the house had been sold. By the late 1970s, the Castletown Foundation assumed ownership of the house from the IGS and numerous original contents were recovered. These were on display when Castletown became the first country house in Leinster to open its doors to the public. [91] The IGS and other small lobby groups of interested parties began to make a real mark in the 1950s in terms of highlighting the importance of retaining country houses (and urban historic properties), and were followed in later decades by figures such as Desmond Fitzgerald, Knight of Glin, and Professor Kevin B. Nowlan. [92] Dooley admits that they continued to face a number of major obstacles, in particular the government's taxation policy toward country houses and their owners. [93] Although the IGS was founded on aesthetic, not political grounds, Comerford has described how it quickly devolved into an organisation that was viewed as having entrenched dogmatic attitudes. In his opinion, these developed in opposition to the challenge they faced from national governments, perhaps understandably, but certainly to their disadvantage. Instead of the commercial ambitions of a government intent of the pursuit of anything that sniffed of modern development, they developed a diametrically opposed, 'uncompromising notion of preservation, or restoration to a supposed pristine state.'[94] Comerford notes how, in fact, 'opposition in these terms suited developers very well because it could be depicted as cranky or simply unrealistic.'[95]

Dooley has similarly maintained that, while there were indications of a change in attitudes toward these houses in this period at least in rhetoric, this was still only a cause being championed, albeit for the first time, by a minority. He argued that there remained a dichotomy in Irish society between 'the minority who viewed historic houses as the creations of master architects and craftsmen, cultural artefacts worth preserving for future generations, and the majority who would quite gladly have seen them razed to the ground' either through apathy or else perceptions of the houses as symbolic of colonial oppression.[96] One figure who continued to represent virulently nationalist ideals in rhetorical flourishes, at least into the early 1960s, was Fine Gael TD for Meath, Captain Giles, who in 1961 argued that a landed estate 'should belong to the Irish people. I hope the Land Commission will take it over and that decent people will be planted on it and that the old house on it will be blown sky-high.'[97] In the same year, referring to the Anglo-Irish class, he argued that 'throughout the country … sons of the exploiters are forming game protection associations in many areas … It is time that we stopped taking our hats off to them and bowing and scraping. Our game laws should be in the hands of the Irish farmers and not under the control of the exploiter.'[98] In a similar vein, in a debate on lands, Michael Donnellan, Clann na Talmhan TD for Galway North, argued: 'that it is not the remnants of the landlord class that count in the country'.[99] Giles was, however, one of the most openly antagonistic deputies toward these houses surviving with their original owners in this period.

On the other hand, calls for an appreciation of the merits of such architecture from An Taisce and the IGS were becoming tarnished, as the latter in particular was gaining a reputation as an upper-class club. In reality, preservation of Georgian architecture, especially concessions for those still used as private mansions, remained, at best, unimportant to the majority of the population. In 1968, the *Irish Times* criticised what it saw as Fianna Fáil's antagonistic party line on preserving Georgian architecture because of the upper class stigma attached to it. They maintained:

This was the kind of shoneen patriotism that gutted rural Ireland of many fine mansions and many valuable collections of old books and manuscripts: today some of the arsonists of those days recognised the artistic vandalism they perpetrated yet their whizz-kid sons, now in the cumainn, see it as no crime against an ancient nation to pull down an architectural heritage of houses or waterways in the interests of an economic society and party political advantage. The Georgian sponsorship of Desmond Guinness was, after all, a blessing: he was comfortably 'Big House' and was only one against the hungry peasant-punters who controlled the political riches at the polling booth.[100]

PERCEPTIONS OF COUNTRY HOUSE OWNERS

Media coverage in this period highlighted that, while there may have been a softening in attitudes towards country houses as historical buildings, there was no such reprieve in antagonistic attitudes towards their owners from some sections of the population. In 1964, General Tom Barry, who had been the commander of a flying column in Cork during the revolutionary period, protested at the Earl of Rosse, owner of Birr Castle, receiving an invitation to open the International Choral Festival in Cork. Barry maintained that he and his supporters were 'making a dignified protest against their betrayal and their history and insult to their people.'[101] He said the Earl was part of 'the lords of conquest' and they did not want him put forward as a representative of the Irish people to visitors from other countries.[102] In spite of this, the *Sunday Independent* reported that the Cork Tóstal Committee were standing by their decision, while in a letter to the editor a correspondent wrote: 'Tom Barry has not and did not object to the worthy Earl (quite an anachronism in this modern age and "Republic") on account of his religion or race. He simply objected to this individual because he represents the ascendancy class, nothing less, nothing more.'[103] Another letter berated the *Irish Times*, stating: 'your leading article on the subject of Tom Barry's objection to Lord Rosse, exemplifies the West British outlook which is expected of you.'[104] The correspondent argued that 'General Barry based his objection on the fact that Lord Rosse is a member of a class which oppressed and exploited the Irish people for centuries, that was and is, socially and culturally, a foreign colonial minority. He contends that the earl is thus an unsuitable person to represent the people of Cork or Ireland on an occasion of international significance.'[105]

Further illustrating that this was not just the particular complaint of one or two individuals, at the opening of the festival it was reported that

some 200 students ... from University College Cork marched from the college to
the City Hall, carrying banners which said: 'Go home Rosse, Cork does not want
you'; 'Lords of the conquest not wanted in Ireland'; 'Who banned our Irish culture? –
British lords'; 'Why not a citizen of Cork to open a Cork festival?'; and '1920 British
murder gang in Cork – 1964 British Earl is welcomed in Cork, why?'[106]

Despite this, the *Irish Times* also recorded that such attitudes were not universal
and 'the entry of the Earl of Rosse and the Lord Mayor to the concert hall was
greeted with loud applause and each was given a big ovation when he spoke
subsequently'.[107] The Earl took the opportunity to counter arguments raised by
the protest. In his address he stated:

> I cannot allow a statement insinuating that I am not an Irishman ... I am Irish, my
> family came here first about twenty years before the Mayflower went to America, and
> if I am not Irish there is no American who is not a Red Indian. Another point I would
> like to make is that my family have never been aggressors. They have always sought
> to work for Ireland according to their best lights, and the only member of my family
> who ever took a prominent part in politics, was my great-grandfather, who was one of
> the leaders against the Act of Union and was a great friend of Wolfe Tone. I mention
> that, because I think I have as good a right to be called an Irish man as anyone else.[108]

It is interesting that many country house families had the luxury of being able to
prove their family lineage extended far back in Irish history, often to plantation
times. In contrast, the ordinary Irish citizen could not prove that their 'Irishness'
went back centuries as they did not have ancestral homes that remained in families for hundreds of years, nor the finances to keep records regarding family
history. What this meant in practice is that country house families could prove
their 'Irishness' through generations, but the average worker could not. While
such organised displays of antagonism were rare, negative attitudes towards
country house owners simmered on, despite changes in attitudes towards these
houses; although, in fact, those of the class who remained in Ireland were
now barely even a perceptible presence. In 1965, the *Irish Times* recounted the
isolation of the class of country house owners that had been highlighted the
previous year at the protest in Cork, stating: 'the Big House of the past symbolised, with its surrounding high wall, the tragic isolation of a class which might
have contributed so much to their country but, with a few notable exceptions,
did not aspire to or rise to leadership'.[109]

Olwen Purdue has shown how different the situation was in Northern
Ireland. By 1960, a majority of landed families had disappeared and their
houses were no longer private homes, but a significant minority were still

living in their ancestral homes and kept their estates running through careful estate management and creative economic activity.[110] In more dramatic contrast to the position of such owners in the Republic, Purdue maintained that those who remained were sufficiently numerous 'to operate as a healthy, active social group. Their numerical density was still sufficient to provide enough social interaction with others of their class to give them a sense of belonging to a wider group, and encouraged them to remain living in Northern Ireland rather than move to Britain or further afield in search of like-minded society.'[111] Purdue has highlighted this continuing sense of living as part of a viable and vibrant group of people as an important factor in the continued survival of this class in the North, particularly compared to their counterparts in the south. This was made possible because, while in the Republic the upper-middle classes were predominately Catholic and nationalist, in Northern Ireland they were largely Protestant and unionist. They shared the same values of the landed class, with a sense of greater understanding and connection, even emulating their way of life. In this regard, Purdue has cited the example of two families, the Mulhollands and the Craigs, who acquired titles, land and country houses, 'thus helping to keep big house society alive by the infusion of new blood to replace those families that had left or died away.'[112]

The contrasting alienation of the landed class from the rest of the population in the south was highlighted in 1959 when the *Irish Farmers Journal* covered a sale of house contents and furniture. The reporter commented: 'although I lived within a townland of this Big House, I had never been inside it and I had never talked to the ladies who were the last owners. They were gentry … The old gentry and generally were a strange, lonely sort of people, living out their lives in isolation surrounded by high walls and with very little communication with the ordinary people.'[113] Interestingly, this sentiment was repeated as late as 2002 when the *Irish Times* covered an auction at Farnham House, Cavan, where it reported that 'much of the interest in the clearance of the mansion's contents stemmed from the "kudos" of owning an item from the residence … A large number of Cavan-registered cars at the event indicated that plenty of local people had come to get a look at the inside of the "big house", which they may have grown up close to, but never visited.'[114] This was the case in many localities where the country house had always been isolated from the local populace and the walls of the demesne kept owners in and locals out. In 1965 the *Irish Times* ran an article on 'West Britons' concluding: 'whatever he may once have had in common with the Britain he's west of, is now a revered illusion. In Wilson's Britain he would be an anachronism; in Lemass' Ireland he is an irrelevance ... these are part of a sub-culture in its death-throes, not only in Ireland, but in the UK ... And their decline is one of privilege, not religion.'[115] Further underlying negative attitudes towards the country house way of life were later unearthed when, in 1969, Charles Haughey, then Fianna Fáil Minister for Finance, bought the Georgian house Abbeville in Kinsealy as his private residence. The *Irish Times* reported that within Fianna Fáil 'some of its older, more Republican members were bitterly affronted by Haughey's enthusiasm for such "ascendancy" past-times [*sic.*] as hunting and horses.'[116] The paper did report, however, that it was the 'older' members of the party who held these views, pointing, perhaps, to a more enlightened new crop of politicians who benefited from their temporal remove from the revolutionary period.

In 1968, a writer to the editor of the *Irish Times* also exhibited historical grievance. In a letter entitled 'Aristocratic Sneer', the correspondent declared that not all mansions were gutted by 'rabble', but were often broken up and sold off by the gentry themselves, with contents

> Hauled off to Sotheby's or broken up *in situ* as the impoverished remnants of a dilapidated and repudiated gentry made off for the shores where the flag still flew and the natives knew their places ... libraries sold off that no 'arsonist' ever laid hands on. It was no 'rabble' broke up Castletown House, one of the marvels of Europe, and then sold the empty shell to the Georgian Society.'[117]

This letter is notable for acknowledging that, while some houses were demolished by government departments or others left to ruin because owners could not afford them, owners often took little or none of the responsibility for this decline. The mismanagement of finances or a lack of ambition and initiative in trying to keep houses going or exploit their potential as an income-producing asset – attempted in numerous inventive ways by some owners, particularly in Britain – also contributed to the demise of some houses. In addition, a refusal to acknowledge that the privileged life that had once sustained these houses had passed away, and its gentlemen and ladies now needed to work, was another factor that contributed to their decline in the early twentieth century. Other owners simply sold up and happily left a country they had never deigned to be part of when it was no longer a desirable place to live. For example, Major Bowes-Daly, the owner of Dunsandle House, County Galway, moved to South Africa and put the house on the market. Dunsandle, which had been abandoned to its fate by its owner, was sold in 1954 and in 1958 mostly demolished with only a few walls left standing.

THE CASE OF BISHOPSCOURT HOUSE

A particularly striking case of a country house that was offered to the state during this period is that of Bishopscourt House in Straffan, County Kildare. This case illuminates how state bodies acted in an individual case, the influence of individual figures at the head of government, and also to what extent the changes in wider society were influential when a country house was actually offered for state ownership. Bishopscourt in particular is useful to analyse in detail as the actions and attitudes of some state departments involved, such as the OPW and the Land Commission, appear atypical in relation to the other cases examined in Chapters Three and Five. The changes in government and extensive delays between departmental and ministerial discussions on the offer of Bishopscourt illustrate how difficult it was to reach a consensus in government when the varying relevant departments had different interests in such a property. The decline in the absolute power that the Department of Finance had held over government decisions until the late 1950s is also evident given that their recommendation was not final in this instance. This was undoubtedly one factor that led to the negotiation of this offer dragging on for many years.

Originally built by John Ponsonby, Bishopscourt had, by the 1950s, passed through numerous sales to Patricia McGillycuddy, who put the property up for sale in June 1955. The advertisements described the house as 'one of the finest Georgian houses in Ireland'.[118] The Land Commission became interested in the property and inspected the estate in September 1955. The Commission's inspector condemned the buildings, which he described as 'a "nightmarish" collection' with the mansion 'old, rambling and cavernous'.[119] He asserted: 'I do not believe any organisation or community would take on this building and … [I] regard it as a subject for the crowbar'.[120] The report found the house 'not likely to prove of much value to the Land Commission and in too poor repair to be converted into any institution at reasonable cost.'[121] It did contain 'valuable lead and saleable slates and fittings', yet the cost of demolition would have been great.[122] Negotiations for purchase began in November 1955, but two years later had not progressed and, in 1957, the property was withdrawn from sale.[123]

Almost ten years later, on 24 March 1966, Patricia McGillycuddy wrote to the Taoiseach, Seán Lemass, to offer Bishopscourt House and lands to the nation, with about 450 acres, 'so that it would be preserved intact for future generations and used for a worthy national purpose'.[124] The next day, Lemass appeared eager to accept, as government departments were asked to consider the offer 'as expeditiously as possible' because, if they saw no objection, 'the Taoiseach would like to convey acceptance ... as soon as possible ... without waiting for the completion of any detailed examination.'[125] The Department of Lands responded, referring to the 1955 Land Commission report of the buildings 'as having many shortcomings and unless they have been redecorated and reconditioned in the meantime, they could prove to be in the "white elephant" class'.[126] Similarly, the Department of Finance replied that it would be to the state's advantage to obtain possession of the lands without having to preserve the house, as reports suggested it was 'in poor condition and not worthwhile taking over'.[127] Finance Minister Jack Lynch recommended examination of the property before taking a decision and the OPW and Department of Agriculture inspected it on 27 May.

The OPW report of the house is significant, coming 11 years after the Land Commission had designated it a 'subject for the crowbar'. Their architect, G. McNicholl, considered the house to be 'extraordinarily attractive ... of considerable architectural interest and ... a splendid place for reception and entertaining ... a very beautiful and valuable property'.[128] McNicholl added that the structure appeared generally sound and concluded that, subject to reservations, it 'could be kept in good shape without excessive expenditure'.[129] In contrast, the Department of Finance noted that the agriculture report found the lands suitable, briefly mentioned the OPW's report, but concentrated on the 1955 report, concluding that a commitment to preserve the house intact for future generations 'could prove to be very onerous and expensive' and recommended that it should not be undertaken.[130] The Taoiseach's Department summarised the responses on 25 August, emphasising that the Department of Finance had highlighted three drawbacks to acceptance, namely the loss of estate duty, the cost of maintaining and staffing the house as a residence, and the liability involved in preserving it 'intact for future generations'.[131] The Taoiseach's Department admitted that 'no one would presumably favour acceptance of the liability' of the third option.[132] Comparison was made with Chevening House and Chequers in Britain which had trust funds, but there was no indication that Bishopscourt would bring a fund with it. This report concluded that acceptance or refusal should be based on whether it would be practical or desirable to maintain it as a residence for the Taoiseach or otherwise.[133]

On 30 August 1966 Lemass wrote to Patricia McGillycuddy seeking clarification on whether the government would have immediate use of the lands and if spending on preservation of the house would be at the Finance Minister's discretion. He concluded: 'subject to clarification on these points, the government are very pleased to accept your offer.'[134] Patricia McGillycuddy replied: 'I am emphatic that the preservation of the house together with its lands ... stay together'.[135] She reiterated that she was offering the entire estate on her death 'as a trust ... for the nation'.[136] In her view, Bishopscourt 'must be its own Trust – with the income from the lands, gardens, woods and their sporting rights, being ploughed back into itself'.[137] Furthermore, a workman from Sibthorpes – a firm of tradesmen and decorators in Dublin who had done some work on the roof of Bishopscourt at this time – estimated, according to Mrs McGillycuddy, that the house was 'good for another 200 years or more'.[138]

On 7 November at a government meeting, the Department of Finance recommended that the government in office at the time of Mrs McGillycuddy's death should decide on the gift, as the lands were not immediately available and such an 'unqualified commitment ... could not be agreed to at this juncture'.[139] The OPW representative agreed as he 'could not quantify the likely cost of preservation of the residence and having had some bad experience with old residences was, on the whole, pessimistic about preservation expense'.[140] As Chapter Three has shown, this attitude was typical of the OPW and their reluctance to become responsible for these houses. The Secretary General at the Department of the Taoiseach believed that Patricia McGillycuddy had not responded in such a way that the Taoiseach should change from acceptance to refusal, but the Department of Finance disagreed.

This memorandum did admit: 'the residence is a gamble. The term for its preservation is not, however, precisely defined. The 200 year ... estimate ... could ... be taken as the maximum length of the term.'[141] This is notable as in no other files on country houses that were offered to the state which have been examined as part of this study is the natural demise of the house considered in a decision on its acceptance. The memorandum also stated that the property would be useful 'if in the life of the residence it should be decided ... to provide a first class week-end or general residence for any office holder or ... accommodation for foreign guests'.[142] While it did recommend acceptance, it noted against this that 'gambles with other large residences – particularly Shelton Abbey and Johnstown Castle – have proved very costly to the state ... and could ... mean ... the liability arising from the residence could outweigh the value of the other assets of Bishopscourt.'[143] As noted previously, these two properties were given as examples in various cases of how governments' attempts to utilise country houses had not paid off, yet both are still being used for the purposes for which they were acquired by the state today. The reference to them here suggests, however, that they are costly burdens on the state to maintain. The memorandum noted additionally that to use Bishopscourt as an official residence would increase expenditure.[144]

Attached to this memorandum was a draft letter accepting the gift, although it was never sent since no agreement was reached.[145] Additionally, only three days later, on 10 November 1966, Lemass resigned as Taoiseach. The former Minister for Finance, Jack Lynch, became Taoiseach, while his post in Finance was taken over by the Minister for Agriculture, Charles Haughey. There was little delay in continuing with this case. The Department of External Affairs suggested the house 'might be used as a sort of Chequers come Blair House', as they had 'on occasion, been conscious of the absence of some such residence for … distinguished visitors'.[146] They noted that, while such occasional use would probably not justify its sole maintenance, if accepted and the lands were used, then the house would certainly be useful.[147] On 21 December a letter to the Department of Finance requested their observations 'as a matter of urgency' as 'the Taoiseach is concerned at the delay in reaching a decision on this matter'.[148]

Despite this, the issue was continually delayed with the Department of Finance[149] and a year later Patricia McGillycuddy wrote again to the Finance Minister stressing: 'if the government do not wish to proceed further with the idea of my "willing" the place to them as a "restricted gift" there is no harm done and I will proceed along an alternative route.'[150] The terms of this 'restricted gift' were 'that it should be preserved intact … for the use of the Taoiseach as is Chequers in England, and that the lands should continue to be farmed and used as one unit.'[151] The following year she wrote again to Haughey[152] and the Minister suggested negotiations were being finalised.[153] In spite of this, the Department of Finance had no record of any further discussions. The next letter from Patricia McGillycuddy was to the Taoiseach a year and a half later in December 1970, seeking his blessing that the place would become property of the nation when she died and that it would be put to use 'as a country home for the Head of Government'.[154] There was no mention that her private negotiations with the Minister for Finance had furthered the acceptance of the gift and this, along with the extremely private nature of these negotiations, is peculiar. In March 1970, Lynch had written to Haughey enquiring about developments, adding that since it had been under consideration for four years 'they should make up their mind',[155] but no response was recorded.

Haughey's involvement in this case is interesting and, in the absence of records, hard to understand. The peculiar point is, in fact, the absence of records and his unusual personal and private involvement in the case. Ordinarily, discussions like this would be handled by civil servants with the minister only advising as to the policy position overall or coming in when final approval was needed. It is unusual that a minister, particularly one with a portfolio as large, important and demanding as Finance, would personally work on this case privately and single-handedly when his brief covered issues like the national budget. One thing both his supporters and detractors would agree on is that Haughey never did things the ordinary way. He remains undoubtedly one of Ireland's most controversial politicians for many reasons and appears to have had disparate motivations and moulding forces in his life. His father was actively involved in the republican movement and Haughey himself almost ended his own political career due to his involvement in the importation of arms into Northern Ireland. On the other hand, he was also criticised for living a lavish lifestyle that often seemed to ape the Anglo-Irish aristocracy, in the end even owning his own private island. This, from a man who had told the population that they were living beyond their means, must certainly have been galling to some. Whether Haughey ever considered negotiating for the purchase of Bishopscourt to acquire it as his own residence is impossible to ascertain and certainly is only conjecture. It was at this time that Haughey bought another Georgian property that was very similar to Bishopscourt – Abbeville in Kinsealy. This means that it can at least be concluded that the purchase of a large country house just outside Dublin with all its esteemed Anglo-Irish history and even an association with horses was undoubtedly on Haughey's mind at the time, and he was obviously in the market for just such a property. While there are no records to suggest Haughey's personal interest in this case, it is interesting that there are no records on the negotiations he undertook at all. Ironically, on resigning as Taoiseach in 1992, Haughey's speech, while not about this issue, encapsulates some of the arguments around the state's involvement with the country house; while decisions on such houses are often made for economic reasons, Haughey reminded the Dáil that the government should always have a broader view of its duty. He said:

> We should always keep in our minds, too, that government has much wider dimensions than merely managing an economy. There must be concern and commitment that all shall participate in the fruits of progress, a caring attitude towards the least advantaged, a love of our heritage and culture, a desire to protect our environment, a deep attachment to the values that are precious to us.[156]

The Bishopscourt case was revisited on 26 August 1971. Following his dismissal on foot of the Arms Trial, Haughey had been replaced as Minister for Finance by George Colley. The Department of Finance suggested further discussion, adding that 'even if the lands were made available for use in a year or so, it is questionable if there is any specific need for them' and that the conditions of the gift 'could prove costly ... to implement'.[157] The Minister for Agriculture maintained that the land was required by his department and would enable them to sell off land elsewhere, the proceeds of which would cover, substantially, the cost of developing Bishopscourt,[158] while the Minister for Lands had thought that the gift had already been accepted.[159] In contrast, the Minister for Finance concluded that his department did not favour acceptance in a time of budgetary difficulty as it was an indeterminate commitment and one for decision on Mrs McGillycuddy's death.[160]

Despite this, cabinet minutes from 9 September 1971 show that 'it was decided that negotiations with a view to the early acceptance of the gift should be pursued'.[161] After further delays, at a meeting with the Attorney General in July 1973, Dermot McGillycuddy explained that his wife still wished to make Bishopscourt a gift to the nation, to be used as an Irish 'Chequers', a residence for the Taoiseach, but maintained that she did not want the state to be in a position to use it for other purposes, such as an old persons home, or for the Forestry department.[162] Dermot McGillycuddy also thought that the government should build a house for him and his wife and provide them with an income, on the basis that the state was obtaining a very valuable income-producing asset.[163] The list of conditions attached to this gift was becoming longer and certainly the absolute restrictions as to the government's use of the land and house would have been influential factors in making a decision, as the needs of governments change over time. Nor would there have been any precedent for the state to provide an income to private individuals and build a property for them in return for the gift of another. Over the next few months, Dermot McGillycuddy became increasingly impatient. He explained: 'my wife feels the situation has radically changed in the past eighteen months with the enormous escalation in the value of agricultural land, which is now making in this area, anything up to £3,000 an acre.'[164] With apparent frustration he added: 'it is difficult to farm this property at a profit in relation to its true capital value, and if the government do not feel inclined to go ahead she would probably put it on the open market.'[165] A number of months later, Dermot McGillycuddy wrote again to the Attorney General stating that his wife

> Quite understands that the government have far more in their minds at the moment than the acquisition of a country residence as a kind of Irish Chequers and that it does not seem worthwhile proceeding with the matter. She finds that life at Bishopscourt is becoming increasingly difficult due to the proximity of the property to Dublin and she is pestered daily with people looking for building sites, but as you know it has always been her main object to keep the whole estate intact.[166]

He revealed that, in an effort to do so, she had applied for planning permission to make a golf course on the field in front of the house, together with a number of houses to be built along the approach.[167] This illustrates how the value of land in the intervening years had changed and was, by 1973, much more valuable for housing development potential than it was for agricultural use.

In September 1975, the Department of the Taoiseach wrote to the Attorney General informing him that, once again, alternative proposals had been forwarded by the owner. These were either to make an outright gift to the nation of the residence and out-offices, together with approximately fifteen acres of land or, alternatively, to offer the entire property to the nation, which comprised the residence, out-offices and approximately 380 acres, on an arrangement to be agreed whereby Patricia McGillycuddy would receive a certain capital sum immediately, together with an annual yearly income.[168] Eventually, after consideration of these proposals, on 28 November 1975, the government decided not to proceed with the acquisition[169] and in February 1976, Bishopscourt was put on the market by the McGillyguddys.[170] Over 20 years after the original critical Land Commission report, the *Irish Times* described it as being 'in good condition throughout' and reported that 'a price in excess of half a million pounds would not be surprising for this property'.[171] It was purchased and, to this day, remains in private ownership, though little is known about its current use or state of repair.

CONCLUSION

Bishopscourt is a particular case study that is illuminating for an assessment of wider governmental and public attitudes to the country house in the period 1957–73. The fact that the Taoiseach, Seán Lemass, was in favour of accepting this gift is interesting and may suggest that he had a personal appreciation for such properties. If this was the case, then it also explains the personal interest he took in Derrynane and the discussions he initiated in government over the use of the long-idle Muckross House. His son-in-law, Charles Haughey, appeared to share his interest and purchased the historic Georgian house Abbeville in this period.

This government, like all others since 1922, primarily decided on such gifts to the state based on the use to which the properties could be put and their economic viability. They knew from experience that these properties were expensive to maintain. It was difficult to justify expenditure on Bishopscourt, for example, as no official residence was required, and no other use was suggested for the house. It is also true that the onerous conditions that were placed on the gift, which in the end would have amounted to the state paying the McGillycuddys a yearly income, were unprecedented and not justifiable to the government or the public. In addition, the limitations that the McGillycuddys would have imposed on the use of the house and lands would have made it difficult for the state itself to decide on the best use of the gift for public benefit without causing undue expense to the Exchequer. There is evidence of the government's progressively outward-looking policy with comparison to the stately homes maintained for such purposes in England, for example. In the case of Derrynane, the cost was also difficult for the government, although they appear to have felt obliged to preserve this property when the responsibility was asked of them and when no one else offered to take it on. This may have owed to its national historical importance and possible resulting tourism value, neither of which were associated with Bishopscourt.

The evidence presented in Chapter Five and previous chapters suggested that, predominantly, the Land Commission had an uncompromisingly practical and utilitarian policy when it came to assessing country houses on acquired lands. When the Land Commission's inspector examined Bishopscourt in 1955, he believed that it was suitable only for demolition. Yet, ten years later, the OPW's architect described it as a house of great historical and architectural significance with little evidence of rot. Chapter Three has shown that this was an unusual stance for the OPW, whose officers mostly took the view in this period that country houses could not be classified as national monuments, although similarly they did not recommend categorising Bishopscourt as a national monument, even though they appreciated its merits. It is also worth noting that while the OPW inspector was appreciative of the house as a building, they did not recommend accepting this gift. Similarly, the OPW had not recommended preserving any country houses documented in Chapter Three as national monuments. The change in staff at both organisations during this time frame must also have been an influential factor in the change of attitude displayed by both organisations in this case.

The contrast between the Land Commission's report of the house and the OPW's is striking. The Land Commission's inspector would not have been viewing the house with the same architectural scrutiny as the OPW's and therefore may have thought that it was not structurally sound when he saw any evidence of rot. If so, their reports in other cases may have been similarly flawed. If the Land Commission acquired the lands at Bishopscourt in

1955, they would have had to take on the house for which they had no use and perhaps then this report would have given them ample justification to demolish the property and get on with their primary work regarding the land. Again, this may also have been an influencing factor in other cases on their books. It is also possible that the McGillycuddys, who were not in financial difficulties, may have restored the house in the intervening ten years between the reports, given that it was their family home. This possibility would also explain why the house would appear to have been in much better condition when the OPW architect inspected it. Alternatively, the differing opinions of the Land Commission and OPW inspectors may have merely been the diverse viewpoints of the two individuals who inspected and attempted to come to a weighty recommendation based in both cases on brief inspections.

It is also significant that the OPW's report came a decade after the Land Commission's. This decade was a defining threshold for the evolution of attitudes towards the country house, not least because of Whitaker's economic plans, the establishment of the IGS and applications for, and accession to, the EEC. These developments created a context where an appreciation for historical and international architecture became more acceptable – even of 'foreign' or 'British' styles. The country house was also viewed and repackaged in a different frame as part of the European built heritage rather than as a remnant of the historically-loaded British domination of Ireland. This representation was also motivated by a new eagerness to assimilate these historical mansions into the national heritage where they were beginning to show their value as tourist attractions – something owners, too, were eager to capitalise on by opening their houses as guesthouses. The development of the tourism industry and the modernisation of the country were also factors in this period of rapidly-changing social history, not least of all with the airing of the first Irish television station in 1961, which opened up the country to outside influences like never before.

Dooley has stressed the importance of this wider context for influencing the perception, and reception, of the country house by politicians and public alike. He has cited economic prosperity, increasing urbanisation and decreasing denominalisation, as well as the introduction of free secondary education for all in 1967, as influential in loosening agrarian and religious preoccupation. These factors gradually widened support for the country-house bid to become part of the national heritage amongst an increasingly educated audience.[172] From 1957, both the temporal remove from the struggle for independence, particularly among politicians, and the psychological remove from insular protectionism and xenophobia, meant that the country house was viewed with much less hostility. The eruption of the Troubles in the North also meant that most citizens of the Republic were eager to distance themselves from any views that could be deemed nationalist – a label becoming increasingly tarred with the brush of radical and violent extremism – and the country house was the beneficiary of such attitudinal changes. Appreciation for these houses was now aired in a more welcoming atmosphere, and a minority began to fight in their corner, although the same could not be said for the original owners.

A period of history … may contain within it several possible narratives … determined by the needs and the demands and expectations of different people and different eras.

—Brian Friel, *Making History*[1]

T his book is an attempt to chart the story of the state and the country house in independent Ireland. George Bernard Shaw maintained: 'things do not happen in the form of stories and dramas and since they must all be told in some form, all reports, even by eye witnesses, all histories, all stories, all dramatic representations, are only attempts to arrange the facts in a faithful, intelligent, interesting form'.[2] After 1973, the narrative of the history of the country house changed once again and the shifts in the way Irish governments viewed them gradually progressed further. Financial relief for houses and their owners materialised in the latter decades of the twentieth century.[3] However, over 90 years after the establishment of the Free State, the threats that faced country houses then continue to challenge their survival across Ireland, Northern Ireland and Britain today. These threats can be lethal if estates are not carefully managed and economically self-sustaining. In 2017, the Beit Foundation at Russborough was forced to sell one of the most significant paintings in its collection in order to satisfy death duties owed to the British Revenue Commissioners. The battle to save these houses is likely to rage on for as long as they stand.

Today, concessions can be made towards these houses because the state is in a secure enough financial position to do so. For example, at the height of the economic boom in 1999, Farmleigh in Dublin's Phoenix Park was purchased for €29 million. Ireland was one of the richest countries in Europe at this time and therefore such an outlay was hardly noticed by the majority of the populace. The country could afford state residences without taking budgetary allocations from issues such as the poverty and lack of sanitation that were rampant in 1940s Ireland.

An examination of the attitudes of the Irish state to the country house in post-independence Ireland cannot be carried out without also charting the political, social and economic changes that took place over this time. This situates a study of the country house within the broader history of the state, and this approach provides a framework within which the changing priority of the country house issue, and public attitudes towards the demise or survival of these houses, can be understood. Throughout this book, part of the methodological approach has been to use case studies to provide an in-depth analysis of what ministers and civil servants thought of the merits of these houses. This approach also centres case studies in an analysis of the wider national issues surrounding country houses.

Most of the correspondence examined in these detailed studies is from government files, many of which have never before been examined. They are valuable primary sources, revealing for their frank appraisals and opinions. In these files, it is notable that generally civil servants and the government illustrated little or no antagonistic attitudes towards these houses. While prejudice was sometimes present, and forward enlightened thinking was often lacking, they were only some of the ingredients in the mix. Above all, in private government discussions and correspondence, practical utility and economics overrode both historical associations and architectural significance and were the most important factors affecting the survival or demise of country houses during this period. In fact, it was not narrow-mindedness that caused their destruction, but apathy and pragmatism: a belief that the issue was not the responsibility of the government. Admittedly, these are much less exciting as a cause of blame than fire, revolution or antagonism. Practical decisions were made based on the limited use of country houses, the limited budgets of the government and a prioritisation of the social and economic problems affecting the majority of citizens at that time: the same criteria in use even today.

For the Cumann na nGaedheal government that came to power in 1922, establishing the new state and its civil authority was its primary task in office and as such the decline of the country house was not considered a priority. The government and, in particular, civil servants in the Department of Finance, faced an enormous task knowing that the fledgling state could fail on financial as well as political grounds. This government would not have had the support of the public had it attempted to tackle this decline. Country houses were thought of as private homes, not national monuments or sites of historic or national heritage, and so the government did not even contemplate making their plight part of its programme. For country houses that had been damaged or destroyed during the War of Independence and Civil War, there was little compensation available; of this, there was never enough to fund the cost of rebuilding those that had been burned to the ground during the revolutionary period. These houses were now outdated and onerously expensive to maintain while their market value had also plummeted. The finances needed to cover the maintenance of country houses, let alone rebuild, were also increasingly unavailable to most owners as the land acts stripped them of their rental income from tenanted land. These acts were introduced in order to appease the wider electorate and political body for whom land redistribution was one of the most politically important issues.

In the new and economically struggling state, funding was scare. J. J. McElligott was one of the most dominant civil servants in the Department of Finance and was Secretary General from 1927 until 1953, thereby influencing government policy in relation to finance for a considerable period of time. His belief in keeping expenditure and borrowing to a minimum made his tenure in the department a time of tight budgetary control. The Department of Finance was the most influential department in government throughout the period from 1922–73 and their judgment on policy and action, made on economic grounds, was largely decisive in most cases. Increased taxation, rates and duties were enforced by the Department of Finance to enable the state to establish itself on a sound economic basis. For the owners of country houses, this proved to be one of the most detrimental factors that led to their demise in large numbers.

The frailty of the economic growth of the state and consequent difficulties for ordinary citizens was a constant throughout the period in question. The 1920s, '30s and '40s were times of great poverty and hardship for the majority of citizens with tenement slums, for example, an accepted feature of urban life. The 1950s saw economic stagnation and mass emigration, but in the 1960s and 1970s the mood improved as new economic thinking allowed the state to loosen the financial noose around its neck. At no time in the period examined in this book were the finances of the state so ebullient as to make a large budgetary allocation to heritage of any kind an easy decision. The Department of Finance was therefore usually against any such scheme, although this was not directed solely at exemptions for historic houses. When tax relief for foreign investment in the country was proposed later in this period, the department was also staunchly opposed to that suggestion.

Additionally, the concept of heritage was not one that garnered much attention, support or cabinet time in the first half of the century. Nonetheless, Cumann na nGaedheal legislated for the 1930 National Monuments Act to provide protections for monuments of national importance. In terms of dates, the legislation was not specific; however in reality it was predominantly only implemented to protect monuments dating from the seventeenth century or earlier. In any case, the OPW's annual budget was restrictively low: in 1929, for example, when it was asked to consider accepting the gift of Russborough House, County Wicklow, its budget was only £2,800 for the acquisition, repair and maintenance of all national monuments. Russborough, by contrast, would have cost an estimated £5,000 in initial acquisition costs and over half the annual budget of the OPW per annum to maintain. This made the acquisition of any country house almost impossible. Thus, the actions of OPW officials in not taking action to preserve any country house in the period from 1930–70, while certainly surprising, should be viewed with an understanding of the reality of the position and limitations within which they carried out their work.

In 1932, the 'Big House problem', as it was described in 1945 by H. G. Leask, Inspector of National Monuments, fell to the newly-elected Fianna Fáil government under Taoiseach Éamon de Valera. This government immediately sought to distance the Free State from Britain, which undoubtedly affected those in the country house who were traditionally seen as representatives of the old regime in Ireland. No act was passed with the aim of heritage protection during this period. Furthermore, while Muckross estate was acquired, chiefly for the amenity value of its parkland, no other country house was procured as a national monument. In terms of social policy, the 1933 Land Act continued, and, in many cases, completed the land division that had already taken place under the 1923 and 1931 Land Acts. The division of land contributed greatly to the decline of the country house as the land on which most were dependent for income was now almost completely gone. Some owners gave up the fight and abandoned their houses to ruin for a number of reasons: they were unable to sustain them; they did not wish to be part of the new state; they felt unwelcome; or even because of apathy toward the fate of their former residences.

Restricted by a very limited budget and staff, the OPW refused to classify any country house brought to its attention during this period as a national monument as it believed they were too modern. This was particularly true of its Inspector of National Monuments, H. G. Leask. Most of the structures that the office had previously preserved dated prior to the seventeenth century and were mostly ruins or sites that took little expenditure in terms of maintenance. The office was also anxious not to set a precedent and subsequently receive a flood of applications. It is also true that the OPW had no real public mandate, like governments, to preserve the country houses, and there was no developed domestic or international tourism industry to support these properties.

Economics were also a factor that limited the OPW in terms of their ability to acquire and preserve such properties. Nonetheless, the OPW was, at times, one of the most unsympathetic bodies to the demise of the houses. Their chairman in the 1940s, Joseph Connolly – a passionate nationalist – took an unflinchingly pragmatic approach to their preservation when he stated that the majority of country houses had to be demolished as the cost of their future maintenance would be prohibitive unless they could be put to some use. This pragmatic attitude may have filtered down through the rest of the organisation as no country house was preserved as a national monument between the advent of the National Monuments Act 1930 and the late 1960s. There were others in the government and the civil service who displayed a nativist bias that affected their views on the importance of these houses, such as the Secretary of the Department of Finance, J. J. McElligott, who was not in favour of the acquisition of Russborough due to the enormous expense involved, but also because he believed neither the house nor its owners had any real historical importance to the Irish nation. It is notable that in none of the OPW's files on country houses does it suggest asking the Department of Finance for an increased budget in light of the destruction that was taking place. The period from 1930 to 1960 was one of the most dramatic in terms of the decline, dereliction and demolition of the country house in Ireland.

The period from 1948 until 1957 was an unstable one in terms of the governance of the country as Fianna Fáil and inter-party governments regained and lost power quickly. It was also a time characterised by soaring levels of emigration. The years from 1950 to 1960 were some of the most destructive of the twentieth century for the country house in Ireland, not least of all because any owners who had attempted to retain their properties in the Free State after the stripping of their lands could no longer sustain them by this time, owing to high taxation, duties, rates, lack of income from land, and often poor returns from stocks and bonds received or invested in since the sale of land. The inter-party governments under Costello were more pro-active than previous administrations in relation to the arts and heritage more generally. During their tenures in office, the 1949 Report into the State of the Arts in Ireland was commissioned, the Arts Council was established and, in 1954, the National Monuments Act was amended. Furthermore, there were moves towards a softening of international economic relations and policy on inward investment. An Taisce and the National Monuments Advisory Council continued to press governments for changes in policy that would allow for the survival and protection of at least some country houses but, for the most part, these suggestions were never followed up by the government. The allocation of the finances or resources of the government on this issue, when the country was crippled by economic stagnation, unemployment and emigration, would have been hugely unpopular. This would have been an influential consideration for these short-lived governments who were frequently facing constituents on the campaign trail and dependent on their allegiance in elections.

An Taisce, the National Trust for Ireland, which was established by private individuals in 1948, was unable to act with regard to acquiring houses throughout this period owing to a lack of funds – they did not receive any financial help from the state – and also because these houses were so expensive to maintain. As has been illustrated, those in An Taisce continually blamed the government for their inability to act, especially as they would have received no reduction on rates on such a building if they took it over. They compared their situation to that of the English National Trust which received grants and exemptions. However, it is worth noting that the English National Trust aimed at being a self-supporting charity and also that it was able to make some of its properties economically viable since there was great interest in visiting such stately homes in England. The same was not true of Ireland at this time and it was not until after the 1970s that tourism began to develop and the government began to encourage it.

The decline, demolition and ruin of the country houses motivated a minority of interested members of the public, journalists and politicians to write to the government in the 1940s, emphasising that these houses could be put to new uses by the state as schools, hospitals or sanatoria. The government's response to this pressure – a report by the Department of Local Government into their possible use – concluded in 1945 that they were overwhelmingly unsuitable for adaptation to any public purpose. Ironically, country houses gained value for the first time in years for their salvaged materials during and after the Emergency, so that destruction and disuse became the fate of many more country houses at this time. This material helped to build factories and roads in the country when raw materials were in short supply. Alternatively, new use was often the only other salvation for the many houses that were pouring onto the market by the 1950s when governments were unwilling to preserve them on their own merits and no substantial section of the public was pressurising them to do so.

The initial break-up of landed estates under the Land Acts from 1881–1909, and subsequently the acquisition and redistribution of land, as legislated for by independent governments in the 1923, 1931 and 1933 Land Acts, made the country house in Ireland unsustainable unless another source of income could be found to adequately replace the income once generated by enormous tracts of land. Hence, the work of the Land Commission was undoubtedly one of the most significant factors in the demise of the country house in Ireland. The acquisition and redistribution policy as legislated for by the land acts, and which the Land Commission had the responsibility to enforce, made the decline of the country house inevitable.

The Land Commission frequently came into possession of country houses during its land division work. While some Ministers for Lands, such as Fianna Fáil's Seán Moylan, were not enthusiastic about the continued presence of the country house and their owners in the country, in the 1958 memorandum, the Department of Lands and the Land Commission outlined to government departments their ostensible practical policy in relation to such houses. This policy was to inform other government departments of the Commission's acquisition of a country house during the course of their land division work in case it was needed for some state use. Alternatively, the Commission attempted to sell it with a small piece of land around it, although not enough to make the house economically viable through income from lands alone. It was only when all these options failed that the Land Commission demolished a country house.

Evidence suggests that such demolition took place in a minority of cases, at least during the short number of years for which Land Commission statistics are available, and it was not the Commission's first preference or a matter of policy to do so. In such cases, the Commission could not keep these country houses as it had not the mandate, remit or resources to do so, nor had they any use for them and no other organisation committed to take them on. The 1958 memorandum also shows that, predominantly, the houses that were demolished were in too poor a repair to be sold on or used. It is possible, though, that, as in the case of Bishopscourt, reporting that the house was in 'poor repair' would have made demolition a more justifiable course of action for the Land Commission. In addition, apart from the 1958 memorandum, the other sources for the evidence of the practical policy of the Commission are mainly the speeches of ministers or the correspondence of the Commission with other government departments. They must therefore be viewed carefully, given the fact that civil servants in the Department of Lands or Land Commission may have been saying what their minister or the opposition wanted to hear rather than outlining an accurate statement of policy. Even so, the fact that multiple different sources repeated the same line of policy, and that the same practical policy is outlined in internal departmental correspondence, illustrates that it most likely was the policy position of the Land Commission. Unfortunately, there are no statistics or sources available to the public documenting the Land Commission's policy in relation to country houses in the earlier decades of independence when land division was at its peak.

The period from 1957–73 was a defining threshold for the evolution of attitudes towards the country house, not least because of the new Department of Finance Secretary, T. K. Whitaker. His economic plans for an expansion of foreign trade and investment and accession to the EEC created a context where an appreciation for the country house, once viewed as foreign, became more acceptable.[4] The country house began to be viewed and repackaged as part of the European built heritage rather than as a remnant of the historically-loaded British domination of Ireland. This representation was also motivated by a new eagerness to assimilate these historical mansions into the national heritage where they were beginning to show their value as tourist attractions. The development of the tourism industry and the modernisation of the country were also factors in this period of rapidly changing social history that influenced a shift in attitudes toward the country house and its value to the nation and heritage. In later years, some country houses were taken over as hotels and the demesne land was converted into golf courses. While these ventures have ensured that many houses can be maintained and restored and become, once again, centres for luxury and entertainment, this re-imagining also has its critics. Sir Charles Colthurst of Blarney Castle has been one such opponent. In his opinion, when country houses have been taken over by hotel chains, 'sadly the life has gone out of them. Maybe that was always the political intention. I really don't mean to sound bitter, but very few houses are now looked after by the families who owned them, and there's absolutely no grant-aid whatsoever'.[5] On the other hand, hotels have been the saviours of many country houses, including Carton House, County Kildare and, as Christopher Ridgway has argued:

> Country estates have always functioned as places of leisure and work, and today Carton may operate in very different ways to before, but in this era (as in previous times) if estates are not economically sustainable they simply have no future.[6]

Many of the political and economic movements of this period, attributed to the Fianna Fáil government, had actually been initiated by the previous inter-party government, proving how gradual and difficult these shifts in perceptions and attitudes toward the country house are to define. Even as far back as the late 1950s and 1960s, one can see the beginnings of tentative attitudinal changes. Importantly, this developing appreciation of their heritage value and historic importance coincided with, and was made possible by, governments' changing economic outlooks, upward economic turns and increasing stability with regard to the state's finances.

The same attitudinal change could not be observed when it came to original owners, however, who remained an isolated group. By the mid-century, owners of such houses were increasingly perceived as eccentrics and caricatured in the national press and literary forms. In addition, their diminishing numbers heightened their sense of isolation. In local communities, they were often viewed as a different class. The lack of integration experienced by some was also exacerbated by those country house families who continued older traditions, such as sending their children to school in England, for example. This often meant that no matter how many years they had lived in Ireland, they were still differentiated from other citizens, not least by their accent. Their position in Ireland was, however, a complex one to navigate, infused as it was with historical association, class tensions and, in some cases, a sense of isolation or rejection. The ambiguous nature of this position is in evidence in Blarney Castle's Sir Charles Colthurst's thoughts on his own sense of identity. He maintained: 'Personally, I feel more Irish than I do English, and as I was born in Dublin, I always did, even in prep school, public school and at university. I've never supported England in any sporting event in my life, but have always shouted for Ireland. None of my friends would consider me English, though I'd need to be pretty drunk to attempt an Irish accent! I would say that as a family, we've always integrated locally, though maybe discreetly …'.[7] Similarly Dan (Christopher) Somerville of Drishane House, Castletownshend, County Cork, stated: 'I feel Irish once I'm in Ireland and I feel English once I'm back in Somerset. I seem to be able to respond to both identities.'[8] Hence, when the country house was reimagined as part of national heritage from the late 1960s and 1970s, because of the popular perceptions of the houses' owners as Anglo-Irish or eccentrics, it was more difficult for them to be incorporated in this process of inclusion.

A growing realization of the tourism potential of these houses, among other factors, stimulated a change in how the country house was presented, but it does not show that private government attitudes to the country house were radically different to what they were in the 1920s. In the case of Bishopscourt, County Kildare, for example, many of the departments' viewpoints were very similar to those expressed in discussions surrounding one of the very first houses offered to the state, Russborough House, County Wicklow. Furthermore, no country house had been preserved as a national monument up to the 1970s and so, in many ways, governments' attitudes that motivated policy on country houses remained somewhat static throughout this period. The only gifts of country houses accepted by the state in this period were Muckross, County Kerry, in 1932 and later, in 1975, Barretstown, County Kildare. Importantly, the latter house was offered as a viable gift with endowments and rents receivable, while Muckross, too, had gate receipts and livestock on a well-kept property in one of the most popular tourist spots in the country. The state also took over Derrynane, County Kerry, in the period from 1957 to 1973. In this case, the government in power was concerned about expenditure in relation to Derrynane and judged that, if the Trust could not maintain the house properly, then it would be preferable to acquire it themselves and thus ensure public funds were being properly appropriated. Nonetheless, they were still unsure if Derrynane could be used as a viable tourist attraction. In contrast, the perceived value of the house to the country and its position in relation to the nation and its heritage had begun to be re-appraised in the 1960s and 1970s, but it was not until after 1970 that this resulted in changes in government policy.

The similarity in governments' views and the attitudes of various departments throughout this period is remarkable. For example, despite the various changes in government during this time, in most cases of country houses gifted to the state, the consideration of the offer was the same, with the Department of Finance's recommendation the most important factor for determining the government's decision. Until recently, the notable importance of civil servants in government was all too frequently ignored in historiography.[9] High-ranking officers in departments – who were in such positions for long periods of time while the various appointed ministers changed much more frequently – were really the ones pulling the strings and influencing policy. Ministers usually only entered discussions when final authorisation was needed. In 1953, influential civil servant, McElligott was replaced as Secretary of the Department of Finance by the next-in-line in the department, Owen Joseph Redmond. Redmond exercised similar policy principles, and so he, McElligott and the civil servants of the Department of Finance were hugely influential in forming the government policy of keeping expenditure to a minimum. It was not until a new crop of civil servants, most particularly T. K. Whitaker, ascended to the most important roles in the department in the late 1950s that policy began to change, with significant ripple effects for the country's economic and political outlook and for society at large.

For the few country houses that did survive, historical associations were often important, i.e. the preservation of Avondale, Derrynane or the Pearse Museum. However, historical associations do not appear to have been significant reasons behind their destruction, abandonment, refusal as gifts, or demolition. Predominantly it was not narrow-mindedness that caused the destruction of country houses, but practical decisions based on limited use, inadequate budgets and a concern for the more urgent social problems affecting citizens throughout this period.

In the final analysis, this story is a difficult one to tell. There are contradictions between individuals in government departments, between public bodies, between public rhetoric and private views, and between what was said and what was done. It is challenging to understand fully how the state viewed these houses. Certainly it seems that, for most of this period, they were focussed on other more widespread or critical issues. Some of the difficulties in piecing together a coherent story arise from the fact that many of these houses, when they appeared as problems on departments' desks, were dealt with on a case-by-case basis without there ever having been a whole of government policy with regard to their survival. Simply put, this issue was never important enough in this period, nor did it affect the daily lives of the majority of citizens. There were no clear lines as to whose brief it would have been to voluntarily investigate the issue. The Land Commission looked at country houses when they were disposing of land, the Taoiseach's Department or Finance investigated cases of gifts to the state, while the OPW became involved mainly when they were asked by local committees, the Land Commission or the NMAC to examine particular cases from a point of view of recording the building before demolition or considering its preservation as a national monuments. As with many other issues, when absolute responsibility for an issue is not clear, no department wants to become to embroiled in the affair for fear that it would then be entirely responsible for that problem. If the OPW did not consider these houses national monuments – and evidence shows that it overwhelmingly did not – then the government had no real justification for aiding private owners with their preservation. It would most appropriately have fallen to the OPW, which has, in recent years, taken on a number of country houses. In such instances, it has done an admirable job of restoring and preserving them and trying to make them an accessible amenity to all, including Castletown House, Country Kildare, and Emo Court, County Laois. Ironically, the primary reasons for the lack of government policy on country houses during this period continue to dog their fate today: limited budgets amid other pressing issues and little viable use for the large number of country houses dotted around the country.

From 1957, the temporal remove from the struggle for independence and the psychological remove from insular protectionism and xenophobia meant that the country house was regarded with less hostility and the virulent rhetorical flourishes against these houses in the Oireachtas became old-fashioned views. The Troubles in the North, which flared in the 1970s, also tarred nationalistic views with associations of violent extremism. The Republic sought to distance itself from this past by moving in the opposite direction. This was in evidence in the language surrounding the house that began to be used by politicians, private interest groups and organisations established by owners themselves. Colonial or British associations were often ignored and the houses were hailed as if they were entirely designed, built and furnished by local Irish craftsmen and labour. The difficulty with this is that the pendulum had swung too far in the other direction and this portrayal of country houses does not accurately reflect their full history and role in the Irish story either. It is instead closer to a rewriting of the past to suit the present and, as David Lowenthal has argued, 'credence in a mythic past crafted for some present cause suppresses history's impartial complexity'.[10] Instead, as Hugh Maguire has contended, their role in the convoluted historical process should be fully acknowledged. In fact, Maguire has maintained that an acknowledgment of attitudes toward the country house as a colonial symbol is essential to finally coming to terms with it, and ultimately to its possible acceptance as national heritage. He argued:

> that the Irish house was indeed part of a colonial perception of space is never fully acknowledged by preservationists and to allude to such is to be branded a quasi-terrorist. And yet a fuller analysis of the role of the house as a consolidating element in the colonial process would actually acknowledge a more honest reality, not necessarily engender hostility.[11]

Therefore, in terms of finally coming to terms with the complex historical position of the country house in Ireland, as well as acknowledging their value, worth and beauty today, there is still a long way to go and the story is not yet over. Records and departmental files that will be released in the coming years will undoubtedly shed new light on this aspect of their history and continue to enrich the historiography in this field.

NOTES

INTRODUCTION

1 Allen Warren, 'The twilight of the ascendancy and the big house: A view from the twenty-first century', in Terence Dooley and Christopher Ridgeway (eds), *The Irish Country House: Its Past, Present and Future* (Dublin, 2011), pp 244–56.

2 Terence Dooley, *The Decline of the Big House in Ireland: A Study of Irish Landed Families, 1860–1960* (Dublin, 2001), p. 9; the term was also used by Olwen Purdue in *The Big House in the North of Ireland: Land, Power and Social Elites, 1878–1960* (Dublin, 2009).

3 Dooley, *The Decline of the Big House in Ireland*, p. 9.

4 Ibid.

5 Purdue, *The Big House in the North of Ireland*, p. 146.

6 R. V. Comerford, *Ireland: Inventing the Nation* (London, 2003), p. 46.

7 Danielle O'Donovan and Jennifer McCrea, 'Education and the historic house: Where the past has a value for the future', in Dooley and Ridgway, *The Irish Country House*, p. 185.

8 Sandra Murphy, OPW, email to the author, 16 Aug. 2018

9 Benedict Anderson, *Imagined Communities: Reflections on the Origin and Spread of Nationalism* (Revised edn, London, 1991), p. 6.

10 Comerford, *Inventing the Nation*, p. 2.

11 Mark Thatcher, 'Introduction: The State and historic buildings: Preserving "the national past"', in *Nations and Nationalism*, xxiv:1, Jan. 2018, pp 22–42; available at https://onlinelibrary.wiley.com/doi/full/10.1111/nana.12372, 17 June 2018.

12 Terence Dooley, *The Big House and Landed Estates of Ireland: A Research Guide* (Dublin, 2007), p. 115.

13 These included: Mark Bence-Jones, *Twilight of the Ascendancy* (Edinburgh, 1987) and *A Guide To the Irish Country House* (Edinburgh, 1988); Desmond Fitzgerald, David Griffin & Nicholas Robinson, *Vanishing Country Houses of Ireland* (London, 1988); Desmond Guinness & William Ryan, *Irish Houses and Castles* (London, 1971); Simon Marsden's *In Ruins: The Once Great Houses of Ireland* (London, 1997); and Randal MacDonnell's *The Lost Houses of Ireland* (London, 2002), among others.

14 Purdue, *The Big House in the North of Ireland*.

15 Terence Dooley, 'National patrimony and political perceptions of the Irish country house in post-independence Ireland', in Dooley (ed), *Ireland's Polemical Past: Views of Irish History in Honour of R. V. Comerford* (Dublin, 2010), pp 192–212.

16 Warren, 'The twilight of the ascendancy', pp 244–5.

17 The change in attitudes, widely accepted, is charted in Dooley, 'National patrimony and political perceptions', pp 192–212.

18 Amanda Mc Evoy, Records Branch, Legal Services Division, Department of Agriculture, Food and the Marine, letter/email to the author, 8 June 2017.

19 Given the lack of names in certain files and the many illegibly signed handwritten notes, this interdepartmental correspondence will be referenced simply by department when it is not possible to accurately identify the writer of the document.

20 Elaine A. Byrne, 'A unique experiment in idealism: The Irish senate 1922–28', in Mel Farrell, Jason Knirck and Ciara Meehan (eds), *A Formative Decade: Ireland in the 1920s* (Sallins, 2015), p. 60.

21 Ibid., p. 64.

22 Ibid., p. 69.

23 Mark O'Brien, *The Irish Times: A History* (Dublin, 2008), p. 58.

24 Ibid.

CHAPTER ONE

1 Terence Dooley, *The Decline of the Big House in Ireland: A Study of Irish Landed Families, 1860–1960* (Dublin, 2001), p. 171.

2 *Anglo-Irish Treaty*, 6 Dec. 1921.

3 The President of the Executive Council was the head of government before the creation of the position of Taoiseach. For a discussion of the free state under Cosgrave see John A. Murphy, *Ireland in the Twentieth-Century* (2nd edn, Dublin, 1989), pp 61–75.

4 Frank Murphy, 'Dublin slums in the 1930s', in *Dublin Historical Record*, xxxvii:3 & 4, June–Sept. 1984, p. 111; *Irish Press*, 13 Oct. 1936.

5 R. F. Foster, *Modern Ireland, 1600–1972* (2nd edn, London, 1989), p. 519.

6 Mel Farrell, 'Cumann na nGaedheal: A new 'national party?', in Mel Farrell, Jason Knirck and Ciara Meehan (eds), *A Formative Decade: Ireland in the 1920s* (Sallins, 2015), pp 36–58.

7 For a concise history of the civil war period, see Dermot Keogh, *Twentieth-Century Ireland: Nation and State* (Dublin, 1994), pp 1–63.

8 Dooley, *The Decline of the Big House in Ireland*, p. 185.

9 Ibid., p. 182.

10 Ibid., p. 185.

11 James S. Donnelly Jr., 'Big house burnings in County Cork during the Irish revolution, 1920–21', in Éire–Ireland, xlvii:3 & 4, fall/winter 2012, p. 142.

12 Dooley, *The Decline of the Big House in Ireland*, p. 189.

13 Ibid., p. 191.

14 Elaine A. Byrne, 'A unique experiment in idealism: The Irish Senate 1922–28', in Farrell, Knirck and Meehan, *A Formative Decade*, p. 67.

15 Dooley, *The Decline of the Big House in Ireland*, p. 190.

16 Ibid., pp 171–207. In contrast, Olwen Purdue has written that 'despite the violence raging in the southern provinces, particularly Munster, the early months of 1920 were relatively peaceful in the north-east. While newspapers reported almost daily on the burnings, raids and murder that were taking place in the south and west, reports of incidents in the six counties of the north-east were few and far between.' Olwen Purdue, *The Big House in the North of Ireland: Land, Power and Social Elites, 1878–1960* (Dublin, 2009), p. 145.

17 See, for Example, Keogh, *Twentieth-Century Ireland*, pp 27–39.

18 See Jane O'Hea O'Keeffe, *Voices from the Great Houses of Cork and Kerry* (Cork, 2013), pp 21, 36, 60–1.

19 For a discussion of the revolution in Russia and the violent hatred it engendered toward the aristocratic class, see Douglas Smith, *Former People: The Destruction of the Russian Aristocracy* (Hampshire, 2012).

20 Ibid., p. 8.

21 Ibid., p. 14.

22 O'Hea O'Keeffe, *Voices from the Great Houses of Cork and Kerry*, p. 236.

23 Ibid., p. 256.

24 Charles Lysaght, 'Foreword', in ibid.

25 *Damage to Property (Compensation) Act, 1923. An Act to Alter the Law Relating to Compensation for Criminal injuries*, 12 May 1923.

26 Dooley, *The Decline of the Big House in Ireland*, pp 202–4.

27 Ibid.

28 Ibid., pp 197–207.

29 Ibid., I, 2020, 1 Nov. 1922.

30 Ibid., I, 2028, 1 Nov. 1922.

31 Ibid.

32 Ibid.

33 *Dáil Éireann Deb.*, ii, 1855–6, 1 Mar. 1923.

34 Ibid., ii, 1858, 1 Mar. 1923.

35 Ibid.

36 *Dáil Éireann Deb.*, ii, 1896 (1 Mar. 1923).

37 *Irish Times* (hereafter *IT*), 14 Apr. 1923.

38 Ibid.

39 Ibid.

40 *Dáil Éireann Deb.*, xiv, 11, 28 May 1925.

41 *IT*, 17 Aug. 1925.

42　Dooley, *The Decline of the Big House in Ireland*, p. 160. For a discussion of servant life in the Big House, see this work, pp 146–70.

43　Eugenio F. Biagini has given a concise overview of the situation for Protestants generally in the south, that is, of all social classes, in his review article 'The Protestant minority in southern Ireland', in *the Historical Journal*, lv:4, Dec. 2012, pp 1161–84. The alienation of the Anglo–Irish landed class even before partition is evident in works by authors from this background themselves, such as the memoirs of Elizabeth Plunkett, Countess of Fingall, in *Seventy Years Young: Memories of Elizabeth, Countess of Fingall* (London, 1937), Or the works of Elizabeth Bowen, most famously capturing the decline of the country house in *The Last September* (London, 1998).

44　Charles Lysaght, 'Foreword', in O'Hea O'Keeffe, *Voices from the Great Houses of Cork and Kerry*, p. 8.

45　Terence Dooley, *The Decline of the Big House in Ireland*, p. 113.

46　Terence Dooley, 'The Fitzgeralds: A survey history, 1169–2013', in Patrick Cosgrove, Terence Dooley and Karol Mullaney-Dignam (eds), *Aspects of Irish Aristocratic Life: Essays on the Fitzgeralds and Carton House* (Dublin 2014), p. 28.

47　Myrtle Hill and John Lynch, 'Movements for political & social reform, 1870–1914', available at University College Cork, multitext project in Irish history, http://Multitext.Ucc.Ie/D/Ireland_Society_Economy_1870–1914, 14 Nov. 2012.

48　Purdue, *The Big House in the North of Ireland*, pp 94–5.

49　*Land Act, 1923. An Act to amend the law relating to the occupation and ownership of land and for other purposes relating thereto*, 9 Aug. 1923.

50　Ibid.; in 1923 ministerial responsibility for the Land Commission lay with the Department of Agriculture and then Minister for Agriculture, Patrick Hogan, but by 1927 it was realised that this was too big a portfolio to lump with agriculture, and so the Department of Lands and Fisheries was created. Over the following decades, Land was often included with portfolios such as fisheries, industry and commerce, and the Gaeltacht.

51　Terence Dooley, *'The Land for the People': The Land Question in Independent Ireland* (Dublin, 2004), p. 18.

52　Ibid., p. 90.

53　Dooley, *The Decline of the Big House in Ireland*, pp 131–2.

54　*Northern Ireland Land Act, 1925. An Act to amend the law relating to the occupation and ownership of land in Northern Ireland; and for other purposes relating thereto*, 28 May 1925.

55　Purdue, *The Big House in the North of Ireland*, p. 100.

56　*Land Act, 1931. An Act to make provision for the early vesting of holdings in the purchasers thereof under the Land Purchase Acts and for that and other purposes to amend those Acts and the Local Registration of Title (Ireland) Act, 1891, and also to make provision in respect of the variation of certain tithe rentcharges and variable rents*, 30 Apr. 1931; *Land Act, 1933. An Act to amend generally the law, finance, and practice relating to land purchase, and in particular to make further and better provision for the execution of the functions of the judicial and lay commissioners of the Land Commission and to provide for the revision of purchase annuities and certain other annual payments and for the funding of arrears thereof, and to provide for other matters connected with the matters aforesaid*, 13 Oct. 1933.

57 Patrick J. Sammon, *In the Land Commission: A Memoir, 1933–1978* (Dublin, 1997), p. 9.

58 Dooley, '*The Land for the People*', p. 67.

59 *Land Act, 1965. An Act to Amend and Extend the Land Purchase Acts*, 9 Mar. 1965.

60 Alvin Jackson, *Ireland 1798–1998* (Oxford, 1999), p. 226.

61 Ibid.

62 Dooley, '*The Land for the People*', p. 45.

63 O'Hea O'Keeffe, *Voices from the Great Houses of Cork and Kerry*, pp 21–2.

64 Terence Dooley, *The Big House and Landed Estates of Ireland: A Research Guide* (Dublin, 2007), p. 62.

65 *United Irishman*, 6 May 1848.

66 R. V. Comerford, *Ireland: Inventing the Nation* (London, 2003), p. 9.

67 'William Cosgrave proceeded to appoint 16 former unionists of different descriptions … but for those who emerged, dazed, into the more settled conditions of the mid-1920s, the Irish free state offered a home: a home where there were some restrictions and some threats, where some territory was out of bounds, but a home nonetheless.' Jackson, *Ireland*, p. 277.

68 For further discussion of landowners and the changes in hunting and shooting, see Dooley, *The Decline of the Big House in Ireland*, pp 258–64.

69 *Seanad Éireann Deb.*, xiii, 337, 12 Dec. 1929.

70 Ibid.

71 *Seanad Éireann Deb.*, i, 718, 28 Mar. 1923.

72 Ibid.

73 Dooley, *The Decline of the Big House in Ireland*, pp 118–22.

74 See Ibid., pp 242–60.

75 Ibid., p. 141.

76 For more information on this, see Chapter Five: The Irish Land Commission, 1940–65.

77 Dooley, *The Decline of the Big House in Ireland*, p. 16.

78 *Dáil Éireann Deb.*, xxxvii, 1736, 18 Mar. 1931.

79 Ibid., viii, 1583, 17 July 1924.

80 O'Hea O'Keeffe, *Voices from the Great Houses of Cork and Kerry*, p. 252.

81 Dooley, *The Decline of the Big House in Ireland*, p. 136.

82 Ibid.

83 Ibid., p. 137.

84 Ibid.

85 Purdue, *The Big House in the North of Ireland*, p. 111.

86 Ibid., p. 115.

87 Ibid.

88 *Weekly Irish Times*, 25 Apr. 1931.

89 Keogh, *Twentieth-Century Ireland*, p. 91.

90 Enda Delaney, 'Emigration, political cultures and the evolution of post-war society', in Brian Girvin and Gary Murphy (eds), *The Lemass Era: Politics and Society in the Ireland of Seán Lemass* (Dublin, 2005), p. 49.

91 Ibid.

92 *Irish Times*, 5 Feb. 1975.

93 Christopher Ridgway, 'The Fitzgerald legacy', in Cosgrove, Dooley and Mullaney-Dignam, *Aspects of Irish Aristocratic Life*, p. 222.

94 Allen Warren 'The twilight of the ascendancy and the big house: A view from the twenty-first century', in Terence Dooley and Christopher Ridgeway (eds), *The Irish Country House: Its Past, Present and Future* (Dublin, 2011), pp 244–56.

95 File on Ancient and National Monuments Acts addressed to Commissioner Kent, 16 Apr. 1928, National Archives of Ireland (hereafter NAI), Office of Public Works (hereafter OPW) files, F94/289/1/1.

96 'Powers of Commissioners of Public Works', undated, NAI, OPW files, F94/289/1/1.

97 Memorandum, undated, NAI, Dept of the Taoiseach files (hereafter DoTF), S5004A.

98 Ibid.

99 Ibid.

100 *Dáil Éireann Deb.*, xxxii, 267, 24 Oct. 1929.

101 *National Monuments Act, 1930. An Act to make provision for the protection and preservation of national monuments and for the preservation of archaeological objects in Saorstát Éireann and to make provision for other matters connected with the matters aforesaid*, 26 Feb. 1930.

102 Ibid.

103 Mairéad Carew, 'Politics and the definition of national monuments: The "Big House problem"', in *The Journal of Irish Archaeology*, xviii, 2009, p. 132.

104 National Monuments Act, 1930: Amendments Recommended by NMAC, NAI, OPW files, F94/289/1/1.

105 OPW internal minute, 'Notes on amendments proposed by National Monuments Advisory Council', 14 June 1938, NAI, OPW files, F94/289/1/1.

106 Ibid.

107 *National Monuments (Amendment) Act, 1954. An Act to amend the National Monuments Act, 1930*, 22 Dec. 1954.

108 Anne Carey, 'Harold G. Leask: Aspects of his work as inspector of national monuments', in *the Journal of the Royal Society of Antiquaries of Ireland*, cxxxiii, 2003, p. 25.

109 Signed internal note in reply to Division C of the OPW's handwritten note, 18 Jan. 1944, NAI, OPW files, F94/574/1.

110 Draft letter from the OPW to Tipperary District Council, Apr. 1944, NAI, OPW files, F94/574/1.

111 Department of Finance to the Secretary to the President of the Executive Council, 2 Nov. 1930, NAI, DoTF, S5935.

112 Peter Mandler, *The Fall and Rise of the Stately Home* (New Haven & London, 1997), p. 256.

113 Ibid., p. 272.

114 Ibid., p. 298.

115 Ibid.

116 Ibid.

117 Ibid.

118 Ibid.

119 Mark Bence-Jones, *A Guide to Irish Country Houses* (Revised edn, London, 1988), p. 250.

120 Sir Edward Eliot to Sir Walter Nugent, 12 Oct. 1929, NAI, DoTF, S5935.

121 Ibid.

122 Ibid., 10 Dec. 1929, NAI, DoTF, S5935.

123 Ibid.

124 Ibid.

125 Ibid.

126 Ibid.

127 Department of the President to Senator Sir Walter Nugent, 27 Jan. 1930, NAI, DoTF, S5935.

128 Ibid.

129 W. T. Cosgrave to Sir Charles Barrington, 29 July 1925. *Glenstal Abbey Archives*. Boxfile No 1: 'Origins of Glenstal Abbey' Cit. in Mark Tierney OSB, 'The origins and early days of Glenstal Abbey', in Martin Browne OSB and Colmán O Clabaigh (eds), *The Irish Benedictines: A History* (Dublin, 2005), http://www.catholicireland.net/Pages/index.Php?Art=1026, 24 Oct. 2012.

130 Ibid.

131 Department of the President to Senator Sir Walter Nugent, 27 Jan. 1930, NAI, DoTF, S5935.

132 Ibid.

133 Copy of President's Note on Visit to 'Russboro', 11 Feb. 1930, NAI, DoTF, S5935.

134 Ibid.

135 Attached to a letter from Edward Eliot to President Cosgrave, 1 Mar. 1930, NAI, DoTF, S5935.

136 Raftery for the Secretary of the OPW to the Secretary of the Department of the President, 2 Apr. 1930, NAI, DoTF, S5935.

137 T. Cassedy, Secretary of the OPW, to the Secretary to the Department of the President, 30 July 1930, NAI, DoTF, S5935.

138 OPW's Principal Architect Mr Byrne's Report on Russborough House, County Wicklow, 25 July 1930, NAI, DoTF, S5935.

139 Ibid.

140 Ibid.

141 Assistant Secretary to the Private Secretary to the Minister for Finance, 3 Sept. 1930, NAI, DoTF, S5935.

142 Ibid.

143 Signed for the Private Secretary to the President of the Executive Council to Hon. Edward G. Eliot, 15 Oct. 1930, NAI, DoTF, S5935.

144 Ibid.

145 Ibid.

146 J. J. McElligott, Secretary of the Department of Finance, to the Secretary to the President of the Executive Council, 24 Oct. 1930, NAI, DoTF, S5935.

147 Ibid.

148 Ibid.

149 John Paul McCarthy and Tomás O'Riordan, 'James J. MacElligott', in *The Pursuit of Sovereignty & the Impact of Partition, 1912–1949*', University College Cork multitext project in Irish History, http://multitext.ucc.ie/D/James_J_Macelligott, 1 Dec. 2012.

150 Ibid.

151 Ibid.

152 Handwritten note on letter from J. J. McElligott, Secretary of the Department of Finance, to the Secretary to the President of the Executive Council, 24 Oct. 1930, NAI, DoTF, S5935.

153 J. J. McElligott, Secretary of the Department of Finance, to the Secretary to the President of the Executive Council, 24 Oct. 1930, NAI, DoTF, S5935.

154 Ibid.

155 Ibid.

156 Sir Edward Eliot to Sir Walter Nugent, 12 Oct. 1929, NAI, DoTF, S5935.

157 J. J. McElligott, Secretary of the Department of Finance, to the Secretary to the President of the Executive Council, 24 Oct. 1930, NAI, DoTF, S5935.

158 Ibid.

159 Ibid.

160 Ibid.

161 Ibid.

162 Ibid.

163 Ibid.

164 Ibid.

165 Ibid.

166 Ibid.

167 Department of Finance draft letter to President of the Executive Council submitted to Minister for Finance for Approval, 22 Oct. 1930, NAI, Dept of Finance, S 2/11/30.

168 Department of Finance minute addressed to Mr Codling, 20 Sept. 1930, NAI, Dept of Finance S 2/11/30. Arthur Codling was an Assistant Secretary in the Department of Finance.

169 Ibid.

170 Handwritten note to the Secretary, 15 Sept. 1930, on Department of Finance minute addressed to Mr Codling, 20 Sept. 1930, NAI, Dept of Finance S 2/11/30.

171 Extract from cabinet minutes, 2 Dec. 1930, NAI, DoTF, S5935.

172 President Cosgrave to Sir Edward Eliot, 5 Dec. 1930, NAI, DoTF, S5935.

173 Assistant Secretary of the Department of the President to the Secretary of the OPW, 15 Dec. 1930, NAI, DoTF, S5935.

174 President William Cosgrave to Sir Edward Eliot, 15 Jan. 1931 NAI, DoTF, S5935.

175 Sir Edward Eliot to President Cosgrave, 16 Jan. 1931, NAI, DoTF, S5935.

176 *IT*, 3 June 1931.

177 Ibid.

178 Russborough House website, http://www.russborough.ie/, 31 May 2017.

179 Speech given by former Taoiseach Dr Garret Fitzgerald at An Taisce, the National Trust for Ireland's Heritage, in Trust Corporate Breakfast, 17 Nov. 2008, http://www.antaisce.org/Articles/speech–given–former–taoiseach–dr–garret –fitzgerald–taisce–national–trust–ireland%E2%80%99s–Heritage, 24 May 2017.

180 Terence Dooley, 'Land and politics in independent Ireland, 1923–1948: The case for reappraisal', in *Irish Historical Studies*, xxxiv:134, Nov. 2004, p. 183.

181 Fianna Fáil Frank Lawlor Cumann to the President, 17 Dec. 1932, NAI, DoTF, S2353.

182 *Seanad Éireann Deb.*, lxxxiii, 1744–5, 7 Apr. 1976.

183 Ibid., lxxxiii, 1745, 7 Apr. 1976.

CHAPTER TWO

1 The title was changed to Taoiseach in 1937.

2 *Irish Press*, 13 Oct. 1936.

3 Ibid.

4 Ibid.

5 Frank Murphy, 'Dublin slums in the 1930s', in *Dublin Historical Record*, xxxvii:3/4, June-Sept. 1984, p. 111.

6 *Irish Independent*, 14 May 1937.

7 The Labour Party gave Fianna Fáil the five extra votes it needed to have an overall majority in the Dáil. For more on the election campaign, see Dermot Keogh, *Twentieth-Century Ireland: Nation and State* (Dublin, 1994), pp 59–63.

8 Keogh has argued that the hard-line Anglo-Irish policy that de Valera 'drifted into within weeks of coming to power ... was against the best advice of the most senior member of the Department of External Affairs'. Keogh, *Twentieth-Century Ireland*, p. 67.

9 Kevin O'Rourke, 'Burn everything British but their coal: The Anglo-Irish economic war of the 1930s', in *The Journal of Economic History*, li:2, June 1991, p. 358.

10 R. F. Foster, *Modern Ireland, 1600–1972* (2nd edn, London, 1989), p. 552.

11 The agreements were enshrined in a new Anglo-Irish agreement, which was signed on 25 Apr. 1958. Keogh, *Twentieth-Century Ireland*, p. 104; O'Rourke, 'Burn everything British but their coal', p. 358.

12 For a discussion of Bunreacht na hÉireann, see Ibid., pp 96–104.

13 Ibid., p. 96.

14 *Bunreacht na hÉireann* (1937), article 400.

15 *Irish Times* (hereafter *IT*), 17 May 1932.

16 Ibid.

17 Terence Dooley, *The Decline of the Big House in Ireland: A Study of Irish Landed Families, 1860–1960* (Dublin, 2001), p. 137.

18 Ibid., p. 136.

19 Ibid., p. 137.

20 Ibid.

21 This did not always work out due to economic factors such as the worldwide economic depression of the 1920s but also because of some landowners' inexperience and naivety in the business of investments. See Dooley, *The Decline of the Big House in Ireland*, pp 118–22.

22 See Olwen Purdue, *The Big House in the North of Ireland: Land, Power And Social Elites, 1878–1960* (Dublin, 2009), pp 103–9.

23 See Dooley, *The Decline of the Big House in Ireland*, pp 121–2.

24 *IT*, 7 Nov. 1932.

25 Mark O'Brien, *The Irish Times: A History* (Dublin, 2008), p. 66.

26 Ibid.

27 Ibid., pp 66–7.

28 Figures are estimated by the author from houses listed as having been demolished specifically in these two decades by Mark Bence-Jones in his *A Guide to Irish Country Houses* (Revised edn, London, 1988).

29 Ibid., p. vii.

30 This would be a very useful study that would be hugely beneficial for the historiography surrounding the country house in Ireland.

31 These are estimates subject to human error. They were compiled by the author

working through each entry and what was listed as the fate of each house. Not included in these figures were houses which were damaged or destroyed by fire, accidental or deliberate, houses which fell into ruin or dereliction and were demolished afterwards, and houses located in the six counties of Northern Ireland. Furthermore, many entries did not say what fate befell the house so these were excluded. In addition, in relation to the boundaries of study here, the details given in this book from 1988 are interesting. The fate of any houses listed may have changed since, although the numbers for those ruined, derelict or demolished after 1970, as listed in this work, are rare.

32 The number taken over by religious orders necessitates a study on this aspect of the survival of the country house, which once again will add tremendous value to the historiography of this field. Houses taken on by religious orders include: Mount Anville, County Dublin, which became a girls' convent school; Moore Abbey, County Kildare, which became a hospital run by the Sisters of Jesus and Mary; Gallen Priory, Offaly, which became a convent; Loftus Hall, County Wexford, which became a convent; Kylemore Abbey, County Galway, which became a convent and school; Glenstal Castle, County Limerick, which became a Benedictine Abbey and a boys' private school; Blayney Castle, Monaghan, which became a convent; Faithlegg House, County Waterford, which became a school run by the De la Salle brothers; Gormanstown Castle, County Meath, which became a Franciscan school; Cloonamahon, County Sligo, which was bought by the Passionist fathers; Dromcar, County Louth, taken over by the Society of St John of God's; Myross Wood, County Cork, which became property of the Sacred Heart Fathers; Donamon Castle, County Roscommon, which was bought by the Divine Word missionaries, among many others.

33 Purdue, *The Big House in the North of Ireland*, p. 119.

34 *Seanad Éireann Deb.*, xxvii, 2133, 19 May 1943.

35 In fact, as noted in the previous chapter, many of the staff working in the country house, and particularly in the most important posts, were English or Scottish Protestants; therefore Dooley has illustrated that 'big houses were not of great economic benefit to locals seeking employment on a permanent basis'. Dooley, *The Decline of the Big House in Ireland*, p. 160. However, locals were employed on demesnes and farms. Ibid., p. 272.

36 *Seanad Éireann Deb.*, xxvii, 2134, 19 May 1943.

37 Ibid.

38 Ibid., xxvii, 2134–5, 19 May 1943.

39 Ibid., xxvii, 2135, 19 May 1943.

40 The Commissioner of Valuation made this point to the Land Commission in 1958 when the L. C. suggested a reduction of rates on historic mansions. The letter read: 'the commissioner does not think the suggestion is practicable. There are more occupied than unoccupied mansions and large houses. An increase in

rate poundages would inevitably follow the legislator's unwillingness to offer to future occupiers of currently unoccupied mansions a relief which was to be withheld from, say, religious communities caring for mental defectives or epileptics in similar mansions. How could the legislator defend derating of the native, not to mention the foreign, occupier of a mansion to the cottier, the widow or the father who gets no relief from a burden which normally represents a higher proportion of net income the lower the income group to which the ratepayer belongs?' Observations of the Commissioner of Valuation on the memorandum for the Government from Oifig an Aire Tailte regarding the preservation of mansions and large houses, 21 Oct. 1958, National Archives of Ireland (hereafter NAI), Dept of Finance files (hereafter DoFF), FIN/F63/8/58.

41 *Irish Independent*, 8 July 1946.

42 Sarah Connolly-Carew, *The Children of Castletown House* (Dublin, 2012), p. 106.

43 *Nenagh Guardian*, 6 July 1946.

44 Ibid.

45 *IT*, 24 July 1937.

46 Ibid.

47 Conor A. Maguire, Attorney General, to Senator Arthur Vincent, 5 Sept. 1932, NAI, Attorney General files, AGO/2005/77/34.

48 Conor A. Maguire, Attorney General, to the President of the Executive Council, 19 Oct. 1932, NAI, Attorney General files, AGO/2005/77/34; Unfortunately, this name for the park has now been dropped.

49 Messrs Whitney, Moore & Keller solicitors to Conor A. Maguire, Attorney General, 16 Nov. 1932, NAI, Attorney General files, AGO/2005/77/34.

50 Draft press release forwarded to the Attorney General by Messrs Whitney, Moore and Keller solicitors for Senator Vincent, 16 Nov. 1932, NAI, Attorney General files, AGO/2005/77/34.

51 Ibid.

52 Handwritten note on draft government announcement on the Bourn Vincent Memorial Park NAI, Attorney General files, AGO/2005/77/34.

53 Department of Environment, Heritage and Local Government: National Parks and Wildlife Service, 'Management plan for Killarney National Park, 2005–2009', p. 38, http://www.npws.ie/publications/archive/KNPMP.pdf, 27 Mar. 2013.

54 Liam Irwin to the Taoiseach, 13 Feb. 1974, NAI, Dept of the Taoiseach files, S2005/7/415.

55 Peter Mandler, *The Fall and Rise of The Stately Home* (New Haven & London, 1997), p. 256.

56 Ibid., p. 245.

57 *Dáil Éireann Deb.*, xlviii, 2391, 13 July 1933.

58 Ibid.

59 *Land Act, 1933. An act to amend, generally, the law, finance, and practice relating to land purchase, and in particular to make further and better provision for the execution of the functions of the judicial and lay commissioners of the Land Commission and to provide for the revision of purchase annuities and certain other annual payments and for the funding of arrears thereof, and to provide for other matters connected with the matters aforesaid*, 13 Oct. 1933.

60 Dooley, *The Decline of the Big House in Ireland*, p. 134.

61 Ibid.

62 *Seanad Éireann Deb.*, xxiii, 955, 26 July 1939.

63 Ibid.

64 Ibid.

65 See, for example, *Weekly Irish Times*, 9 Nov. 1940.

66 Dooley, *The Decline of the Big House in Ireland*, p. 258

67 Elizabeth Bowen, 'The Big House', in Hermione Lee (ed.), *The Mulberry Tree: Writings on Elizabeth Bowen* (London, 1986), p. 30.

68 Jane O'Hea O'Keeffe, *Voices from the Great Houses of Cork and Kerry* (Cork, 2013), p. 11.

69 *Dáil Éireann Deb.*, lxxxvii, 851, 2 June 1942.

70 Ibid.

71 *IT*, 21 July 1934.

72 *Dáil Éireann Deb.*, lxxv, 1239, 27 Apr. 1939.

73 Ibid., xci, 1410, 28 Oct. 1943.

74 Ibid., lxx, 1020, 24 Mar. 1938.

75 Mandler, *The Fall and Rise of the Stately Home*, p. 246.

76 *IT*, 21 Mar. 1933.

77 *Dáil Éireann Deb.*, lxxxii, 1435, 3 Apr. 1941.

78 Ibid., lxxxii, 2006–2007 30 Apr. 1941.

79 Ibid., cxci, 1330, 19 July 1961.

80 Ibid., xciii, 52, 2 May 1944.

81 Dooley, *The Big House and Landed Estates of Ireland: A Research Guide* (Dublin, 2007), p. 137.

82 *Dáil Éireann Deb.*, xcii, 1518, 23 Feb. 1944.

83 *Irish Press*, 15 July 1944.

84 Ibid.

85 In 1939 Bord Cuartaíochta na hÉireann was established by an act of the Dáil. This organisation took over from the Irish Tourists Association. It was then succeeded by Bord Fáilte Éireann, which was created in 1955 under the Tourist Traffic Act.

86 *Irish Press*, 19 July 1944.

87 Ibid.

88 Ibid.

89 Ibid.

90 *Irish Independent*, 1 Sept. 1944.

91 Ibid.

92 Ibid.

93 *IT*, 15 Aug. 1944.

94 *Irish Press*, 31 Aug. 1944.

95 *IT*, 18 Sept. 1944.

96 Westmeath County Council to An Taoiseach Eamonn de Valera, 28 June 1944, NAI, Dept of the Taoiseach files (hereafter DoTF) S13344B.

97 Allen Warren, 'The twilight of the ascendancy and the big house: A view from the twenty-first century', in Terence Dooley and Christopher Ridgway (eds), *The Irish Country House: Its Past, Present and Future* (Dublin, 2011), p. 251.

98 Dooley, *The Big House and Landed Estates of Ireland*, p. 138.

99 David Cannadine, *The Decline and Fall of the British Aristocracy* (Revised edn, London, 2005), p. 643.

100 Department of the Taoiseach, cabinet minutes, 30 Sept. 1943, NAI, DoTF, S13344A.

101 'Disused country mansions', 8 Dec. 1943, NAI, DoTF, S13344A.

102 Department of Local Government and Public Health memorandum for Government, 17 May 1945, NAI, DoTF, S13344B.

103 Ibid.

104 Ibid.

105 Department of Local Government and Public Health to Secretary for Government, 23 May 1945, NAI, DoTF, S13344B.

106 Department of the Taoiseach, cabinet minutes, 29 May 1945, NAI, DoTF, S13344B.

107 Dooley, *The Big House and Landed Estates of Ireland*, p. 139.

108 Mandler, *The Fall and Rise of the Stately Home*, p. 254.

109 Terence Dooley, 'National patrimony and political perceptions of the Irish country house in post-independence Ireland', in Dooley (ed.), *Ireland's Polemical Past: Views of Irish History in Honour of R. V. Comerford* (Dublin, 2010), p. 196.

110 John Gaze, *Figures in A Landscape: A History of the National Trust* (London, 1988), pp 92–3.

111 Mandler, *The Fall and Rise of the Stately Home*, p. 245.

112 Ibid.

113 Department of the Taoiseach, memorandum for Government, 16 June 1945, NAI, DoTF, S13649A.

114 Ibid.

115 Ibid.

116 Department of Industry and Commerce to Department of the Taoiseach, 23 May 1945, NAI, DoTF, S13649A.

117 Department of the Taoiseach, cabinet minutes, 3 July 1945, NAI, DoTF, S13649A.

118 Department of the Taoiseach, minute, 20 Aug. 1945, NAI, DoTF, S13649A.

119 Commissioners of Public Works to Department of Finance, 27 Sept. 1945, NAI, DoTF, S13649A.

120 Ibid.

121 Department of Finance to the Department of the Taoiseach, 8 Oct. 1945, NAI, DoTF, S13649A.

122 Ibid.

123 Ibid.

124 Ibid.

125 Department of the Taoiseach, minute, 9 Oct. 1945, NAI, DoTF, S13649A.

126 Ibid.

127 Ibid.

128 Finance solicitor to the Secretary of the Department of the Taoiseach, 22 June 1946, NAI, DoTF, S13649A.

129 Ibid.

130 Ibid.

131 Ibid.

132 Ibid.

133 Department of the Taoiseach memorandum for Government, 22 Aug. 1946, NAI, DoTF, S13649A.

134 *IT*, 12 Jan. 1946.

135 Ibid.

136 Ibid.

137 Ibid.

138 Ibid.

139 Ibid.

140 Mandler, *The Fall and Rise of the Stately Home*, pp 254–5.

141 *IT*, 12 Jan. 1946.

142 Ibid.

143 Ibid.

144 Ibid.

145 Ibid.

146 *IT*, 16 Jan. 1946, NAI, OPW files, F94/574/1.

147 Ibid.

148 Ibid.

149 Ibid.

150 Ibid.

151 *Evening Mail*, 18 Jan. 1946.

152 Ibid.

153 *IT*, 19 Jan. 1946.

154 For more on Butler, see Robert Tobin, *The Minority Voice: Hubert Butler and Southern Irish Protestanism, 1900–1991* (Oxford, 2012).

155 *IT*, 21 Jan. 1946.

156 Ibid.

157 Ibid.

158 For example, the rubble from Tubberdaly House and Ballylin House, both County Offaly, was used to build power stations at Rhode and Ferbane, County Offaly, respectively.

CHAPTER THREE

1 The National Archives have also acknowledged this difficulty, noting: 'the exact original title of the office of public works is obscure. it has been known as the Office of Public Works, The Board of Works and The Board of Public Works. All of these titles have appeared on letter-heads and registration stamps from 1830'. Rena Lohan, 'The archives of the office of public works and their value as a source for local history', The National Archives of Ireland (hereafter NAI), http://www.nationalarchives.ie/topics/OPW/LH_Archives.html, 8 Apr.2013.

2 *National Monuments Act, 1930. An Act to make provision for the protection and preservation of national monuments and for the preservation of archaeological objects in Saorstát Éireann and to make provision for other matters connected with the matters aforesaid*, 26 Feb. 1930.

3 Ibid.

4 The Commissioners of Public Works, along with the other heads of divisions, made up the senior management of the Office of Public Works (hereafter OPW). The chairman and administrative head of the OPW was also the Chairman of the Board of Commissioners.

5 Anne Carey, 'Harold G. Leask: Aspects of his work as Inspector of National Monuments', in *the Journal of the Royal Society of Antiquaries of Ireland*, cxxxiii, 2003, p. 26.

6 *Irish Independent*, 20 Oct. 1953

7 Ibid.

8 Ibid.

9 *An Act to make further and better provision for the encouragement and development of the tourist traffic and, in particular, to establish a body to engage in publicity in connection with such traffic, to amend and extend the tourist traffic acts, 1939 and 1946, to amend the law relating to the licensing of hotels and holiday camps for the sale of intoxicating liquor, and to provide for other matters connected with the matters aforesaid*, 3 July 1952.

10 *Irish Independent*, 20 Oct. 1953

11 Ibid.

12 Ibid.

13 Ibid.

14 Ibid.

15 Carey, 'Harold G. Leask', p. 25.

16 Ibid., p. 31.

17 Ibid., p. 28.

18 Ibid., p. 29.

19 Allen and Townsend Chartered Surveyors to H. G. Leask, 13 Jan. 1943, NAI, OPW files, F94/544/1.

20 Note from H. G. Leask to Division C, OPW, 14 Jan. 1943, NAI, OPW files, F94/544/1.

21 Other divisions of the OPW were Division A: New Works; Division B: Contracts; Division D: Property; Division E: Personnel; Divisions G, H and J were later divisions and covered new works also.

22 Note from H. G. Leask to Division C, OPW, 14 Jan. 1943, NAI, OPW files, F94/544/1.

23 OPW to Messrs. Allen and Townsend, 3 Mar. 1943, NAI, OPW files, F94/544/1.

24 *Irish Independent*, 19 July 1943.

25 H. G. Leask and J. Raftery, Joint Honorary Secretaries of the National Monuments Advisory Council (hereafter NMAC), to the Secretary of the OPW, 26 Mar. 1945, NAI, OPW files, F94/574/1.

26 Ibid.

27 Carey, 'Harold G. Leask', pp 24–35.

28 W. J. Veale, A/S Secretary of the OPW to the Secretary of the Land Commission, 12 Apr. 1945, NAI, OPW files, F94/574/1.

29 [D. F.] Nally, Secretary of the Department of Lands to the Secretary of the OPW, 25 Apr. 1945, NAI, OPW files, F94/574/1.

30 K. L. Schorman of the Department of Lands to the NMAC, 3 May 1945, NAI, OPW files, F94/574/1.

31 Ibid.

32 Ibid.

33 Ibid.

34 H. G. Leask internal note to Division C, OPW, 8 May 1945, NAI, OPW files, F94/574/1.

35 Ibid.

36 H. G. Leask And J. Raftery, Joint Honorary Secretaries of the NMAC to the Secretary of the Department of Lands (Forestry Division), 15 June 1945, NAI, OPW files, F94/574/1.

37 J. Darby, Department of Lands, to the Secretary of the NMAC, 10 May 1945, NAI, OPW files, F94/574/1.

38 H. G. Leask handwritten note to Division C, OPW, 17 May 1945, on letter from J. Darby, Department of Lands to the NMAC, 10 May 1945, NAI, OPW files, F94/574/1.

39 Ibid.

40 The Land Commission to the OPW, 16 Mar. 1954, NAI, OPW files, F94/1084/1/57.

41 Ibid.

42 Ibid.

43 OPW to the Land Commission, 26 Mar. 1954, NAI, OPW files, F94/1084/1/57.

44 The Land Commission to the OPW, 26 Oct. 1957, NAI, OPW files, F94/1084/1/57.

45 Handwritten note addressed to the Inspector of National Monuments, 5 Nov. 1957, NAI, OPW files, F94/1084/1/57.

46 The Land Commission to the OPW, 30 Nov. 1957; 31 Dec. 1957, NAI, OPW files, F94/1084/1/57.

47 Handwritten note Addressed to the Inspector of National Monuments, 5 Dec. 1957; 2 Jan. 1958; 28 Jan. 1958, NAI, OPW files, F94/1084/1/57.

48 The Land Commission to the OPW, 27 Jan. 1958, NAI, OPW files, F94/1084/1/57.

49 OPW to the Land Commission, 10 Feb. 1958, NAI, OPW files, F94/1084/1/57.

50 Handwritten note in OPW files, signed H. G., entitled: 'Mote Park, County Roscommon', 27 Feb. 1958, NAI, OPW files, F94/1084/1/57.

51 Ibid.

52 OPW to the Land Commission, 8 Mar. 1958, NAI, OPW files, F94/1084/1/57.

53 *Irish Independent*, 6 Sept. 1958.

54 Ibid.

55 Carey, 'Harold G. Leask', p. 28.

56 [Proinnsias Ó Udéada] Honorary Secretary of Limerick City Executive to the Secretary of the Board of Works, 9 Oct. 1943, NAI, OPW files, F94/574/1.

57 H. G. Leask, Inspector of National Monuments, to Division C, OPW, 18 Oct. 1943, NAI, OPW files, F94/574/1.

58 Ibid.

59 Ibid.

60 Ibid.

61 Ibid.

62 Ibid.

63 Ibid.

64 Handwritten notes detailing reply to be sent, approval given and letter acknowledged by Limerick Executive Council On 1 Nov. 1943, NAI, OPW files, F94/574/1.

65 This aspect of the subject area warrants its own study and, as such, falls outside the scope of this study, which concentrates on the attitudes and actions of central government and line departments.

66 H. G. Leask, handwritten note to Division C, OPW, 31 Dec. 1943, NAI, OPW files, F94/574/1.

67 Ibid.

68 J. P. O'Brien, Chairman of the Irish Tourist Board to the Secretary of the Department of Supplies, 6 Nov. 1943; forwarded from the Department of

Industry and Commerce to the Secretary of the OPW, 22 Dec. 1943, NAI, OPW files, F94/574/1.

69 Ibid.

70 Ibid.

71 H. G. Leask, handwritten note to Division C, OPW, 31 Dec. 1943, NAI, OPW files, F94/574/1.

72 Draft letter from OPW to the Department of Industry and Commerce, Jan. 1944, NAI, OPW files, F94/574/1.

73 Ibid.

74 Ibid.

75 Signed internal note in reply to Division C of the OPW's handwritten note, 18 Jan. 1944, NAI, OPW files, F94/574/1.

76 Town Clerk of Tipperary Urban District Council to the OPW, 4 Apr. 1944, NAI, OPW files, F94/574/1.

77 Ibid; *Muintir Na Tíre* is the national association for the promotion of community development in Ireland.

78 H. G. Leask, handwritten note to Division C, OPW, 31 Dec. 1943, NAI, OPW files, F94/574/1.

79 Handwritten note from H. G. Leask, 12 Apr. 1944, on letter from town clerk of Tipperary Urban District Council to the OPW, 4 Apr. 1944, NAI, OPW files, F94/574/1.

80 Draft letter from OPW to Tipperary Urban District Council, Apr. 1944, NAI, OPW files, F94/574/1.

81 *National Monuments Act, 1930. An act to make provision for the protection and preservation of national monuments and for the preservation of archaeological objects in Saorstát Éireann and to make provision for other matters connected with the matters aforesaid*, 26 Feb. 1930.

82 Handwritten OPW internal note, 20 Apr. 1944, NAI, OPW files, F94/574/1.

83 H. G. Leask and Joseph Raftery, Joint Honorary Secretaries of the NMAC to the Secretary of the OPW, 5 Oct. 1945, NAI, OPW files, F94/574/1.

84 Ibid.

85 Ibid.

86 Handwritten note from Division C, OPW, to the Inspector of National Monuments, 15 Oct. 1945, NAI, OPW files, F94/574/1.

87 H. G. Leask to Division C, OPW, 30 Oct. 1945, NAI, OPW files, F94/574/1.

88 Ibid.

89 Ibid.

90 Ibid.

91 Ibid.

92 Ibid.

93 OPW departmental minute, undated, unsigned, NAI, OPW files, F94/574/1.

94 Ibid.

95 OPW internal handwritten note, 5 Dec. 1945, NAI, OPW files, F94/574/1.

96 Ibid.

97 OPW internal letter to Mr Cullinane, 24 Jan. 1958, NAI, OPW files, F94/1085/1/57.

98 Ibid.

99 Ibid.

100 Ibid.

101 Ibid.

102 Chairman of the OPW's notes for 'a board conference on old mansions and big houses', 1 Jan. 1946, NAI, OPW files, F94/574/1.

103 Ibid.

104 Ibid.

105 Ibid.

106 Ibid.

107 Ibid.

108 Department of Local Government and Public Health, memorandum for the government, 17 May 1945, NAI, Dept of the Taoiseach files (hereafter DoTF), S13344B.

109 Chairman of the OPW's notes for 'a board conference on old mansions and big houses', 1 Jan. 1946, NAI, OPW files, F94/574/1.

110 Ibid.

111 Ibid.

112 Ibid.

113 OPW minute to Division F, 4 June 1954, NAI, OPW files, F94:940/1/54.

114 Draft preservation order for Dunsandle House, NAI, OPW files, F94:940/1/54.

115 Internal minute to Mr O'Donnellan, June 1954, NAI, OPW files, F94:940/1/54.

116 Submission in OPW files, unsigned, undated, NAI, OPW files, F94:940/1/54.

117 OPW internal minute to Division F, 7 July 1954, NAI, OPW files, F94:940/1/54.

118 Ibid.

119 OPW internal minute submitted to Mr Cullinane, 15 July 1954, NAI, OPW files, F94:940/1/54.

120 Ibid.

121 OPW internal minute submitted to Mr Cullinane, 26 July 1954, NAI, OPW files, F94:940/1/54.

122 Ibid.

123 Handwritten note to the Commissioners and Chairman of the OPW, 28 July 1954, NAI, OPW files, F94:940/1/54.

124 *Irish Times*, 24 July 1954.

125 Ibid.

126 Ibid.

127 Handwritten note submitted to OPW, 12 Aug. 1954, NAI, OPW files, F94:940/1/54.

128 Ibid.

129 NMAC to OPW, 15 Oct. 1954, NAI, OPW files, F94:940/1/54.

130 Ibid.

131 OPW to NMAC, Nov. 1954, NAI, OPW files, F94:940/1/54.

132 Galway County Council to the OPW, 11 Dec. 1954, NAI, OPW files, F94:940/1/54.

133 Ibid.

134 *Connacht Tribune*, 21 Sept. 1957.

135 *Irish Press*, 26 Sept. 1957.

136 *Connacht Tribune*, 14 Dec. 1957.

137 Ibid.

138 Department of Finance to the Secretary to the President of the Executive Council, 2 Nov. 1930, NAI, DoTF, S5935.

139 Department of Finance to the Secretary to the President of the Executive Council, 2 Nov. 1930, NAI, DoTF, S5935.

140 A. T. Lucas, 'Harold G. Leask, M. Arch., Litt.D., Past President', in *the Journal of the Royal Society of Antiquaries of Ireland*, xcvi, No. 1, 1966, pp 1–2.

141 Carey, 'Harold G. Leask', pp 24–35.

142 For published works see Lucas, 'Harold G. Leask, M. Arch., Litt.D., Past President', pp 3–6.

143 Carey, 'Harold G. Leask', p. 28.

144 Ibid.

145 Terence Dooley, *The Decline of the Big House in Ireland: A Study of Irish Landed Families, 1860–1960* (Dublin, 2001), pp 254–5.

146 Quoted in Jane O'Hea O'Keeffe, *Voices from the Great Houses of Cork and Kerry* (Cork, 2013), p. 48.

147 Dooley, *The Decline of the Big House in Ireland*, p. 278.

CHAPTER FOUR

1 Dermot Keogh, *Twentieth-Century Ireland: Nation and State* (Dublin, 1994), p. 185.

2 Olwen Purdue, *The Big House in the North of Ireland: Land, Power and Social Elites, 1878–1960* (Dublin, 2009), pp 197–8.

3 Ibid., p. 231.

4 F. J. McEvoy, 'Canada, Ireland and the Commonwealth: The declaration of the Irish Republic, 1948–9', in *Irish Historical Studies*, xxiv: 96, Nov. 1985, p. 508.

5 Ibid.

6 Keogh, *Twentieth-Century Ireland*, p. 191.

7 Ibid.

8 McEvoy, 'Canada, Ireland and the Commonwealth', p. 506.

9 Ibid.

10 Ibid., p. 521.

11 Ibid.

12 *Dáil Éireann Deb.*, cxliii, 1828, 9 Dec. 1953.

13 Ibid.

14 *Dáil Éireann Deb.*, cxxxvii, 687, 19 Mar. 1953.

15 *Irish Times* (hereafter *IT*), 6 Oct. 1952.

16 Ibid.

17 Ibid., 8 Nov. 1955.

18 Ibid.

19 Terence Dooley, *The Decline of the Big House in Ireland: A Study of Irish Landed Families, 1860–1960* (Dublin, 2001), p. 268.

20 Ibid., p. 269.

21 Brian Joseph Casey, 'Land, politics and religion on the Clancarty Estate, east Galway, 1851–1914', unpublished PhD thesis, National University of Ireland, Maynooth, 2011, pp 293–4.

22 *IT*, 10 Dec. 1952.

23 Robert M. Smyllie was editor of the *Irish Times* from 1934 until 1954.

24 *IT*, 13 Sept. 1954; quoted in Mark O'Brien, *The Irish Times: A History* (Dublin, 2008), p. 80–1.

25 Ibid.

26 *IT*, 3 Nov. 1953.

27 Ibid.

28 Ibid.

29 For a discussion of the club life of the landed class from 1914–50, See Dooley, *The Decline of the Big House in Ireland*, pp 267–8.

30 *IT*, 7 Sept. 1954.

31 L. P. Curtis, Jr., 'Demonising the Irish landlords since the famine', in Brian Casey (ed.), *Defying the Law of the Land: Agrarian Radicals in Irish History* (Dublin, 2013), p. 21.

32 Ibid., p. 22.

33 For more on this subject see Otto Rauchbauer (ed.), *Ancestral Voices: The Big House in Anglo-Irish Literature: A Collection of Interpretations* (Dublin, 1992); Vera Kreilkamp, *The Anglo-Irish Novel and the Big House* (Syracuse, 1998).

34 *IT*, 1 Feb. 1949.

35 Jane O'Hea O'Keeffe, *Voices from the Great Houses of Cork and Kerry* (Cork, 2013), p. 124.

36 Sarah Connolly-Carew, *The Children of Castletown House* (Dublin, 2012), p. 68.

37 *IT*, 10 May 1950.

38 Dooley, *The Decline of the Big House in Ireland*, p. 170.

39 Figures compiled by author from houses listed by Mark Bence-Jones as having been demolished specifically in these decades. Mark Bence-Jones, *A Guide to Irish Country Houses* (Revised edn, London, 1988). For more information on these estimates and figures, see Chapter Two.

40 O'Hea O'Keeffe, *Voices from the Great Houses of Cork and Kerry*, p. 221.

41 Connolly-Carew, *The Children of Castletown House*, p. 192.

42 Ibid, p. 193.

43 Ibid.

44 Connolly–Carew, *The Children of Castletown House*, p. 200.

45 Ibid.

46 *Irish Independent*, 2 Oct. 1952.

47 Ibid.

48 Ibid.

49 Ibid.

50 Peter Mandler, *The Fall and Rise of the Stately Home* (New Haven & London, 1997), p. 340.

51 Ibid.

52 Ibid., p. 348.

53 *IT*, 11 Jan. 1957.

54 Ibid.

55 Ibid.

56 Ibid.

57 Keogh, *Twentieth-Century Ireland*, p. 200.

58 Extract from report to the government of Ireland on various institutions and activities concerned with the arts in Ireland, 30 Sept. 1949, National Archives of Ireland (hereafter NAI), Dept of the Taoiseach files (hereafter DoTF), S8488B.

59 Ibid.

60 Ibid.

61 *Arts Act, 1951. An Act to stimulate public interest in, and to promote the knowledge, appreciation, and practice of, the arts and, for these and other purposes, to establish an arts council, and to provide for other matters in connection with the matters aforesaid,* 8 May 1951.

62 *National Monuments (Amendment) Act, 1954. An Act to amend the National Monuments Act, 1930,* 22 Dec., 1954.

63 Keogh, *Twentieth-Century Ireland*, p. 213.

64 Ibid., p. 215.

65 O'Brien, *The Irish Times*, p. 154.

66 Ibid.

67 Copy of letter from the NMAC to the OPW re: Dunsandle House, County Galway, 26 May 1955, NAI, Office of Public Works (hereafter OPW) files, F94/574/1.

68 Ibid.

69 National Monuments Council: Report of committee on lands and buildings of architectural and historic interest ineligible for preservation under the National Monuments Act, attached to a letter from the NMAC to the OPW, 4 July 1955, NAI, OPW files, F94/574/1.

70 Ibid.

71 Ibid.

72 Ibid.

73 Ibid.

74 Ibid.

75 Ibid.

76 Ibid.

77 Justin Green, 'Introduction', in Mary Leland, *At Home in Ireland* (Cork, 2012), p. xi.

78 *Cara*, Apr./May 2011, pp 78–80.

79 National Monuments Council: report of committee on lands and buildings of architectural and historic interest ineligible for preservation under the National Monuments Act attached to a letter from the NMAC to the OPW, 4 July 1955 (NAI, OPW files, F94/574/1).

80 Ibid.

81 Ibid.

82 Ibid.

83 Ibid.

84 OPW to the NMAC, 17 Aug. 1955, NAI, OPW files, F94/574/1.

85 *IT*, 10 Aug. 1956.

86 Ibid., 12 June 1956.

87 Ibid.

88 Ibid.

89 Ibid.

90 *Irish Independent*, 16 June 1956.

91 *National Parks and Access to the Countryside Act, 1949. An Act to make provision for national parks and the establishment of a National Parks Commission; to confer on the nature conservancy and local authorities powers for the establishment and maintenance of nature reserves; to make further provision for the recording, creation, maintenance and improvement of public paths and for securing access to open country, and to amend the law relating to rights of way; to confer further powers for preserving and enhancing natural beauty; and for matters connected with the purposes aforesaid*, 16 Dec. 1949.

92 *Finance Act (Northern Ireland) 1948. An Act to alter certain duties of excise (including entertainments duty and duties on licences for mechanically-propelled vehicles) and stamp duties; to amend the law relating to the duties aforesaid and to death duties; to abolish certain duties; to provide for certain payments; and to make further provision in connection with finance*, 10 Aug. 1948.

93 *Irish Independent*, 16 June 1956.

94 OPW memorandum on the proposed sale of the Kenmare Estate and of the middle and lower lakes of Killarney, 24 July 1956, NAI, DOTF, S16047A.

95 Ibid.

96 *IT*, 7 Aug. 1956.

97 Ibid.

98 Ibid., 10 Aug. 1956.

99 Ibid.

100 *Kerryman*, 11 Aug. 1956.

101 Ibid.

102 Ibid.

103 '€7 m Restoration for Killarney House announced', RTÉ News, http://www.rte .ie/News/2011/0730/304417-Kenmare/, 6 Apr. 2013.

104 See for example, article in *IT*, 3 Nov. 1953.

CHAPTER FIVE

1 Patrick Kavanagh, 'Epic', in *Patrick Kavanagh: Collected Poems* (2nd edn, London, 1972), p. 136.

2 Terence Dooley, *'The Land for the People': The Land Question in Independent Ireland* (Dublin, 2004), p. 67.

3 Patrick J. Sammon, *In the Land Commission: A Memoir, 1933–1978* (Dublin, 1997), p. 9.

4 Ibid.

5 Ibid.

6 This is reflected in the fact that Patrick J. Sammon has dedicated a section of his memoir of the Land Commission to discussing his tenure as Minister; the only one chosen among all Ministers for Land. See ibid., pp 48–57.

7 Ibid., p. 48.

8 Ibid., pp 295–6.

9 Dooley, *'The Land for the People'*, p. 11.

10 Sammon, *In the Land Commission*, p. 296.

11 Erskine Childers, Minister for Posts and Telegraphs, to T. Ó Deirg, Minister for Lands, 5 Nov. 1953, National Archives of Ireland (hereafter NAI), Dept of the Taoiseach files (hereafter DoTF), S5004B.

12 Ibid.

13 T. Ó Deirg, Minister for Lands, to Erskine Childers, Minster for Posts and Telegraphs, 10 Nov. 1953, NAI, DoTF, S5004B.

14 Sammon, *In the Land Commission*, p. 86.

15 Ibid.

16 The interior of French Park was dismantled in the 1950s and the ruins demolished in the 1970s, although it was not property of the Land Commission.

17 See Chapter Two: Figures compiled by the author from houses listed by Mark Bence-Jones as having been demolished specifically in this decade in Mark Bence-Jones, *A Guide to Irish Country Houses* (Revised edn, London, 1988).

18 T. K. Whitaker was Secretary of the Department of Finance from 30 May 1956 until 28 Feb. 1969.

19 E. Ó Dálaigh, Secretary of the Department of Lands, to the Secretary of the Department of Finance, 5 Aug. 1958, NAI, Dept of Finance files (hereafter DoFF), FIN/F63/8/58.

20 Oifig An Aire Tailte Summary of Memorandum for Government: Preservation of Mansions and Large Houses, 5 Aug. 1958, NAI, DoFF, FIN/F63/8/58.

21 Ibid.

22 Erskine Childers, Minister for Posts and Telegraphs, to T. Ó Deirg, Minister for Lands, 5 Nov. 1953, NAI, DoTF, S5004B.

23 Oifig An Aire Tailte, Summary of Memorandum for Government: Preservation of Mansions and Large Houses, 5 Aug. 1958, NAI, DoFF, FIN/F63/8/58.

24 Ibid.

25 The net result of the investigations into the possible usefulness of these mansions was that five (as a provisional number) were suitable for accommodation and 325 were unsuitable for any public purpose. Department of Local Government and Public Health Memorandum for Government, 17 May 1945, NAI, DoTF, S13344B.

26 Oifig An Aire Tailte, Summary of Memorandum for Government, 5 Aug. 1958.

27 Ibid; migrants were those who were given an allotment of land in a different county to where they lived, causing them to migrate there.

28 Ibid.

29 Ibid.

30 Ibid.

31 Ibid.

32 See Appendix One for tables.

33 Table A, Appendix to Oifig An Aire Tailte, Summary of Memorandum for Government, 5 Aug. 1958.

34 Ibid.

35 Ibid.

36 Table B, Appendix to Oifig An Aire Tailte, Summary of Memorandum for Government, 5 Aug. 1958.

37 Ibid.

38 Sammon, *In the Land Commission*, p. 45.

39 Table C, Appendix to Oifig An Aire Tailte, Summary of Memorandum for Government, 5 Aug. 1958.

40 Ibid.

41 Appendix to Oifig An Aire Tailte, Summary of Memorandum for Government, 5 Aug. 1958.

42 See Chapter Two: Figures compiled by the author from houses listed as having been demolished specifically in Bence-Jones, *A Guide to Irish Country Houses*.

43 Appendix to Oifig An Aire Tailte, Summary of Memorandum for Government, 5 Aug. 1958.

44 [J. McMahon] Land Commission to the Secretary of the Department of Finance, 30 Sept. 1958, NAI, DoFF, FIN/F63/8/58.

45 J. Mooney, Department of Finance to the Secretary of the OPW, 7 Oct. 1958, NAI, DoFF, FIN/F63/8/58.

46 Handwritten note on letter, J. Mooney, Department of Finance to the Secretary of the OPW, 7 Oct. 1958, Dated 21 Nov. 1958, NAI, DoFF, FIN/F63/8/58.

47 The Secretary of the Commissioners of Public Works, OPW, to the Secretary of the Department of Finance, 30 Dec. 1958, NAI, DoFF, FIN/F63/8/58.

48 Ibid.

49 *Dáil Éireann Deb.*, xciii, 52, 2 May 1944; Moylan was Minister for Lands from July 1943 until Feb. 1948.

50 *Irish Times* (hereafter *IT*), 16 Jan. 1946.

51 The Secretary of the Commissioners of Public Works, OPW, to the Secretary of the Department of Finance, 30 Dec. 1958, NAI, DoFF, FIN/F63/8/58.

52 Ibid.

53 Draft letter from J. W., Department of Finance, to the Department of Lands, Feb. 1959, NAI, DoFF, FIN/F63/8/58.

54 Oifig An Aire Tailte, Summary of Memorandum for Government, 5 Aug. 1958.

55 Ibid.

56 Ibid.

57 Office of the Revenue Commissioners to the Department of Finance, 2 Sept. 1958, NAI, DoFF, FIN/F63/8/58.

58 Ibid.

59 Department of Finance, handwritten note on letter from the Commissioners of Public Works to the Department of Finance, 30 Dec. 1958, NAI, DoFF, FIN/F63/8/58.

60 The Secretary of the Commissioners of Public Works, OPW, to the Secretary of the Department of Finance, 30 Dec. 1958, NAI, DoFF, FIN/F63/8/58.

61 Ibid.

62 Ibid.

63 Ibid.

64 Ibid.

65 Draft letter from J. W., Department of Finance, to the Department of Lands, Feb. 1959, NAI, DoFF, FIN/F63/8/58.

66 Ibid.

67 The only information that could be obtained on these officials were their initials from the sources.

68 J. M., Department of Finance, to Mr Hogan, Department of Finance, 10 Feb. 1959, NAI, DoFF, FIN/F63/8/58.

69 Valuation Office to the Secretary of the Department of Finance, 21 Oct. 1958, NAI, DoFF, FIN/F63/8/58.

70 Observations of the Commissioner of Valuation on Oifig An Aire Tailte's Summary of Memorandum for Government: Preservation of Mansions and Large Houses, 21 Oct. 1958, NAI, DoFF, FIN/F63/8/58.

71 Ibid.

72 Ibid.

73 Ibid.

74 Ibid.

75 Draft letter from J. W., Department of Finance, to the Department of Lands, Feb. 1959, NAI, DoFF, FIN/F63/8/58.

76 Ibid.

77 Ibid.

78 Ibid.

79 J. M., Department of Finance, to Mr Hogan, Department of Finance, 10 Feb. 1959, NAI, DoFF, FIN/F63/8/58.

80 Ibid.

81 Ibid.

82 Ibid.

83 Ibid.

84 Draft letter from Department of Finance to the Department of Lands, undated, NAI, DoFF, FIN/F63/8/58.

85 J. M., Department of Finance, to Mr Hogan, Department of Finance, 10 Feb. 1959, NAI, DoFF, FIN/F63/8/58.

86 Ibid.

87 Handwritten note from L. Ó N to Mr Mooney [J. M.], Department of Finance, 10 Feb. 1959, on letter from J. M., Department of Finance, to Mr Hogan, Department of Finance, 10 Feb. 1959, NAI, DoFF, FIN/F63/8/58.

88 Department of Finance to the Department of Lands, 16 Feb. 1959, NAI, DoFF, FIN/F63/8/58.

89 Sammon, *In the Land Commission*, pp 54–5.

90 Ibid., p. 55.

91 Ibid., p. 56.

92 Ibid., p. 57.

93 *Irish Independent*, 26 Oct. 1953.

94 Ibid.

95 S. Mac Piarais, Department of Lands, to Mr Doyle, 30 Oct. 1953, NAI, DoTF, S5004B.

96 Ibid.

97 Ibid.

98 Terence Dooley, *The Decline of the Big House in Ireland: A Study of Irish Landed Families, 1860–1960* (Dublin, 2001), p. 143.

99 Desmond Guinness, quoted in Ibid., p. 143.

100 Dooley, *'The Land for the People'*, p. 90.

101 *Dáil Éireann Deb.*, xcii, 1518, 23 Feb. 1944.

102 Ibid., xciii, 52, 2 May 1944.

103 Department of Lands (Land Commission), draft letter to Lord Mountbatten, NAI, DoTF, 98/6/677.

104 Ibid.

105 *Dáil Éireann Deb.*, lviii, 835, 12 Feb. 1965.

106 Ibid.

107 *Dáil Éireann Deb.*, lviii, 835–6, 12 Feb. 1965.

108 Ibid., lviii, 838, 12 Feb. 1965.

109 *IT*, 20 June 1992.

110 *Irish Land Commission (Dissolution) Act, 1992. An Act to provide for the dissolution of the Irish Land Commission, for the winding up of the system of land purchase, for the transfer of certain functions exercisable under the Land Purchase Acts, and for other connected matters*, 11 Nov. 1992.

CHAPTER SIX

1 Frank Barry, 'Foreign investment and the politics of export profits tax relief 1956', in *Institute for International Integration Studies (IIIS) Discussion Paper*, 357, Feb. 2011, p. 2. Trinity College, http://www.tcd.ie/iiis/Documents/Discussion/pdfs/iiisdp357.pdf, 21 Nov. 2012.

2 Ibid.

3 Ibid.

4 Ibid., p. 6.

5 Ibid., p. 11.

6 Ibid., pp 16–17.

7 Ibid., p. 17.

8 Dermot Keogh, *Twentieth-Century Ireland: Nation and State* (Dublin, 1994), p. 245.

9 Ibid.

10 Alvin Jackson, *Ireland 1798–1998* (Oxford, 1999), pp 317–18.

11 Ibid., pp 318–19.

12 Ibid., p. 320.

13 John A. Murphy, *Ireland in the Twentieth Century* (2nd edn, Dublin, 1989), pp 143–4.

14 Ibid., p. 145.

15 Ibid.

16 Ibid.

17 *Seanad Éireann Deb.*, lxi, 1233, 29 June 1966.

18 Ibid.

19 *Seanad Éireann Deb.*, lxvii, 78, 12 Nov. 1969.

20 Ibid., lxix, 100–1, 16 Dec. 1970.

21 Observations of the Commissioner of Valuation on Oifig An Aire Tailte's Summary of Memorandum for Government: Preservation of Mansions and Large Houses, 21 Oct. 1958, National Archives of Ireland (hereafter NAI), Dept of Finance files (hereafter DoFF), FIN/F63/8/58.

22 J. M., Department of Finance, to Mr Hogan, Department of Finance, 10 Feb. 1959, NAI, DoFF, FIN/F63/8/58.

23 Patrick J. Sammon, *In the Land Commission: A Memoir, 1933–1978* (Dublin, 1997), p. 86.

24 Harry Teggin, '*Domus Britannicus*: What future for the country house?', in *The Architect's Journal*, 24 Jan. 1979, p. 166; quoted in Terence Dooley, 'National patrimony and political perceptions of the Irish country house in post-independence Ireland', in Dooley (ed), *Ireland's Polemical Past: Views of Irish History in Honour of R. V. Comerford* (Dublin, 2010), p. 199.

25 Dooley, 'National patrimony and political perceptions of the Irish country house', p. 199.

26 Keogh, *Twentieth-Century Ireland*, p. 247.

27 Ibid.

28 Enda Delaney, 'Emigration, political cultures and the evolution of post-war society', in Brian Girvin and Gary Murphy (eds), *The Lemass Era: Politics and Society in the Ireland of Seán Lemass* (Dublin, 2005), p. 87.

29 Keogh, *Twentieth-Century Ireland*, p. 318.

30 See for example Terence Dooley, 'National patrimony and political perceptions of the Irish country house', pp 192–212.

31 *Seanad Éireann Deb.*, liv, 1581, 2 Aug. 1961.

32 Ibid.

33 The endurance of this rhetorical re-presentation of the house is evidenced by the fact that, many years later in 2004, then Taoiseach, Bertie Ahern, opened the Third Annual Historic Houses of Ireland Conference at the National University of Ireland, Maynooth, with the following words: 'for too long the historic house was not seen by many as part of a shared Irish heritage – nor indeed was it viewed as a heritage worth preserving. Fortunately, times and opinions have changed radically since then. The Irish Big House is increasingly valued today for its architectural significance; for the wealth of design created for the most part by Irish craftspeople; and for the valuable insight it offers us into an era that had had such an influence on shaping our history.' An Taoiseach, Bertie Ahern's speech at the Third Annual Historic Houses of Ireland Conference, NUI Maynooth, Sept. 2004; www.taoiseach.gov.ie/index.Asp?Docid=2145, 5 July 2012.

34 See, for example, R. V. Comerford, *Ireland: Inventing the Nation* (London, 2003), p. 2.

35 *Dáil Éireann Deb.*, cxciv, 352–4, 22 Mar. 1962.

36 *Irish Independent*, 13 June 2009.

37 *Dáil Éireann Deb.*, ccii, 1475, 14 May 1963.

38 See for example Dooley, 'National patrimony and political perceptions of the Irish country house', p. 202.

39 Ibid., p. 203.

40 *Connaught Tribune* 3 June 1977.

41 Ibid.

42 *Dáil Éireann Deb.*, cccv, 676, 13 Apr. 1978.

43 Girvin and Murphy, 'Whose Ireland? The Lemass Era', in *The Lemass Era*, p. 6.

44 *Dáil Éireann Deb.*, ccii, 1470, 14 May 1963.

45 Luke Gibbons, *Transformations in Irish Culture* (Cork, 1996), p. 171.

46 *Irish Times* (hereafter *IT*), 16 May. 1970.

47 Ibid., 20 Oct. 1970.

48 Keogh, *Twentieth-Century Ireland*, p. 245

49 Dooley, 'National patrimony and political perceptions of the Irish country house', p. 200.

50 *IT*, 16 Jan. 1971.

51 Peter Mandler, *The Fall and Rise of the Stately Home* (New Haven & London, 1997), p. 403.

52 Seán Lemass to Donough O'Malley, 30 Apr. 1962, NAI, Dept of the Taoiseach files (hereafter DoTF), S6355 C/62.

53 Ibid.

54 Ibid.

55 Donough O'Malley to Seán Lemass, 2 May 1962, NAI, DoTF, S6355 C/62.

56 Ibid.

57 Erskine Childers to Seán Lemass, 16 May 1962, NAI, DoTF, S6355 C/62.

58 Ibid.

59 Ibid.

60 Institute of Public Administration, Centre for Administrative Studies memorandum, June 1962, NAI, DoTF, S6355 C/62.

61 Ibid.

62 Ibid.

63 'The Trustees of Muckross House', Muckross House website, http://www.muckross-house.ie/trustees.htm, 29 Nov. 2011.

64 Ibid.

65 Ibid.

66 *Irish Press*, 31 Oct. 1964.

67 Sylvester O'Brien to Mr Dillon, 8 Oct. 1949, NAI, DoTF, S3649B.

68 Ibid.

69 M. A. Purcell, Secretary of Bord Fáilte Éireann, to Dr N. Ó Nualláin, Assistant Secretary of the Department of the Taoiseach, 29 Sept. 1959, NAI, DoTF, S3649B.

70 Ibid.

71 Ibid.

72 Ibid.

73 M. J. O'Connor to An Taoiseach, Seán Lemass, 14 Oct. 1959, NAI, DoTF, S3649B.

74 M. A. Purcell, Secretary Bord Fáilte Éireann, to Dr N. Ó Nualláin, Assistant Secretary of the Department of the Taoiseach, 29 Sept. 1959, NAI, DoTF, S3649B.

75 *Irish Press*, 21 Aug. 1967.

76 Ibid., 7 Dec. 1964; Ibid., 7 Dec. 1964; Mark O'Brien has described how 'The *Irish Independent* was traditionally deferential to the Catholic Church, and the *Irish Press* was essentially the mouthpiece of Fianna Fáil', in Mark O'Brien, *The Irish Times: A History* (Dublin, 2008), p. 133.

77 Ibid.

78 Ibid.

79 *Dáil Éireann Deb.*, ccxlv, 167, 11 Mar. 1970.

80 Dooley, 'National patrimony and political perceptions of the Irish country house', pp 200–1.

81 *Dáil Éireann Deb.*, ccxlv, 167, 11 Mar. 1970.

82 Ibid., ccxlv, 168, 11 Mar. 1970.

83 See Keogh, *Twentieth-Century* Ireland, pp 243–4.

84 Girvin and Murphy, 'Whose Ireland? The Lemass era', p. 2.

85 Ibid., p. 5.

86 Ibid., p. 11.

87 John Horgan, 'Foreword', in *The Lemass Era*, p. xi.

88 *Irish Independent*, 13 June 2009.

89 Ibid.

90 Later works include Mark Bence-Jones, *Life in An Irish Country House* (London, 1996) and Simon Marsden, *In Ruins: The Once Great Houses of Ireland* (Boston & London, 1997), among many others.

91 Terence Dooley, *The Decline of the Big House in Ireland: A Study of Irish Landed Families, 1860–1960, 1860–1960* (Dublin, 2001), p. 253.

92 Terence Dooley, *The Big House and Landed Estates of Ireland: A Research Guide* (Dublin, 2007), p. 141.

93 Ibid.

94 R. V. Comerford, 'Foreword', in Terence Dooley and Christopher Ridgway (eds), *The Irish Country House: Its Past, Present and Future* (Dublin, 2011), p. 12.

95 Ibid.

96 Dooley, *The Big House and Landed Estates of Ireland*, p. 141.

97 *Dáil Éireann Deb.*, cxci, 1331, 19 July 1961.

98 Ibid., cxci, 1332, 19 July 1961.

99 Ibid., clxi, 218, 24 Apr. 1957.

100 *IT*, 6 Feb. 1968.

101 Ibid., 20 May 1964.

102 Ibid.

103 *Sunday Independent*, 7 June 1964.

104 *IT*, 22 May 1964.

105 Ibid.

106 Ibid., 21 May. 1964.

107 Ibid.

108 Ibid.

109 Ibid., 2 Feb. 1965.

110 Olwen Purdue, *The Big House in the North of Ireland: Land, Power and Social Elites, 1878–1960* (Dublin, 2009), p. 237.

111 Ibid.

112 Ibid., pp 237–8.

113 *Irish Farmers Journal*, 21 Mar. 1959.

114 *IT*, 31 Jan. 2002.

115 Ibid., 26 Mar. 1965.

116 Ibid., 11 June 1969.

117 Ibid., 24 Feb. 1968.

118 Ibid., 9 July 1955.

119 Land Commission Report on inspection of Bishopscourt Estate, Sept. 1955, quoted in letter from the Department of Lands to Department of the Taoiseach, 31 Mar. 1966, NAI, DoTF, 99/1/466.

120 Ibid.

121 Ibid.

122 Ibid.

123 Land Commission Report on negotiations for Bishopscourt purchase, Apr. 1955, quoted in letter from the Department of Lands to the Department of the Taoiseach, 31 Mar. 1966, NAI, DoTF, 99/1/466; McMahon & Tweedy Solicitors to the Land Commission, 1 Oct. 1957, NAI, DoTF, 99/1/466.

124 Patricia McGillycuddy to Seán Lemass, 24 Mar. 1966, NAI, DoTF, 99/1/466.

125 Department of the Taoiseach to other government departments, 25 Mar. 1966, NAI, DoTF, 99/1/466.

126 Department of Lands to the Department of the Taoiseach, 31 Mar. 1966, NAI, DoTF, 99/1/466.

127 Department of Finance to the Department of the Taoiseach, 21 Apr. 1966, NAI, DoTF, 99/1/466.

128 G. McNicholl, Office of Public Works report on examination of Bishopscourt House, 2 June 1966, NAI, DoTF, 99/1/466.

129 Ibid.

130 Department of Finance to the Department of the Taoiseach, 3 Aug. 1966, NAI, DoTF, 99/1/466.

131 Department of the Taoiseach memorandum, 25 Aug. 1966, NAI, DoTF, 99/1/466.

132 Ibid.

133 Ibid.

134 Seán Lemass to Mrs Dermot McGillycuddy, 30 Aug. 1966, NAI, DoTF, 99/1/466.

135 Patricia McGillycuddy to Seán Lemass, 6 Oct. 1966, NAI, DoTF, 2002/8/353.

136 Ibid.

137 Ibid.

138 Ibid.

139 Department of the Taoiseach minutes of departmental meeting, 7 Nov. 1966, NAI, DoTF, 99/1/466.

140 Ibid.

141 Ibid.

142 Ibid.

143 Ibid.

144 Ibid.

145 Draft letter to Mrs McGillycuddy submitted for approval, 7 Nov. 1966, NAI, DoTF, 99/1/466.

146 Department of External Affairs to the Department of the Taoiseach, 6 Dec. 1966, NAI, DoTF, 99/1/466; Blair House is the guest house of the President of the United States; Chequers is the country house retreat of the Prime Minister of the United Kingdom.

147 Department of External Affairs to the Department of the Taoiseach, 6 Dec. 1966, NAI, DoTF, 99/1/466.

148 Department of the Taoiseach to the Department of Finance, 21 Dec.1966, NAI, DoTF, 99/1/466.

149 Handwritten notes of 26 Apr. 1967, 28 Mar. 1967 and 15 Mar. 1967, NAI, DoTF, 99/1/466.

150 Patricia McGillycuddy to Charles Haughey, 24 June 1968, NAI, DoTF, 2002/8/353.

151 Ibid.

152 Patricia McGillycuddy to Charles Haughey, 1 Aug. 1969, NAI, DoTF, 2002/8/353.

153 Reported letter from Charles Haughey to Patricia McGillycuddy, 26 Aug. 1969, referred to in memorandum for the government, 'Bishopscourt House and lands: Offer as gift to the nation', 26 Aug. 1971, NAI, DoTF, 2002/8/353.

154 Patricia McGillycuddy to Jack Lynch, 11 Dec. 1970, NAI, DoTF, 2002/8/353.

155 Jack Lynch to Charles Haughey, 19 Mar. 1970, NAI, DoTF, 99/1/466.

156 *Dáil Éireann Deb.*, cdxv, 1511, 11 Feb. 1992.

157 Memorandum for the government, 'Bishopscourt House and lands: Offer as gift to the nation', 26 Aug. 1971, NAI, DoTF, 2002/8/353.

158 Ibid.

159 Ibid.

160 Ibid.

161 Cabinet minutes, 'Bishopscourt House and lands: Offer as gift to nation', 9 Sept. 1971, NAI, DoTF, 2002/8/353.

162 Attorney General record of meeting with Dermot McGillycuddy, 27 July 1973, NAI, Attorney General Files, AGO/2005/77/151.

163 Ibid.

164 Dermot McGillycuddy to the Attorney General, 9 Oct. 1973, NAI, Attorney General Files, AGO/2005/77/151.

165 Ibid.

166 Ibid., 16 Jan. 1973.

167 Ibid.

168 Department of the Taoiseach to the Attorney General, 9 Sept. 1975, NAI, Attorney General Files, AGO/2005/77/151).

169 Letter from Assistant Secretary to Government to the Private Secretary to the Minister for Finance, 28 Nov. 1975, forwarded to the Attorney General, 2 Dec. 1975, NAI, Attorney General Files, AGO/2005/77/151).

170 *IT*, 13 Feb. 1976.

171 Ibid., 25 June 1976.

172 Dooley, 'National patrimony and political perceptions of the Irish country house', p. 203.

CONCLUSION

1 Brian Friel, *Making History* (London, 1989), pp 15–16.

2 G. B. Shaw, quoted in Richard Pine, *The Diviner: The Art of Brian Friel* (2nd edn, Dublin, 1999), p. 209.

3 Rates were abolished in 1977. Furthermore, the 1982 Finance Act introduced by the short-lived Fine Gael/Labour coalition under Garret Fitzgerald recognised specifically, and for the first time in an independent government's finance act, the special position of historic houses. Section 19 legislated for reliefs in respect of properties determined to have scientific, historical, architectural or aesthetic interest according to the Commissioners of Public Works. A house was deemed to qualify for these reliefs if this interest was ascertained and if, more significantly, the building itself was open for reasonable access to the public for not less than thirty days in a year and at reasonable times and prices so that the public could visit. *Finance Act, 1982. An Act to charge and impose certain duties of customs and inland revenue (including excise), to amend the law relating to customs and inland revenue (including excise) and to make further provisions in connection with finance*, 17 July 1982, Section 19; the most beneficial concession for the country house in the late twentieth century is commonly referred to as Section 482. This

was part of the Taxes Consolidation Act, 1997, which legislated for tax relief on maintenance and repairs on historic buildings or gardens declared to be of 'significant scientific, historical, architectural or aesthetic interest' and open to the public for at least sixty days of the year, or in the case of properties used as guest houses, for at least six months of the year, and could be advertised as tourist attractions by Bord Fáilte. *Taxes Consolidation Act, 1997. An Act to consolidate enactments relating to income tax, corporation tax and capital gains tax, including certain enactments relating also to other taxes and duties*, 30 Nov. 1997, Section 482. Furthermore, in 1995 the Heritage Council was established as a statutory body under the Heritage Act. *Heritage Act, 1995. An act to promote public interest in and knowledge, appreciation and protection of the national heritage, to establish a body to be known as An Chomhairle Oidhreachta, to define its functions, to provide for the exercise by the Minister for Arts, Culture and the Gaeltacht of functions in relation to the national heritage and to provide for other matters connected with the matters aforesaid*, 10 Apr. 1995.

4 In addition, affiliation with the European Union (formerly the EEC) also required the Irish government to come in line with EU policy on heritage protections. As such, they were required, among other moves, to sign up to the *Convention for the Protection of the Architectural Heritage of Europe* (the Granada Convention). This was established in 1985 with the aim to protect and promote common European heritage, but was only ratified by the Irish government in 1994. Furthermore, UNESCO's *Convention Concerning the Protection of the World Cultural and Natural Heritage* was drawn up in 1972, but not ratified in Ireland until 1991. Dooley has maintained that Ireland's participation in the regulations of the Granada Convention, albeit late, meant that the government was committed 'to safeguarding the built heritage of Ireland for the wider good of the future generations of Europeans'. Terence Dooley, *A Future for Irish Historic Houses? A Study of Fifty Houses* (2003), p. 4.

5 Jane O'Hea O'Keeffe, *Voices from the Great Houses of Cork and Kerry* (Cork, 2013), p. 60.

6 Christopher Ridgway, 'The Fitzgerald legacy', in Patrick Cosgrove, Terence Dooley and Karol Mullaney-Dignam (eds), *Aspects of Irish Aristocratic Life: Essays on the Fitzgeralds and Carton House* (Dublin 2014), p. 227.

7 O'Hea O'Keeffe, *Voices from the Great Houses of Cork and Kerry*, pp 60–1.

8 Ibid., p. 109.

9 Recent works redressing the balance include: Eda Sagarra, *Kevin O'Shiel: Tyrone Nationalist and Irish State-Builder* (Kildare, 2013); Martin Maguire, *The Civil Service and the Revolution in Ireland, 1912–38: 'Shaking the Blood-Stained Hand of Mr Collins'* (Manchester, 2008).

10 David Lowenthal, *The Heritage Crusade and the Spoils of History* (Cambridge, 2003).

11 Hugh Maguire, 'Ireland and the house of invented memory', in Mark McCarthy (ed.), *Ireland's Heritages: Critical Perspectives on Memory and Identity* (Hants, 2005), p. 159.

APPENDIX

Source: National Archives of Ireland, Dept of Finance files, FIN/F63/8/58.

BIBLIOGRAPHY

PRIMARY SOURCES

I. MANUSCRIPTS
Attorney General files
Department of the Taoiseach files
Department of Education files
Department of Environment, Heritage and Local Government files
Department of Finance files
Department of Foreign Affairs files
Department of Health files
Department of Industry and Commerce files
National Archives of Ireland, Dublin
Office of Public Works files

II. OIREACHTAS DEBATES
Dáil Éireann
Seanad Éireann

III. NEWSPAPERS AND CONTEMPORARY PERIODICALS
Architect's Journal
Catholic Herald Group
Connaught Tribune
Evening Herald
Evening Mail
Freeman's Journal
Irish Architect and Contractor
Irish Farmers Journal
Irish Independent
Irish Press
Irish Tatler and Sketch
Irish Times
Kerryman

Nenagh Guardian
Sunday Independent
Sunday Press
United Irishman
Weekly Irish Times

IV. WORKS OF REFERENCE AND CONTEMPORARY PUBLISHED WORKS

Bence-Jones, Mark, *A Guide to Irish Country Houses* (revised edn, London, 1988).

Dooley, Terence, *The Big Houses and Landed Estates of Ireland: A Research Guide* (Dublin, 2007).

Sammon, Patrick J., *In the Land Commission:A Memoir, 1933–1978* (Dublin, 1997).

V. PUBLISHED REPORTS

Department of Environment, Heritage and Local Government: National Parks and Wildlife Service, 'Management plan for Killarney National Park, 2005–2009'.

Dooley, Terence, *A Future for Irish Historic Houses? A Study of Fifty Houses* (2003).

McParland, Edward and Nicholas Robinson, eds, *Heritage at Risk: A Digest of An Taisce's Report on the Future of Historic Houses, Gardens and Collections in the Republic of Ireland* (1977).

Walsh, Paul, 'The archaeological survey of Ireland: A historical overview', in *Surveying Our Heritage: The National Monuments Service: Marking 50 Years of the Archaeological Survey of Ireland*, Department of Arts, Heritage and the Gaeltacht (Dublin, 2013), pp S4–S13.

VI. GOVERNMENT LEGISLATION

i. Free State and Republic of Ireland

Anglo-Irish Treaty (6 Dec. 1921).

Arts Act, 1951. An act to stimulate public interest in, and to promote the knowledge, appreciation, and practice of, the arts and, for these and other purposes, to establish an Arts Council, and to provide for other matters in connection with the matters aforesaid (8 May 1951).

Bunreacht na hÉireann (1937).

Convention for the protection of the architectural heritage of Europe (3 Oct. 1985).

Damage to Property (Compensation) Act, 1923. An act to alter the law relating to compensation for criminal injuries (12 May 1923).

Executive Authority (External Relations) Act, 1936. An act to make provision, in accordance with the Constitution, for the exercise of the executive authority of Saorstát Éireann in relation to certain matters in the domain of external relations and for other matters connected with the matters aforesaid (12 Dec. 1936).

Finance Act, 1982. An act to charge and impose certain duties of customs and inland revenue (including excise), to amend the law relating to customs and inland revenue (including excise) and to make further provisions in connection with finance (17 July 1982).

Heritage Act, *1995. An act to promote public interest in and knowledge, appreciation and protection of the national heritage, to establish a body to be known as An Chomhairle Oidhreachta, to define its functions, to provide for the exercise by the Minister for Arts, Culture and the Gaeltacht of functions in relation to the national heritage and to provide for other matters connected with the matters aforesaid* (10 Apr. 1995).

Industrial Development (Encouragement of External Investment) Act, *1958. An act to amend the Control of Manufactures Acts, 1932 and 1934* (2 July 1958).

Irish Land Commission (Dissolution) Act, *1992. An act to provide for the dissolution of the Irish Land Commission, for the winding up of the system of land purchase, for the transfer of certain functions exercisable under the land purchase acts, and for other connected matters* (11 Nov. 1992).

Land Act, *1923. An act to amend the law relating to the occupation and ownership of land and for other purposes relating thereto* (9 Aug. 1923).

Land Act, *1931. An act to make provision for the early vesting of holdings in the purchasers thereof under the land purchase acts and for that and other purposes to amend those acts and the local Registration of Title (Ireland) Act, 1891, and also to make provision in respect of the variation of certain tithe rent charges and variable rents* (30 Apr. 1931).

Land Act, *1933. An act to amend generally the law, finance, and practice relating to land purchase, and in particular to make further and better provision for the execution of the functions of the judicial and lay commissioners of the Land Commission and to provide for the revision of purchase annuities and certain other annual payments and for the funding of arrears thereof, and to provide for other matters connected with the matters aforesaid* (13 Oct. 1933).

Land Act, *1965. An act to amend and extend the land purchase acts* (9 Mar. 1965).

Local Government (Planning and Development) Act, *1963. An act to make provision, in the interests of the common good, for the proper planning and development of cities, towns and other areas, whether urban or rural (including the preservation and improvement of the amenities thereof), to make certain provisions with respect to acquisition of land, to repeal the town and regional planning acts, 1934 and 1939, and certain other enactments and to make provision for other matters connected with the matters aforesaid* (7 Aug. 1963).

National Monuments Act, *1930. An act to make provision for the protection and preservation of national monuments and for the preservation of archaeological objects in Saorstát Éireann and to make provision for other matters connected with the matters aforesaid* (26 Feb. 1930).

National Monuments (Amendment) Act, *1954. An act to amend the National Monuments Act, 1930* (22 Dec. 1954).

Taxes Consolidation Act, *1997. An act to consolidate enactments relating to income tax, corporation tax and capital gains tax, including certain enactments relating also to other taxes and duties* (30 Nov. 1997).

The Republic of Ireland Act, 1948. An act to repeal the Executive Authority (External Relations) Act, 1936, to declare that the description of the state shall be the Republic of Ireland, and to enable the President to exercise the executive power or any executive function of the state in or in connection with its external relations (21 Dec. 1948).

Tourist Traffic Act, 1955. An Act to dissolve Fógra Fáilte and transfer its functions to *An Bord Fáilte* and to provide for other matters connected therewith (21 Mar. 1955).

UNESCO Convention concerning the protection of the world cultural and natural heritage (16 Nov. 1972).

Wealth Tax Act, 1975. An Act to charge and impose on certain wealth a duty of inland revenue to be known as wealth tax, to amend the law relating to inland revenue and to make further provisions in connection with finance (16 Aug. 1975).

ii. Northern Ireland and United Kingdom

Finance Act (Northern Ireland) 1948. An Act to alter certain duties of excise (including entertainments duty and duties on licences for mechanically-propelled vehicles) and stamp duties: to amend the law relating to the duties aforesaid and to death duties: to abolish certain duties: to provide for certain payments: and to make further provision in connection with finance (10 Aug. 1948).

Ireland Act, 1949. An Act to recognise and declare the constitutional position as to the part of Ireland heretofore known as Éire, and to make provision as to the name by which it may be known and the manner in which the law is to apply in relation to it: to declare and affirm the constitutional position and the territorial integrity of Northern Ireland and to amend, as respects the Parliament of the United Kingdom, the law relating to the qualifications of electors in constituencies in Northern Ireland: and for purposes connected with the matters aforesaid (2 June 1949).

National Parks and Access to the Countryside Act, 1949. An Act to make provision for national parks and the establishment of a national parks commission: to confer on the nature conservancy and local authorities powers for the establishment and maintenance of nature reserves: to make further provision for the recording, creation, maintenance and improvement of public paths and for securing access to open country, and to amend the law relating to rights of way: to confer further powers for preserving and enhancing natural beauty: and for matters connected with the purposes aforesaid (16 Dec. 1949).

Northern Ireland Land Act, 1925. An Act to amend the law relating to the occupation and ownership of land in Northern Ireland: and for other purposes relating thereto (28 May 1925).

SECONDARY SOURCES

I.PUBLISHED WORKS

Ashcroft, Bill, *Post-colonial Transformation* (London, 2001).

Anderson, Benedict, *Imagined Communities: Reflections on the Origin and Spread of Nationalism* (revised edn, London, 1991).

Barry, Frank, 'Foreign investment and the politics of export profits tax relief 1956', in *Institute for International Integration Studies (I.I.I.S.) Discussion Paper*, 357, Feb. 2011, pp 1–18; Trinity College website, http://www.tcd.ie/iiis/documents/discussion/pdfs/iiisdp357.pdf/ (28 Apr. 2013).

Bence-Jones, Mark, *Life in an Irish Country House* (London, 1996).

___, *Twilight of the Ascendancy* (London, 1987).

Biagini, Eugenio F., 'The Protestant minority in southern Ireland', in *The Historical Journal*, lv.4, Dec. 2012, pp 1161–84.

Bowen, Elizabeth, 'The Big House', in Hermione Lee, ed., *The Mulberry Tree: Writings On Elizabeth Bowen* (London, 1986), pp 25–30.

___, *The Last September* (London, 1998).

Byrne, Elaine A., 'A unique experiment in idealism: The Irish Senate 1922–28', in Mel Farrell, Jason Knirck and Ciara Meehan, eds, *A Formative Decade: Ireland in the 1920s* (Sallins, 2015), pp 59–85.

Cannadine, David, *The Decline and Fall of the British Aristocracy* (2nd edn, London, 2005).

Carew, Mairéad, 'Politics and the definition of national monuments: The 'big house problem', in *The Journal of Irish Archaeology*, xviii, 2009, pp 129–39.

Carey, Anne, 'Harold G. Leask: Aspects of his work as Inspector of National Monuments', in *The Journal of the Royal Society of Antiquaries of Ireland*, cxxxiii, 2003, pp 24–35.

Casey, Brian, 'The decline and fall of the Clancarty estate, east Galway, 1891–1923', in *Journal of the Galway Archaeological and Historical Society*, 2013.

Chambers, Anne, *At Arm's Length* (2nd edn, Dublin, 2004).

Comerford, R. V., *Ireland: Inventing the Nation* (London, 2003).

___, 'Foreword', in Terence Dooley and Christopher Ridgway, eds, *The Irish Country House: Its Past, Present and Future* (Dublin, 2011), pp 11–13.

Curtis, Jr, L. P., 'Demonising the Irish landlords since the Famine', in Brian Casey, ed., *Defying the Law of the Land: Agrarian Radicals in Irish History* (Dublin, 2013), pp 20–43.

Delaney, Enda 'Emigration, political cultures and the evolution of post-war society', in Brian Girvin and Gary Murphy, eds, *The Lemass Era: Politics and Society in the Ireland of Seán Lemass* (Dublin, 2005), pp 49–65.

Donnelly Jr, James S., 'Big house burnings in County Cork during the Irish revolution, 1920–21', in *Éire-Ireland*, xlvii.3&4, fall/winter 2012, pp 141–97.

Dooley, Terence, *The Decline of the Big House in Ireland: A Study of Irish Landed Families, 1860–1960* (Dublin, 2001).

___, *The Land for the People: The Land Question in Independent Ireland* (Dublin, 2004).

___, 'Land and politics in independent Ireland, 1923–1948: The case for reappraisal', in *Irish Historical Studies*, xxxiv.134, Nov. 2004, p. 183.

___, *The Big House and Landed Estates of Ireland* (Dublin, 2007).

___, 'National patrimony and political perceptions of the Irish country house in post-independence Ireland', in idem, ed., *Ireland's Polemical Past: Views of Irish History in Honour of R. V. Comerford* (Dublin, 2010), pp 192–212.

___ and Christopher Ridgway, eds, *The Irish Country House: Its Past, Present and Future* (Dublin, 2011).

___, 'The Fitzgeralds: A survey history, 1169–2013', in Patrick Cosgrove, Terence Dooley and Karol Mullaney-Dignam, eds, *Aspects of Irish Aristocratic Life: Essays on the Fitzgeralds and Carton House* (Dublin 2014), pp 19–33.

Dwan, David, '*The Great Community*': Culture and Nationalism in Ireland* (Dublin, 2008).

Farrell, Mel, 'Cumann na nGaedheal: A new "National Party"?', in Mel Farrell, Jason Knirck and Ciara Meehan, eds, *A Formative Decade: Ireland in the 1920s* (Sallins, 2015), pp 36–58.

FitzGerald, Desmond, David Griffin and Nicholas Robinson, *Vanishing Country Houses of Ireland* (Dublin, 1988).

Foster, R. F. *The Irish Story: Telling Tales and Making it up in Ireland* (London, 2001).

___, *Modern Ireland, 1600–1972* (2nd edn, London, 1989).

Friel, Brian, *Making History* (London, 1989).

Furlong, Irene, *Irish Tourism, 1880–1980* (Dublin, 2009).

Gaze, John, *Figures in a Landscape: A History of the National Trust* (London, 1988).

Genet, Jacqueline, *The Big House in Ireland: Reality and Representation* (Dingle, 1991).

Gibbons, Luke, *Transformations in Irish Culture* (Cork, 1996).

Girvin, Brian and Gary Murphy, 'Whose Ireland? The Lemass era', in idem, eds, *The Lemass Era: Politics and Society in the Ireland of Seán Lemass* (Dublin, 2005).

Goff, Annabel, *Walled Gardens* (2nd edn, London, 1994).

Guinness, Desmond and William Ryan, *Irish Houses and Castles* (London, 1971).

Hill, Myrtle and John Lynch, 'Movements for political & social reform, 1870–1914', University College Cork multitext project in Irish history, http://multitext.ucc.ie/d/Ireland_society__economy_1870–191 (14 Nov. 2012).

Horgan, John, 'Foreword', in Brian Girvin and Gary Murphy, eds, *The Lemass Era: Politics and Society in the Ireland of Seán Lemass* (Dublin, 2005), pp ix–xi.

Howes, Marjorie, *Yeats' Nations: Gender, Class and Irishness* (Cambridge, 1996).

Inchiquin, Lord, 'Irish Chief, English Accent', in Patrick O'Dea, ed., *A Class of Our Own* (Dublin, 1994), pp 169–88.

Jackson, Alvin, *Ireland, 1798–1998: Politics and War* (Oxford, 1999).

Kavanagh, Patrick, 'Epic', in *Patrick Kavanagh: Collected Poems* (2nd edn, London, 1972), p. 136.

Kelsall, Malcolm, *Literary Representations of the Irish Country House: Civilisation and Savagery Under the Union* (Virginia, 2003).

Keogh, Dermot, *Twentieth-century Ireland: Nation and State* (Dublin, 1994).

Lazarus, Neil, *Nationalism and Cultural Practice in the Postcolonial World* (Cambridge, 1999).

Lucas, A. T., 'Harold G. Leask, M. Arch., Litt. D., past president', in *The Journal of the Royal Society of Antiquaries of Ireland*, xcvi.1, 1966, pp 1–6.

Lyons, F. S. L., *Ireland Since the Famine* (2nd edn, London, 1985).

MacSharry, Ray and Pádraic White, *The Making of the Celtic Tiger: The Inside Story of Ireland's Booming Economy* (Cork, 2000).

Maguire, Hugh, 'Ireland and the house of invented memory', in Mark McCarthy, ed., *Ireland's Heritages: Critical Perspectives on Memory and Identity* (Hants, 2005), pp 153–68.

Mandler, Peter, *The Fall and Rise of the Stately Home* (New Haven & London, 1997).

Marsden, Simon, *In Ruins: The Once Great Houses of Ireland* (Boston & London, 1997).

McCarthy, John Paul and Tomás O' Riordan, 'James J. MacElligott', in *The Pursuit of Sovereignty & the Impact of Partition, 1912–49*, University College Cork multitext project in Irish history, http://multitext.ucc.ie/d/James_J_MacElligott (28 Apr. 2013).

McEvoy, F. J. 'Canada, Ireland and the Commonwealth: The declaration of the Irish Republic, 1948–9', in *Irish Historical Studies*, xxiv.96, Nov., 1985, pp 506–27.

Moran, D. P., *The Philosophy of Irish Ireland*, ed. Patrick Maume (Dublin, 2006).

Murphy, Frank, 'Dublin slums in the 1930s', in *Dublin Historical Record*, xxxvii. 3&4, June–Sept. 1984, pp 104–11.

Murphy, John A., *Ireland in the Twentieth Century* (2nd edn, Dublin, 1989).

Murphy, J. H., *Abject Loyalty: Nationalism and Monarchy During the Reign of Queen Victoria* (Cork, 2001).

O'Donovan, Danielle and Jennifer McCrea, 'Education and the historic house: Where the past has a value for the future', in Terence Dooley and Christopher Ridgway, eds, *The Irish Country House: Its Past, Present and Future* (Dublin, 2011), pp 184–202.

O'Farrell, Patrick, *Ireland's English Question* (London, 1971).

O'Rourke, Kevin, 'Burn everything British but their coal: The Anglo-Irish Economic War of the 1930s', in *The Journal of Economic History*, li.2, June 1991, pp 357–66.

Pine, Richard, *The Diviner: The Art of Brian Friel* (2nd edn, Dublin, 1999).

Plunkett, Elizabeth Mary Margaret Burke, Countess of Fingall, *Seventy Years Young: Memories of Elizabeth, Countess of Fingall* (London, 1937).

Purdue, Olwen, *The Big House in the North of Ireland: Land, Power and Social Elites, 1878–1960* (Dublin, 2009).

___, *The MacGeough Bonds of the Argory: Challenge and Change on a Small County Armagh Estate, 1880–1* (Dublin, 2005).

Regan, John M., 'Southern Irish nationalism as a historical problem', in *The Historical Journal*, l.1, Mar., 2007, pp 197–223.

Ridgway, Christopher 'The Fitzgerald legacy', in Patrick Cosgrove, Terence Dooley and Karol Mullaney-Dignam, eds, *Aspects of Irish Aristocratic Life: Essays on the Fitzgeralds and Carton House* (Dublin 2014), pp 220–8.

Sagarra, Eda, *Kevin O'Shiel: Tyrone Nationalist and Irish State-builder* (Kildare, 2013).

Douglas Smith, *Former People: The Destruction of the Russian Aristocracy* (Hampshire, 2012).

Thatcher, Mark, 'Introduction: The state and historic buildings: Preserving "the national past"', in *Nations and Nationalism*, xxiv, Jan. 2018, pp 22–42, https://onlinelibrary.wiley.com/doi/full/10.1111/nana.12372 (17 June 2018).

Tierney, Mark, OSB, 'The origins and early days of Glenstal Abbey', in Martin Browne OSB and Colmán Ó Clabaigh, eds, *The Irish Benedictines: A History* (Dublin 2005), CatholicIreland.net, http://www.catholicireland.net/pages/index.php?art=102 (28 Apr. 2013).

Tobin, Robert, *The Minority Voice: Hubert Butler and Southern Irish Protestanism, 1990–1991* (Oxford, 2012).

Warren, Allen, 'The twilight of the ascendancy and the big house: A view from the twenty-first century', in Terence Dooley and Christopher Ridgway, eds, *The Irish Country House: Its Past, Present and Future* (Dublin, 2011), pp 244–56.

II.UNPUBLISHED WORKS AND THESES

Casey, Brian Joseph, 'Land, politics and religion on the Clancarty estate, east Galway, 1851–1914', unpublished PhD thesis, National University of Ireland, Maynooth, 2011.

Cosgrove, Patrick John, 'The Wyndham Land Act 1903: The final solution to the Irish land question?', unpublished PhD thesis, National University of Ireland, Maynooth, 2008.

Furlong, Irene, 'State promotion of tourism in independent Ireland, 1925–55', unpublished PhD thesis, National University of Ireland, Maynooth, 2002.

Vandeweghe, Evert, 'Making history: Destruction and (re)construction of old Flemish towns during and after the First World War', delivered at the 'Politics of architectural destruction' conference, 23 May 2011, National University of Ireland, Maynooth.

III.ONLINE SOURCES

Archiseek, archiseek.com

Ahern, Bertie, 'Speech at Historic houses of Ireland Conference', at National University of Ireland, Maynooth, Sept. 2004, Department of the Taoiseach, www.taoiseach.gov.ie/index.asp?docID=2145

Europa: Summaries of EU Legislation, europa.eu/legislation_summaries/institutional_affairs/treaties/treaties_eec_en.htm

FitzGerald, Dr. Garret, 'Speech given by former Taoiseach at An Taisce The
    National Trust for Ireland's Heritage', at Trust corporate breakfast, 17 Nov. 2008,
    http://www.antaisce.org/articles/speech-given-former-taoiseach-dr-garret-
    fitzgerald-taisce-national-trust-ireland%E2%80%99s-heritage/ (24 May 2017).
Heritage Council, www.heritagecouncil.ie
Irish Georgian Society, www.igs.ie
Irish Statute Book, www.irishstatutebook.ie
Landed Estates Database, Moore Institute, National University of Ireland, Galway,
    www.landedestates.ie
Muckross House, www.muckross-house.ie
Multitext Project in Irish History, University College Cork, multitext.ucc.ie
National Archives of Ireland, www.nationalarchives.ie
National Parks and Wildlife Service, www.npws.ie
Nobody Home; Forgotten Buildings of Ireland, www.nobodyhome.ie
Revised Enacted UK Legislation, 1267-present, www.legislation.gov.uk
RTÉ News, www.rte.ie/news
Russborough House, www.russborough.ie
Sligo Today, www.sligotoday.ie

APPENDIX

This appendix has been reproduced verbatim from the source. No further details are currently available regarding codes mentioned within.

Appendix to the Office of the Minister for Lands, memorandum for the government, 'Preservation of mansions and large houses', 5 Aug. 1958

TABLE A: Big Houses on hands of Land Commission

NAME	STYLE	DESCRIPTION	CONDITION	DISPOSAL
LARGE				
Westfield House (Laois)	Modern	Adjacent to Castletown village, 2 miles S. W. Mountrath; stone-built (1929) 54' x 54', 2 storey tiled roof, 21 aparts. (e. 1. h. & c. water).	Very good	May be used for migrant or else offered for sale.
Mote Park House (Roscommon)	Georgian	2 ¾ miles S. Roscommon town. 3 storeys and basement, 23 rooms.	Good repair	Auction of house and 112 acres accommodation lands proved abortive. To be offered for sale at an early date by tender – (a) with accommodation lands and alternatively (b) buildings only for demolition.
Dalystown House (Galway)	Georgian	7 mls. S. E. Loughrea, 56' x 27', 4 storey.	Reasonably good	Considered to be suitable only for demolition and is therefore unlikely to be available for sale.

NAME	STYLE	DESCRIPTION	CONDITION	DISPOSAL
Residence on Atkinson Estate (Offaly)	Georgian	½ ml. N. W. Shinrone, 8 mls. S. W. Birr; Rubble-slated, 29 aparts.	Fair	May be used for Land Commission purposes or offered for sale publicly.
Castle-lough House (Tipperary)	Non-descript	9 mls. N. Nenagh on shores of Lough Derg. Large mansion, masonry built, 2 storey, basement and attic; 30 aparts. Rere [*sic.*] portion old and in poor repair. Front portion built in more recent times and is in fairly sound state of preservation.	Front portion in fairly good condition, Rere portion in poor condition.	–
Strancally Castle (Waterford)	Early pre-Victorian	10 mls. Cappoquin/Youghal. Castellated in imitation Tudor style; 3 storeys and basement (floor space 18,500 sq. ft.) 25 rooms, wired for electricity. £10,000 spent on renovation in 1950.	Fair	Will be offered for sale with 161 acres by tender at an early date.
Franckfort Castle	12th century approx.	5 mls. S. E. Roscrea, 90' x 37', 3 storey and basement, 27 aparts.	Very bad	Unlikely to be available for public sale with accommo-dation lands, (suitable only for demolition).
Castle-bellingham (Louth)	Georgian	Adjoining Castlebellingham village on banks of River Glyde, 2 storey in front, 3 storey in rere, some 30 aparts. (extensive farm bdgs. Including cottages, gardener's hse., etc.) Unoccupied 10–15 yrs. and deteriorating.	Poor	Will be offered for sale with 56A by tender at an early date.

NAME	STYLE	DESCRIPTION	CONDITION	DISPOSAL
MEDIUM				
Coolamber House (Longford)	Georgian	5 ½ mls. N. E. Edgeworth-stown; 14 main rooms, e. l., central heating, out-offices.	Very good	Proposed for sale by auction but now being considered for allot-ment to institution.
Thomas-town House (Offaly)	Do.	4 ½ mls. N. E. Birr, 2 storey non-basement, stone-built, slated; 12 rooms mod-ernised kitchen, wired for electricity, out-offices.	Do.	May be used for Land Commission purposes or offered for sale publicly.
Lissanode House (West-meath)	Modern	6 mls. S. W. Ballymore, 2 storey, slated, floor space 6,000 sq. ft. 14 rooms and domestic offices.	Good	Will likely be allotted to a migrant.
Newforest House (Galway)	Non-de-script	7 ½ mls. Mountbellew, 2 storey rubble-masonry, extensive out-buildings, ESB.	Fair	–
Dwelling-house on Bennett Estate (Offaly)	Georgian	6 mls. E. Birr; 2 storey, basement; 11 rooms and domestic offices.	Poor	Unlikely to be avail-able for public sale with accommodation lands (Suitable only for demolition).
SMALL				
Morris-townbiller House (Kildare)	Georgian	1 ml. Newbridge, 2 storey, stone built, 8 main rooms, electric light, telephone, etc.	Very good	Possibly for public sale with accommodation lands.
Mullacash House (Kildare)	Non-descript	3 mls. S. E. Naas, 4 mls. N. E. Kilcullen, 2 storey, stone-built, slated, e. l.	Good	Will likely be offered for sale publicly with accommodation lands.
Residence adjoining Ardpatrick village (Limerick)	Non-descript	Small mansion-type; 5 mls. S. Kilmallock, 15 rooms.	Fair	Will probably be available for sale with small area.
Fern Hill (Donegal)	Georgian	4 mls. E. Kilmacrennan, 2 storey, 7 rooms.	Poor	Offered for sale by auction – abortive. Still on auctioneer's books.

TABLE B: Results of auctions and sales by tender of Land Commission houses and accommodation plots over past 4 years approximately

NAME	STYLE	DESCRIPTION	DISPOSAL
LARGE			
Glenmalyre House (Laois)	Georgian	4 mls. Portarlington, 2 storey and basement, 16 rooms.	Sold with 50A. accommodation lands in June 1953.
Isercleran (Galway)	Do.	9 mils. Loughrea, 2 storey over semi-basement in front, 3 storey in rere, 19 main rooms, out-offices, lodge etc.	Sold with 75A. in August 1955.
Gowran Castle (Kilkenny)	Do. (with wing)	3 mls. Goresbridge, 2 storey semi-basement, 22 rooms, etc. Very good repair.	Sold with 73A. in May 1956.
MEDIUM/SMALL			
Cooper Hill (Meath)	Built about 1930	3 mls. Drogheda, 2 storey, 7 rooms, very good repair.	Sold with 19A. in October, 1956.
1. Sales by tender (Including private treaty after abortive auction)			
LARGE			
Garretstown House (Cork)	Non-descript	2 storey, stone-built, slated, 23 rooms, out-offices.	Sold with 49A. (February 1954) – tender.
Newpark House (Roscommon)	Georgian	½ ml. Kiltoom, 6 ½ mls. Athlone. 3 storey and basement, 18 rooms, out-offices and 10 roomed house.	Sold with 57A. in March 1955 by private treaty after abortive auction.
2. Abortive auction or tender			
SMALL			
Fern Hill (Donegal)	Georgian	4 mls. E. Kilmacrennan, 2 storey, 7 rooms, poor repair.	Auctioned with 13 acres in March 1958. Abortive and auctioneer still seeking offers.

TABLE C: Big Houses on hands of Land Commission demolished over past 4 years approximately

NAME	STYLE	DESCRIPTION
LARGE		
Pallas House (Wexford)	–	Large mansion 7½ mls. N. E. New Ross, 32 rooms, roof very bad and ceilings collapsing.
Castleharrison (Harrison Estate, Cork)	–	2½ mls. Charleville, large 3 storey mansion, stone-built, slated, 27 apartments, together with range of out-offices all in very poor repair.
Lissard House (Longford)	Georgian	39 rooms, suitable only for demolition.
Shanbally Castle (Tipperary)	Late Georgian of imitated Tudor style (150 years old)	3 mls. Clogheen, 10 mls. Cahir, stone-built, slated roof, 20 principal bed and dressing rooms, bathrooms and ample servant accommodation.
Leamlara House (Cork)	–	4 mls. Carrigtwohill. 2 storey – stone-built, slated, large mansion-type residence and range of out-offices, all in poor repair.
MEDIUM/SMALL		
Dundullerick House (Cork)	Small mansion type	Ruinous condition. Very old and unfit for occupation (Creagh-Barry Estate)
Residence on Robinson Estate (Westmeath)	–	2 storey, with annexe [*sic.*], 18 rooms.
Residence on Duan Estate (Galway)	–	2 storey, 33' x 42', 11 rooms.
Residence on Slattery Estate (Tipperary)	–	6 mls. S. W. Nenagh, 2 storey with basement, annexe, 11 rooms.

INDEX